AMAZING
TALES FROM THE
CHICAGO BEARS
SIDELINE

AMAZING
TALES FROM THE
CHICAGO BEARS
SIDELINE

A COLLECTION OF THE GREATEST
BEARS STORIES EVER TOLD

STEVE MCMICHAEL,
JOHN MULLIN,
AND PHIL ARVIA

FOREWORDS BY MIKE DITKA
AND DAN HAMPTON

SPORTS
PUBLISHING

Copyright © 2011 by Steve McMichael, John Mullin, and Phil Arvia
Forewords copyright © 2011 by Mike Ditka and Dan Hampton

All Rights Reserved. No part of this book may be reproduced in any manner
without the express written consent of the publisher, except in the case of brief
excerpts in critical reviews or articles. All inquiries should be addressed to Sports
Publishing, 307 West 36th Street, 11th Floor, New York, NY 10018.

Sports Publishing books may be purchased in bulk at special discounts for sales
promotion, corporate gifts, fund-raising, or educational purposes. Special
editions can also be created to specifications. For details, contact the Special Sales
Department, Sports Publishing, 307 West 36th Street, 11th Floor, New York,
NY 10018 or info@skyhorsepublishing.com.

Sports Publishing® is a registered trademark of Skyhorse Publishing, Inc.®,
a Delaware corporation.

www.skyhorsepublishing.com

10 9 8 7 6 5 4 3

Library of Congress Cataloging-in-Publication Data

McMichael, Steve.
    Amazing tales from the Chicago Bears Sideline : a collection of the greatest
Bears stories ever told / Steve McMichael, John Mullin, and Phil Arvia.
        p. cm.
    Includes bibliographical references.
    ISBN 978-1-61321-026-0 (alk. paper)
    1. Chicago Bears (Football team)--Anecdotes. 2. Chicago Bears (Football
team)--History. I. Mullin, John. II. Arvia, Phil. III. Title.
    GV956.C5M45 2011
    796.332'640977311--dc23
                                2011020904

Printed in the United States of America

To E.V. McMichael, the man who put me on the road, and to all the people who've touched me along the way, helping me become who I am. —S.M.

To Linda and Pam, for teaching me to read; to Chuck, for teaching me to compete, be it in the basement or the field; and to Tammy, for putting up with me spending so many nights and weekends away watching men play boys' games. —P.A.

CONTENTS

Part II

ACKNOWLEDGMENTS

It is impossible to name all the individuals and sources who contributed to this work. Some of them are unknown; there are Bears tales tucked away in memories of everyone who ever followed, covered, played for or coached the team, and those stories always seem to start something like, "I always heard this one story about…" Where they first heard it they sometimes can't remember. Such is the way of lore and legend.

But some special thanks are in order nonetheless: to Hub Arkush, Greg Blache, Mike Brown, Rick Casares, Bobby Douglas, the late Hugh Gallerneau, Dan Hampton, Jim Harbaugh, Mike Hartenstine, Warrick Holdman, Jeff Joniak, Jack Karwales, Frank Kmet, Glen Kozlowski, Erik Kramer, Dale Lindsey, George McAfee, Dave McGinnis, Jim Morrissey, Ray Nolting, Ed O'Bradovich, Bryan Robinson, Marcus Robinson, Jim Schwantz, Ed Sprinkle, Tom Thayer, Bob Thomas, Tom Waddle, and James "Big Cat" Williams.

The Bears organization itself is due thanks and appreciation. The annual Fan Convention is full of stories and includes a session each year with ex-Bears in which fans can step up to the microphone and ask a player, "I always heard this one story about…" NFL Films also has done a superb job of preserving tales of the Bears and others for all time so that future generations can hear Butkus growl, watch Sayers and Payton run, and enjoy the legends that never seem to grow old.

Colleagues and even competitors have my gratitude. Melissa Isaacson and Don Pierson of the *Chicago Tribune* made the job of storytelling and story-swapping fun, and Mike Mulligan of the *Sun-Times* helped keep fresh the memories of some special moments, usually with one of us starting off, "Hey, remember the time in Tampa when…"

No one book could ever hold all the great stories, and there are too many recommended tomes to list in one place. Mike Ditka's autobiography done with Don Pierson is a must for any Bears bookshelf, as are George Halas' *Halas on Halas*, Jim McMahon's autobiography done with Bob Verdi, and the books of Richard Whittingham, more recently his *What Bears They Were*.

This project never happens without the love and support of Kathleen Rude, who kept telling me I should write the stories down in one place and turn them into a book. Not long after she suggested that, Mike Pearson of Sports Publishing called with the same idea. Great minds do indeed think alike. And what book would be complete without help from Griffin, the Wonder Dog? No matter how old you are, if you still feel like a puppy inside, you get it.

Finally, thanks to the readers and listeners who are the real reasons I have a job. What's the fun of having great stories if you don't have someone to share them with?

—John Mullin

The authors would like to thank Scott Hagel and the Chicago Bears for their assistance; the *Daily Southtown* for help with research and photos; and Misty McMichael for the snacks— even the caviar.

—Steve McMichael and Phil Arvia

FOREWORD

By Mike Ditka

When I first came to the Bears as head coach, my wife and I went out to dinner at a place in Lake Forest on a Friday night. We had a game coming on Sunday.

I'd never been to this place, but she wanted to go, so we went. We got seated at the restaurant, and a couple minutes later the waitress came back and said, "A couple of your players would like to buy you and your wife a drink."

I said, "OK," and asked, "Where are they?" She said, "Out in the bar."

So I went out to the bar, and there was Steve McMichael, Dan Hampton and Mike Hartenstine—three of my key players—doing shots of tequila. What could I do?

I said, "I'll see you at practice tomorrow morning." They were all there and they were ready to go.

I never tried to treat those guys like kids. They weren't kids; they were adults, they were men, men who went out and busted their ass. So what am I going to do, get on them because they had a couple beers or whatever?

What can you say? That's the way that group of guys was. They were throwbacks to the old years I had with the Bears as a player. We played hard, we ran hard and we took our chances. That's what I liked about them.

That's what I liked about Steve McMichael.

Steve's a throwback to the old ballplayers. What you see is what you get, whether you like it or not. He's the teal deal. I always liked Steve, because he gave me everything he had on the field. He played like a warrior, and that's what I appreciate most about him.

Vince Lombardi said you'd never have a great player until you get one who knows how to play the game not only with his head, but also with his heart. Steve knew both. When I looked at him, I looked at a guy for whom things didn't come easy, but his work ethic was second to nobody on the football team.

When he went on the field, I don't think he ever got the recognition he deserved because we had a lot of good people on our defense—but our defense would not have been nearly as good without Steve McMichael, believe me. He made everybody else's job a little easier with the way he played the game.

When we had Steve and William Perry playing the tackles, and Dan Hampton, it was as good a group of guys as you could ask for, really. Then you bring Richard Dent on the outside, and of course we had great linebackers with Mike Singletary, Wilber Marshall and Otis Wilson. Add in the secondary led by Gary Fencik, and it was just a great defense.

I think Steve was an integral part of that defense in every way. When you look at our stats and find out how many pressures he had on the quarterback, how many knock downs—he didn't always get the sack, but I know he was there chasing him into somebody else's arms.

He doesn't try to impress anybody with the fact that he is smart, that he knows what he's doing. Steve can sense things, he can feel things out, he can anticipate things on defense.

He wants to give the image that he's the guy digging the ditch, that he's the hard worker. Nobody's ever going to accuse him of being Phi Beta Kappa, yet he's very smart about the way he played the game of football—and he had to be, because our defense demanded players recognize formations and adjust.

A lot of what Buddy Ryan did, what we did, was confusing the offense. If they can't recognize, they can't block. If you're going to screw up their blocking assignments, there's nobody for them to block, they're not going to do a good job. We did that, and we had athletic ability. You can play any defense, but if you don't have the athletes to do it, it's not going to work.

We had the athletes to do it, and that's what made it so much fun.

Of course, there's no question Steve had a lot of fun. Very few people had more fun than Steve McMichael, but that's OK. There's a time to work and a time to play, when it was time to work and practice, he did that, and when it was time to have fun, he did that. I never had a problem with guys like that.

Steve never wanted to give the impression that he did all the right things, but he did a lot of the right things, believe me.

His honesty—you may not like what he says, but he's going to say it. He doesn't pull any punches.

I knew I could count on Steve. On that football team, I was lucky in the sense that there wasn't anybody, really, whom I couldn't count on. They were all guys that kept the other guys in line. Steve, though, was really in that core group of players that controlled the other players—and you do that basically through example.

The example Steve set on and off the field, was good. He was one of the best in practice. He practiced hard. He was a guy who practiced to get better.

Also, I think he was a role model for other guys. Not rhat he did everything in the world right, but he certainly did it at a full-speed pace.

Steve was small for a defensive tackle even then, but he was strong—exceptionally strong. As far as his upper body went, he was as strong as anybody we had on the football team. He spent a lot of time in the weight room.

When I first got there, I realized he was a player. I didn't have a lot of decisions when I looked at some of the other guys we had. Some of the other guys had bigger reputations than Steve, yet when I watched Steve play I liked what I saw. I liked the way he practiced; I like the way he worked. He just went about his job as a man.

Steve was a lot like I was when I played. He liked to raise a little hell, and on occasion I did that myself.

What I looked for from Steve is what I had as a player. I played hard, I didn't want to get beat by anybody, I didn't want to take a back seat to anybody. I think that's the way Steve played the game.

FOREWORD

By Dan Hampton

Author's Note: The newest Bear to step into Pro Football's hallowed pantheon, the Hall of Fame, lived his professional life down amid the sound and fury of the trenches, where the game always was won or lost and always will be. Dan Hamption was voted to the Pro Bowl four times, twice as a defensive end, twice as a tackle, and was the anchor on one of the greatest defensive lines in the history of football. In his 12 seasons, "Danimal," as he was known by teammates and fans alike, played in 157 regular season games, starting 152, and was named defensive Most Valuable Player in 1982 by Pro Football Weekly. He was the fourth player taken in the 1979 draft following a senior season at Arkansas in which he recorded 18 sacks on the way to being named Southwestern Conference defensive player of the year. As long as there is football played in Chicago, they will tell stories of "Hamp," and the author is grateful not only to Dan for his own contributions to this collection, but also for his part in the stories told by others. More than one Bear; talking about his own experiences, insisted, "Hey, you have got to talk to Hamp. He's got the best stories, and besides, he's in em too!"

*   *   *   *

When I was drafted by the Bears in 1979, I was horrified. That's the truth; like all young college players, I wanted to play in Miami, Los Angeles, San Francisco, any place warm. Little did I know that I was on a collision course with destiny.

In 1979 the Bears were going through a down cycle. Everyone knew of Butkus and Sayers and other greats. But that was in the past, and even with Walter Payton here and a decent year here or there, the franchise was down. You almost felt that something of the greatness that had been the Bears was past.

All that was to change when, in one of his final acts, Papa Bear George Halas hired Mike Ditka because of his burning desire to rekindle the flame of the Monsters of the Midway. It didn't happen overnight, but within a few years, with great players like Walter, Mike Singletary, Richard Dent, Steve McMichael, Jim Covert, Mark Bortz, Jay Hilgenberg and others, we had returned the greatness of the tradition to the Chicago Bears.

It doesn't take long in the league to figure out what the Black and Blue Division was all about.

These stories weave in the tales of the greatness that went before with the rekindling that I was privileged to play a part in, and on into the years that followed. The stories are more than just stories. They define and reveal a little about the men who played this brutal game the way it was meant to be played, in a city where it was meant to be played, and in front of fans who are simply the greatest in any town or sport.

INTRODUCTION

In Steven Spielberg's *Raiders of the Lost Ark,* archaeologist Indiana Jones battles to secure the Ark of the Covenant, the repository for the stone tablets given by God to Moses on which were inscribed the Ten Commandments. The Nazis wanted it for its supposed power.

Jones sought to find it as well but was most interested in keeping it from the Nazis. At one point Jones threatens to blow up the Ark with a bazooka.

Jones's adversary, a French archaeologist named Belloc, challenges Jones to go ahead, destroy the Ark. Jones can't. Belloc knows it, and knows why.

"Indiana," Belloc chides, "you and I are just passing through history. The Ark *is* history."

We as fans, media and others watch football history. The Bears in these pages *are* history.

The Chicago Bears are more than a football team. They are part of the civic fabric of a city and its people. Carl Sandburg was close when he titled Chicago as the City of Big Shoulders. He just didn't go far enough; Chicago is the City of Big Shoulder Pads. Chicago fans want to love their Bears because the Bears are much of what Chicagoans like about themselves: Big. Tough. Champions.

And characters. The Bears, like Chicago, are not just people. They are personalities, for better or worse. They have their mean side, their fun side, their quiet side, their tender side. Their stories. Their tales.

The history of the Bears is the history of pro football. Just about everything that could happen to a pro football team has happened to the Bears; just about everything that could happen to a pro football player has happened to a Bear. Or has been done by a Bear.

George Halas founded the Bears in 1920, not as the Bears and not even in Chicago. He and representatives of 12 other clubs met in Canton, Ohio, and worked out plans for their venture into professional football, which was no small gamble at a time when college football was king of the pigskin landscape.

It was the beginning of a litany of adventures, and sometimes misadventures, that would culminate in a sport that, if it couldn't be America's pastime (baseball had already laid claim to that honor), then it certainly became the king of America's sports interest. The Super Bowl trophy is named for Vince Lombardi, winner of the first two. It should be named for Halas, the man who made it all possible and on whose shoulders Lombardi and so many others would stand.

Halas was a Chicago native and three-time letter winner at the University of Illinois playing under legendary coach Robert C. Zuppke. Ironically, "Zup" would also coach Harold "Red" Grange, the player whose signing enabled Halas to truly launch pro football and enabled him to become a charter member of the Roaring '20s Golden Age of Sports. Zuppke advised Grange against signing to play pro football. Fortunately for Halas and America, he didn't have any more success stopping Grange in that effort than most defenders of the era had in stopping Grange with a football in his hands.

What brought Halas to that Canton meeting was a dream of Mr. Arthur E. Staley, who'd gambled on himself and eventually built a highly successful cornstarch manufacturing company in Decatur, a small town 175 miles southwest of Chicago. As a promotional vehicle and to build employee morale, Staley, through the company's Fellowship Club, sponsored the Staley Starchmakers, a semipro football club, and in March 1920 persuaded Halas to coach the team, which traveled to face other semipro clubs in the Midwest.

A problem with scheduling prompted Halas to write a letter to Ralph Hay, manager of the Canton (Ohio) Bulldogs and suggest forming a league. Hay had been thinking the same thing and already had met with representatives of teams from Akron, Dayton, Cleveland and Massillon, all Ohio towns.

On Sept. 17, 1920, representatives of the teams met in Hay's car dealership, in a showroom big enough for only four cars—Hupmobiles and Jordans—and formed a league that would far outlast those present that day, automotive and athletic. There wasn't enough room for chairs. Halas sat on a running board.

From that two-hour meeting, more than a dozen teams joined the new American Professional Football Association. Besides the newly named Decatur Staleys, there were the Buffalo All-Americans, Canton Bulldogs, Cleveland Indians (headed by the great Jim Thorpe), Dayton Triangles, Akron Professionals, Massillon Tigers (the city from which Paul Brown came and the nickname to this day of the local high school gridders), Rochester (N.Y.) Jeffersons, Rock Island (Ill.) Independents, Muncie (Ind.) Flyers, Chicago (Racine) Cardinals, and Hammond (Ind.) Pros.

Not all would even make it into the season that started Oct. 3 with Halas' team defeating the Moline Tractors 20-0, and through the years others would come and go from what Halas and the others created.

That first Halas team set a standard. In its 13 games (10 wins, one loss and two 0-0 ties), only three opponents scored, one being the Chicago Cardinals for a 7-6 win.

But in 1921 Staley told Halas that the company, while basking in the regional exposure the team gave its name, couldn't underwrite the expenses any longer. And Decatur was too small to support a professional franchise. He suggested that Halas take the team to Chicago, where it was drawing its best crowds, and staked Halas to $5,000 seed money, for salaries of $25 per week per player and other expenses, on the condition that Halas call the team the Staleys (officially "The Staley Football Club") for one more season.

Halas happily agreed, then struck a deal with Bill Veeck Sr., president of the Chicago Cubs, to use Cubs Park. Since the park wasn't being used after baseball season—some say it still isn't used much during baseball season—Veeck liked the idea and let Halas play there in exchange for 15 percent of the gate and concessions. Halas bargained back for the program rights, and the verbal agreement between the two stood for 50 years.

After that first Chicago season, the "Staleys" ceased. Halas wanted to show his appreciation for how Veeck and the Cubs had helped him and considered naming his team the Cubs. But he reasoned that football players were bigger, stronger and (except for maybe Ty Cobb) certainly a lot meaner than baseball players, so he went bigger with his name: The Chicago Bears.

Halas' team, like the football league he and the others started, became bigger in many, many ways. But underneath the glitz, the money, the celebrity, it was always still people: young men with fears, hopes and dreams, playing ultimately for themselves and each other.

It was that way in the beginning. Deep down, it still is.

AMAZING
TALES FROM THE
CHICAGO BEARS
SIDELINE

PART I

Chapter 1

THE JAURON ERA

Dick Jauron took over as Bears coach in 1999, beginning a tenure marked by upheaval and changes within the organization itself. The Bears changed presidents, added a general manager and went through quarterback changes on what seemed like an hourly basis. It was a time that left the Bears changed for all time.

NOT MY FAULT

Quarterback Cade McNown made himself an outcast almost from the moment he arrived in training camp; not the way for a future leader to start off, particularly after being the 12th player taken in the 1999 draft. McNown was 11 days late after a contract impasse that was in fact not his fault (the Bears eventually gave him exactly the deal that agent Tom Condon asked for at their first negotiation), but he wasted little time irritating teammates.

Cade McNown   *AP/WWP*

In one of his first practices, he rolled out the way he had at UCLA and cut loose a pass to wide receiver Macey Brooks, who happened to be covered by three defenders.

The ball was intercepted, after which McNown chided Brooks for runnin the wrong route. Not bad for a quarterback who was two days in camp and who'd been the one to cut the ball loose into triple coverage.

In his first preseason game he mishandled the snap from center Casey Wiegmann, now the starter for the Kansas City Chiefs, when McNown simply pulled back from the snap position too soon. McNown had pulled out too soon but blamed Wiegmann for not getting the ball back to him properly.

Because 1999 was his rookie season and Shane Matthews and Jim Miller were much of the quarterback story, McNown's growing problems were overshadowed, particularly because it was also the first Dick Jauron season and there were many events to occupy fans' attention. But the pattern was set for deeper McNown difficulties.

His already shaky relationships within the locker room worsened after a loss to the New York Giants in early 2000. One week earlier he'd been destroyed in a 41-0 loss to the Tampa Bay Buccaneers in the second game of the season, after which offensive linemen were furious over McNown's failure to get rid of the ball on time, his stupidity in the pocket, running his way into sacks, and not being prepared to recognize his responsibilities on plays, a problem that would be his ultimate undoing later in the season.

"He tells everybody in the huddle, 'Look out for the blitz,'" recalled tackle James "Big Cat" Williams. "He drops back and gets hit—BAM!—right in the mouth. We're walking to the sidelines then and he's cussing and fussing, 'Who's fucking guy was that?' We all said to him, 'That was the 'hot' guy. That was YOUR guy.'"

Against the Giants, McNown overthrew Brooks once and Marcus Robinson twice on wide-open deep passes where they were behind the defense. Afterwards, McNown put the blame on the receivers in a unique bit of subtle slam: "I think I just need to be aware that during the game those guys get a little tired and aren't running as fast," McNown told the postgame press corps.

The receivers were incensed at the not-so-subtle shift of blame for McNown's own bad passes. Robinson went to McNown privately and told him he needed to watch his mouth, that he was losing respect and tolerance among his teammates.

It got worse.

McNown hurt his shoulder at Philadelphia, after which the team picked up noticeably under Jim Miller and then Shane Matthews after Miller tore his Achilles at Buffalo. McNown sat out for six weeks, then was judged healthy enough to return. Mysteriously, coach Dick Jauron chose to start McNown at San Francisco right after Matthews had been near-perfect in a win over the New England Patriots.

McNown, despite having six weeks off to study and prepare for a fresh start after a 1-7 record in the games he'd started before the injury, effectively ended his Chicago career that week. Players said the practices leading up to the 49ers game were some of the worst they had ever been part of. McNown not only threw badly but did not know his assignments, reads or anything else. Clearly he had done nothing with his time off and was phoning it in at game 15 of a lost season.

Trouble was, the players were not quitting, even with their 4-10 record. They were determined to prove that they were not a bad team and that the main reason for their problems was McNown, and his performances Wednesday, Thursday and Friday at practice were proving it. At one point, offensive lineman Todd Perry approached Bryan Robinson and members of the defensive line and apologized in advance for the way they were looking.

On Friday afternoon, after the brief practice, the defensive linemen met for their regular Friday huddle. Instead of settling on one last 49ers point or scheme thought, they decided among themselves that above all else, they needed to go into Sunday expecting to play at least 40 minutes, because the offense under McNown was simply not going to stay on the field.

They were prophetic. McNown began calling nonexistent plays and protections for the line, mixing routes and blocking, failing to get his check-off calls correct. The game was a disaster, a 17-0 loss to the 49ers in which the play of McNown and the offense was overshadowed for the moment by Terrell Owens's record-setting 20 receptions.

"He didn't know what he was doing," Big Cat says. "He didn't know his audibles, would come up to the line and at one point audibled to a play that didn't exist. We were up on the line saying to each other, 'What the fuck did he just say?'

"It was so bad that they asked Dick if he wanted to pull him out and Dick said, 'No, let him finish the game.' It was almost like he was smirking and saying to management, 'You want this quarterback? I'll show you what you've got in this quarterback.'

"I think it was more to the people upstairs than to Cade. He already had his opinion of Cade."

Privately the players were enraged. The anger was not at Jauron, whom the players all believed was being pressured by management to play McNown, if for no other reason than to find out whether or not the kid could play, even though the locker room had long ago decided he couldn't.

There was talk that if Jauron insisted in starting McNown at Detroit, more than a few players simply did not want to take the field. McNown's lack of commitment and preparation put them at risk and made all of them look terrible as a group. Because of the players' respect for Jauron, a true rebellion and sit-down strike was unlikely, but as defensive back Frankie Smith and others said privately, "There would have been an awful stretch of 'slight hamstring strains' that week if they stuck with McNown for that last game."

Several players talked with Jauron and let their feelings be known. Jauron was not one to be pressured and the players weren't trying to do that. But Jauron also was a former player himself and knew what they were feeling, and that McNown did not deserve to play, not with a group that was still willing to play hard. Any rebellious thoughts were quelled when Jauron announced that Matthews would again start, and a Paul Edinger field goal gave the Bears a 23-20 win at Detroit, knocking the Lions out of the

Dick Jauron   *AP/WWP*

playoffs and giving the Bears two wins in their last three games and some momentum into next season's 13-3 season.

And McNown? He never made it out of preseason. He was called into a closed-door meeting with Jauron and quietly cut to ribbons for his conduct, unprofessionalism and failure to be an NFL player. When GM Jerry Angelo arrived in June, he familiarized himself with the McNown situation and had his own meeting with McNown. There he told McNown that the quarterback had "taken on too much water in Chicago and with this team." He began shopping McNown in trade and eventually dealt him to Miami for a late-round draft choice. Miami's personnel department was under Rick Spielman, who'd been the pro personnel director in Chicago when the Bears drafted McNown.

After a wasted season, McNown was sent packing, released and sent to the San Francisco 49ers-the very team against whom he'd show he had no business in an NFL uniform.

TOGETHERNESS

Offensive lines are traditionally one of the closest-knit groups on a football team, but the Bears took that to a new level. At one point before the 2002 season, the wives of center Olin Kreutz and guards Rex Tucker and Chris Villarrial all were expecting babies. Joked Kreutz: "We do everything together."

BLACHE BULLETS

Defensive coordinator Greg Blache, whose hobbies include serious hunting, wanted to motivate his players to become more physical. He decided upon a reward system based on high-impact hits that involved presenting a player with one high-powered rifle shell for a major hit on an opponent.

The player who earned the most bullets during the season would receive a color television.

It worked. Players prized the gesture and lobbied for the bullets after big hits. Safety Rashard Cook, a 1999 draft choice who played only in preseason before being cut, still has his one Blache Bullet earned for huge hits delivered on kickoff coverage during the preseason.

The system came to light when cornerback Tom Carter, whom Blache rode hard because of Carter not being a more physical player, was cut in midseason. Carter had won precisely one Blache Bullet before his release, and when he cleaned out his locker, he left absolutely nothing in the stall, only the solitary bullet standing on the shelf, where the world could see it. It was his special "goodbye" to teammates, Carter said.

The problem was that the NFL doesn't allow teams to compensate players without it counting under their salary cap. The story on the bullets reached the NFL office, which promptly called Blache and told him to cease and desist, as did coach Dick Jauron. But not before the incident became a huge topic on talk shows in town, which unfairly portrayed Blache as some gun-toting violence monger in a time when guns and such had become such a huge issue for society.

BLACHE WATCH

Dick Jauron's defensive coordinator Greg Blache rarely has kind words for the media. "You guys would find holes with Mother Theresa," he complained. "If it was up to you she wouldn't get into heaven because she didn't cure cancer."

Blache accused the media of leaking game plan information to the Baltimore Ravens before the Bears played them to open the 2001 season. His source of inside information? Television psychic Miss Cleo.

"Oh yeah, that's where I get my information," Blache dead-panned. "She's more informative than you guys are, I'll tell you that."

Muttered one press room wag: "Yeah, and she's probably a better defensive coordinator than you are, too."

Asked if he was having fun as a defensive coordinator getting ready to face the Minnesota Vikings with Randy Moss and Daunte Culpepper, Greg Blache shook his head: "No, no. I don't know what gave you that idea. The only thing B. B. King's got on me is guitar and sunglasses. I got the blues, trust me."

Things were getting so bad during a seven-game losing streak in 2002 that "we've been getting calls from Division II schools trying to schedule us for Homecoming," Blache moaned. "I turned them down because I didn't want to overschedule."

BAD INTRODUCTION

When Jerry Angelo arrived as general manager in 2001, he wasted no time in angering most of the team, which turned out to have good results, at least initially.

An introductory team meeting was called and coach Dick Jauron made his remarks, then invited Angelo up to address the team. Instead of a welcoming comment, Angelo shocked the room by essentially threatening everyone's job, beginning with Jauron. It was not a great start, given that Jauron had established a bond with the players, who felt he'd taken the fall for management the year before with the McNown fiasco.

The players were angry and there are those who believe a lot of the 13-3 mark in 2001 was their way of denying Angelo the chance to fire Jauron and bring in his own head coach. Others weren't so sure.

"It wasn't so much motivation as far as something he did, more of a 'Fuck you, really don't need you,'" says James "Big Cat" Williams. "Our big thing that year was we stayed healthy and didn't have a lot of people hurt. We had some good bounces that went our way. I don't think it had anything to do with Jerry.

"A lot of people want to say they played for Dick because Dick's job was on the line. He's a good guy a player's coach; I can't take that away from him. But we were just on our game, we stayed healthy and were able to do what we wanted to do."

A lot of that started with a defense that played so well the offense could relax, and with an offense that went to Jim Miller after Shane Matthews was injured in the second game of the season.

"Everybody believed in Miller," Williams says. "He could come into the huddle and might say the dumbest shit as soon as he walks in, but you knew Jim was trying to get you going and he was 'real' about it. He's one of those quarterbacks like you see in the movies, where everybody is just ready to rally behind him. We know he doesn't have the strongest arm and he's not the most mobile guy. But we knew he was going to get up after a hit and he's not going to make a lot of mistakes."

DANCE FEVER

Minnesota Vikings defensive tackle John Randle found out that center Olin Kreutz was a native Hawaiian. The first time the Bears broke the huddle and Kreutz headed for the line, Randle broke into a hula dance that had the Bears' offense howling and almost calling for a timeout.

Less amused was running back Curtis Enis. He married a former exotic dancer and had to be restrained from going after Randle, who tucked a dollar bill in the belt of his uniform pants and as the Bears came to the line, yelled to Enis, "Hey, how 'bout having your lady do a table dance for us?"

BIG MONEY

With all the money in sports, the numbers that get reported in the news can be pretty numbing. But what do you do, literally, with a check for millions of dollars?

Wide receiver Marcus Robinson signed a contract in 1999 that included a $5 million signing bonus. After taxes, that meant Robinson was handed a check for about $3.5 million at Halas Hall. What does someone do with a check for $3.5 million?

"I walked down the hall into DJ's [Dwayne Joseph's] office and sat down," Robinson said, shaking his head. "I didn't even look at it. I signed and they gave me the envelope. They gave me a folder for it, but I didn't want to be walking around with some folder in my hand, so I took the check and stuck it in the sleeve of my jacket, so I could feel it next to my skin.

"I walked straight to DJ's office. I said, 'DJ, open it.'" He knew I had signed but he didn't know how much. I went and bought a car, that day."

Fellow wide receiver Marty Booker had "number-shock" when he looked at his own signing bonus check. "I just opened it up, looked at it and went 'Wow, would I ever see this many numbers on one check?'" Booker marveled. "Oh, my goodness. I just put it in my pocket in case I needed security getting out of the parking lot."

GOOD IMPRESSION

Coach Dick Jauron was a former standout NFL player, a fact that was not lost on his players, who sensed in him an understanding of the little things that made pro football tough and thus an awareness of when to push and when to ease off.

Jauron also lived by "The Code" of playing the best player. If you were the best at your position, you played, not someone who was there just because he was a high draft choice. One exception was Jauron's playing of Cade McNown through the first half of the 2000 season despite it being obvious every Sunday and every day in practice that McNown was not the best at his position. The reason Jauron never lost the respect of the rest of the players: "We knew that Cade wasn't the best guy," says tackle James "Big Cat" Williams. "We knew it wasn't Dick [pushing him into the lineup]. It was the front office."

Jauron delegated full responsibility to his assistants and did not insist on hands-on coaching for himself. Instead, he was simply a presence that the players understood and appreciated, sometimes more than others."

"Dick will walk around all the time with this serious look on his face, and then walk up beside you and crack a little joke," Williams says. "A stupid joke, but it cracks him up. And you stand there and laugh because you have to, and then he'll walk off laughing, and two of you are standing there asking, 'What the hell was he talking about?'

"That was just him. He didn't talk to you that much like he was trying to buddy up or be one of the guys. But he is a good guy."

RIVALS

The Bears-Packers rivalry is not the only one with some bad blood and tradition among the Bears. Former defensive end Trace Armstrong was once asked who his most-hated player ever was. "Tim Irwin," Armstrong answered immediately, identifying the longtime right tackle for the Minnesota Vikings. "If I ran over him with my car, I'd back up to make sure I got him."

The Vikings disliked the Bears back in the 1980s when a very talented Minnesota group was being upstaged by the Ditka Bears, not only for division titles but also for Pro Bowl honors. That dislike was fueled in 1998 when linebacker Dwayne Rudd returned a fumble recovery for a touchdown and backpedaled across the goal line with the ball extended, taunting running back Edgar Bennett, who was pursuing on the play.

But not all the "rivalry" thoughts are bitter.

"The only reason I really felt that rivalry was because of Korey Stringer," said defensive lineman Bryan Robinson, referring to the outstanding right tackle who died during training camp 2001. "That was my most intense, because we were both from the same state, I watched him come up and followed him through high school and I know he followed me. It was just an honor. "When I finally got to start, it was against Korey Stringer. Then the situation with him dying, its tough for me to look at it like that now. They've got a different guy in there and, not saying Korey was better, but that was something special, we were good friends, and it was an honorable rivalry.

"We did talk off the field and were pretty good friends. That whole thing kind of screwed me up. And I was here when Dwayne Rudd did his thing and when they went 15-1. When we go up there, it's sold out and they hate the Bears.

"I don't think it compares to the Green Bay-Chicago rivalry because that's so old. But any team that's in your division, you want that extra edge to beat that team. And they hate you."

LOOKING AHEAD

Few coaches have taken as much criticism as offensive coordinator John Shoop did in 2002. Injuries gutted the line and took No. 1 quarterback Jim Miller out for sizeable chunks of the season, but fans weren't interested in the problems; they wanted offense.

But even while players sometimes grumbled about excessive conservatism, they also understood that Shoop had a plan, like it or not.

"Shoop has to call his game, get to a point where he's comfortable calling his plays," says "Big Cat" Williams. "He won't score a lot of points early but he needs time. But you will have the opportunity to score points later because he is very good at making one thing look like another."

THE MCGINNIS FIASCO: THE REAL STORY

The disastrous hiring-then-not-hiring of Dave McGinnis to coach the Bears in 1999 was a turning point in the organization and led to the hiring of Dick Jauron. The McGinnis debacle led to the "firing" of Michael McCaskey by his mother and the installation of Ted Phillips as president of the team. But what really happened that day?

McGinnis was one of five finalists screened by personnel VP Mark Hatley and McCaskey. The others: Gunther Cunningham, then defensive coordinator for the Kansas City Chiefs; McGinnis, the former linebackers coach under Mike Ditka; Sherman Lewis, offensive coordinator for Mike Holmgren in Green Bay; Jauron, defensive coordinator at Jacksonville; and Joe Pendry, offensive coordinator at Buffalo and the Bears' running backs coach from 1993-94 under Dave Wannstedt.

McGinnis was McCaskey's first choice. He was popular in Chicago, and when Ed and Virginia McCaskey visited the Phoenix area, they stayed with Dave and his wife Kim. So there was a special bond and comfort level.

That started changing almost from the moment McGinnis woke up on Friday morning, Jan. 22, 1999. First, based on Michael McCaskey's directives, the Bears put out a press release announcing

McGinnis's hiring as the new head coach. It wasn't true; McGinnis hadn't worked out a contract, and in fact was in Chicago to get that done, but it wasn't a *fait accompli*. McGinnis heard about his hiring while he was shaving and getting ready at his hotel to meet with the Bears.

But the premature news announcement was not the real story of the disaster.

McGinnis was extremely upset at the news release but went to talk contract anyway. Significantly, McCaskey convinced McGinnis not to bring his agent with him, that the special relationship between McGinnis and the Bears made that unnecessary.

It turned out to be quite necessary. McCaskey immediately began playing hardball as the meeting got under way. The dollars were way below market rate for a head coach, and McGinnis several times was set to walk out. But finally the money was close enough to where McGinnis wanted on a four-year deal, and it looked like McCaskey would have his head coach in place after all.

But McCaskey in early 1995 had given Wannstedt a multiyear contract extension that shocked everyone. McCaskey was concerned that Wannstedt would be too hot a coaching property for him to afford if it came to bidding against other owners. Wannstedt had in fact chosen the Bears' top job over the New York Giants' offer when he left the Dallas Cowboys and Jimmy Johnson.

McCaskey hadn't negotiated a buyout into Wannstedt's deal and was on the hook for the final two years of Wannstedt's contract when he fired him, a $2.5 million hook. McCaskey was determined not to be in the same bind if things didn't work out with McGinnis.

So McCaskey wanted a clause that let him buy out the McGinnis deal after two years. Absolutely not, McGinnis said, correctly noting that such an arrangement made the contract basically just a two-year pact. Then came the dealkiller.

McGinnis: "And Michael, how can I convince assistant coaches to leave jobs or move families here for a coach with just a two-year contract?"

McCaskey: "Do they have to know?"

At that moment, McGinnis would say later, he knew he could never work for Michael McCaskey.

McGinnis would go on to succeed Vince Tobin, another Bears coach, the defensive coordinator under Mike Ditka, as coach of the Arizona Cardinals. McCaskey, rebuffed in his push for McGinnis, turned his attention to another alternative. He put in a call to Steve Mariucci, the head coach of the San Francisco 49ers and who was on vacation in Mexico, and got a final opinion on Dick Jauron. This time the agent, Don Yee, was involved in the negotiations, which were done by 9 p.m. after McGinnis had left to return to Arizona.

Dick Jauron was not McCaskey's second choice. Michael wanted then-Green Bay Packers offensive coordinator Sherman Lewis. Mark Hatley, whose first choice was Joe Pendry, whom Hatley knew from their days with the Kansas City Chiefs, was adamant that if McCaskey hired Lewis, Hatley would resign immediately.

The mutually agreeable compromise: Dick Jauron.

McGinnis's four-year contract started at about $800,000 and went up each year. The deal Yee worked out for Jauron was $1 million per season. So McCaskey lost money as well as his coach. And several weeks later, after the franchise was dubbed the laughingstock of the NFL, McCaskey lost his job.

GET TO THE POINT

Middle linebacker Brian Urlacher is in charge of the defensive huddle, the eyes, ears and voice of defensive coordinator Greg Blache. But that doesn't mean teammates don't get a little scratchy with him.

The routine is for Blache to signal in the defensive call to Urlacher, who then silences all talk in the huddle—there's often a lot of it between plays, not all for family listening—with one word that ends all chatter: "Listen."

"One of the things that irks me about Brian," says defensive lineman Bryan Robinson with a laugh, "is that he'll know the huddle call and we'll be sitting out there during the timeout and I'll say, 'Did he give you the call?' And he goes, 'Yeah, I got the call.' And I'm like, 'Well ^%#$, give it to me, so I can get it in my mind, know what I'm going to do.'

"I'm always trying to get out of the huddle. I can't wait to get out. I've got to get this call and then I've got to walk around and dissect the play. Brian'll sit there and he'll probably be thinking of his child at home, some good moments, and I'm like, 'Excuse me, can you please give us the %$#@# call?'"

"Oh yeah," says Urlacher. "Yeah, B-Rob, I got it. Listen."

GETTING STARTED

Brian Urlacher had been a safety while at New Mexico but starred at middle linebacker in the Senior Bowl prior to the 2000 draft, making that his projected NFL position. But the Bears weren't eager to just throw their prized rookie out at one of the game's most difficult positions, so they put him at the strong-side linebacker position, where his responsibilities would be primarily to play over the tight end and he could ease into the NFL game.

Urlacher lost that starting job to Roosevelt Colvin before the preseason was half over. But he would prove to be a far faster learner than anyone thought. When Barry Minter was injured in the second game of the season, Urlacher became the starting middle linebacker and never looked back.

Brian Urlacher   *AP/WWP*

"He fooled us all," said Dale Lindsey, then the Bears' line-backers coach, now the defensive coordinator for the San Diego Chargers. "He caught on a lot faster than we thought he would. Anyone tells you different is lying to you.

"We started him at outside linebacker because that required the least amount of changes from college. We felt to take a rookie and put him at middle linebacker the first day training camp would be overwhelming. We didn't want to have what happens to quarterbacks put in there right away: lose confidence. But he kept showing us more intelligence, that he was more instinctive. We thought he could command respect."

"The difference between Brian and an average player, and it's the same with [perennial All-Pro linebacker Junior] Seau," says Lindsey, "is that Brian is so quick that he can screw up and still go make a play that the normal guy couldn't even make if he hadn't screwed up."

In the huddle, "we tell them put your hands on your knees and rest," Lindsey says. "Stare at the ground and be an idiot for a second, but when he says 'Listen,' we want your eyes up looking at him so you can hear and see him talking to you. That's what he does. He says 'Listen.' Everybody is alert; they know the defensive huddle call is coming."

HEARING THINGS

Because of their helmets, it's sometimes difficult for players to make out some of the conversations taking place on the field. Then again, maybe it's better that way.

"Somebody's cussing usually" laughs Brian Urlacher. "It's not nice. You might tell 'em, 'What are you doing?!' Most of the time you're yelling at them because it's so loud out there."

Urlacher gets his share of the yelling too. "One day in practice, I blew the call totally and did the wrong thing and Mike Brown yells, 'What the fuck are you doing?'" Urlacher says. "And I said, 'Don't get all moist, Mike,' which he always says.

"It's like, 'Shut up, dude. It's no big deal.'

"If you talk, then you're wasting your breath because you're going to get tired from talking too much. Just keep it short and have some fun. And this is a fun group right here, I'm telling you. All of the guys out there have fun.

"Walt [Harris] would say, 'Come on, Big Time.' He calls everyone 'Big Time.'

"Mike Brown will single out someone, even on his own team, even in practice. Once he says to Marty Booker, 'Book, if you step on me, I'll break your arm.' Just something stupid.

"The last time I was talking to the Minnesota Vikings center, Matt Birk, a little bit. He kept cutting my ass. I said, 'Hey, you're 300 pounds, why do you keep cutting me? You're bigger than I am.'"

Sometimes the talk has an edge, either mean-spirited or part of getting oneself to a higher level emotionally. "I'm always standing next to B-Rob [Bryan Robinson] and that's always interesting," Warrick Holdman says, laughing. "He'll say, 'See that guy right there? I'm going to beat him the next play. Look, he's scared.'

"You hear all kind of things during TV timeouts. There might be a guy on the other team you went to college with, you'll hear 'How's your wife doing? How's your little boy doing?' But then they'll blow the whistle and it's all right, now I'm going to try to beat you."

LEVELS OF THE GAME

Players will tell you that the NFL game gets fast by levels and nothing in college can prepare you for what it is like. There is the shock of so much speed at the first minicamps right after the draft. Then training camp starts, when jobs are won and lost, and the speed jumps exponentially.

The first exhibition game, which for many will be the first time playing against another NFL team, takes the intensity to another level entirely. That happens again when the regular season begins and the games count. Waiting for the fortunate ones will be the playoffs and maybe someday the Super Bowl, played by the best against the best.

"It's fast and it stays fast," says Brian Urlacher. "Games are totally different. My rookie year I practiced and I was like, 'I got this, this isn't too bad.' Then you get in the game and it's so fast.

"It's like you're in the middle of traffic, because you have to weave around and avoid people. You don't want to get hit. I'm trying to avoid people. If I have to hit them, I will, but you really don't want to. You're just trying to go get the guy with the ball."

For linebacker Warrick Holdman, "It's like the first time I went to downtown Chicago and I was walking trying to find, say, the Water Tower and I was getting bumped, everyone is rushing past me and was just confusing. On the field, it's organized confusion. Everything is happening but all you can see is your man and what you have to do."

Multitasking at the NFL level carries into the rest of life too. "I can play Play Station, talking to my girl and on the phone with my mom," Holdman says, laughing. "I do that all the time."

Chapter 2

THE WANNSTEDT YEARS

After the Dallas Cowboys won the Super Bowl following the 1992 season, their defensive coordinator, Dave Wannstedt, was the hottest head-coaching prospect in the NFL. The finalists came down to the Bears and the New York Giants, with Dave's wife Jan ultimately voting strongly for Chicago as a better place to raise the couple's two girls.

Michael McCaskey pursued Wannstedt and hired him after Jimmy Johnson haggled for Wannstedt in a speaker-phone phone call with Wannstedt sitting there in the room while Johnson told McCaskey what Wannstedt had to have. It ultimately didn't work out for either McCaskey or Wannstedt. Some times were tougher than others.

Dave Wannstedt   *AP/WWP*

BLOWUP

The 1995 team had the most potent offense in franchise history, with Erik Kramer setting passing records throwing to Curtis Conway and Jeff Graham, and Rashaan Salaam rushing for more than 1,000 yards and 10 TDs as a rookie. They had reached the playoffs and upset the Vikings the year before and were off to a 6-2 start in '95.

But a porous defense and too many mistakes caused the season to unravel, reaching the low point in a bumbling 16-10 loss at Cincinnati that left the Bears 7-7. The blowup came the next morning and it was a monster.

The team watched special teams film all together, and everyone was in a bad mood. Special-teams coach Danny Abramowicz began to make prefilm comments but was cut off by coach Dave Wannstedt, who snarled, "Just run the damn film!" The film ran but with the room in silence, no coach making remarks, the first time any player could remember such a silence. When the film was finished, someone flicked on the lights and the order was given, "Go to your meetings."

Running back Lewis Tillman was outraged. "What the hell was that?!" Tillman yelled. The room turned to stone. Assistant coaches called for Tillman to shut up, but Tillman persisted with the question that was on everyone's mind: "Have you coaches quit on us?"

Order was finally restored but not before Kramer remarked, "It was unbelievable. It was like *The Exorcist* where I thought stuff was just going to start flying around the room." The Bears won their final two games but still missed the playoffs when San Francisco was upset by Atlanta, and they did not have another winning season until 2001 when they went 13-3.

Erik Kramer   *AP/WWP*

'ZO

Alonzo Spellman came to the Bears in 1992 as their No. 1 draft choice. He left in 1998 after one of the more bizarre Chicago careers ever.

Rarely was his tenure without some hitch. He'd gotten a hefty contract in 1996 when the Bears elected to match an offer from the Jacksonville Jaguars and fans held that against Spellman for some reason, that he wasn't worth the money. As Atlanta Hawk Jon Koncak once said after receiving a surprisingly large contract, "What am I supposed to do, give it back?"

As that 1996 season went along, Spellman's relationship with the Bears soured and spiraled perilously downward. He missed a Dec. 4 practice for personal reasons, but the team said the absence was not excused. When Spellman did show up, coach Dave Wannstedt felt betrayed after supporting the Bears' match of the Jacksonville offer. Wannstedt was critical of Spellman in front of the team and held Spellman out of the starting lineup Dec. 8 against St. Louis.

The situation worsened enormously when Spellman then asked for permission to address the team in private, no coaches. But instead of making the anticipated apology for missing practice, Spellman contradicted Wannstedt's version of the situation. Wannstedt became incensed and their relationship deteriorated further.

It was on the way to becoming far worse. Spellman believed that the team had hired an investigator to look into aspects of his personal life, specifically the background of his wife, a mysterious figure in her own right, with stories beginning to circulate that she was involved in a voodoo cult, or some secret group.

If Spellman was becoming more and more distrustful of the organization, so were the Bears of him. Spellman, despite a well-known aversion to needles, suddenly began sporting unexplained tattoos. In the locker room before the Sept. 1, 1997 Green Bay game, Spellman appeared disoriented.

Soldier Field   *AP/WWP*

According to one story, Spellman was persuaded to attend a meeting of a voodoo group. There he was given a potion that rendered him unconscious, after which members of the cult pricked him with needles, drew some blood and mixed it into another potion, which they drank.

In one cataclysmic week in early '98, Spellman stormed through team offices, ranting and cursing after a meeting with Wannstedt. Several days later he appeared in the office of Ted Phillips and announced that he was retiring, a threat the Bears dismissed.

But the following Monday, Spellman was involved in what was treated as a hostage situation at the home of his publicist, Nancy Mitchell. The incident was resolved with the help of Mike Singletary and Spellman went to Lake Forest Hospital diagnosed as suffering from bipolar disorder, which produces wide extremes in behavior. His stay was brief, ending with him leaving late at night, wandering around in pajama bottoms and no top before police found him.

Trouble dogged the former No. 1 pick, although he did have stints with the Dallas Cowboys, where he had flashes of good play, and the Detroit Lions.

Ironically, the headlines behind his misadventures were drawing attention to the problem of bipolar disorder. 'Zo's difficulties, in the end, unquestionably helped others.

CHECKING OUT

John Thierry was the Bears' No. 1 draft choice in 1994, the 11th player taken overall, which meant some big money for someone not quite used to it yet.

Thierry's rookie contract paid him a signing bonus of $2.5 million, the up-front money of the deal. Linemen Frank Kmet and Todd Burger were in the weight room lifting when Thierry, a country kid from rural Alabama, came in with an envelope and said he needed to know how to open a checking account.

Burger and Kmet along with other players received work-out money, usually $500-$600. So Burger said sure and took Thierry's envelope and opened it as he told Thierry how to go to a bank, fill out a deposit slip and take it to one of the tellers.

Then Burger saw the check. "Holy shit!!!" he yelled.

The amount of the check Thierry was about to walk up to a new-accounts teller with: $1.3 million.

BYE-BYE

Character is always a difficult issue for NFL teams. The Bears, to their credit, have tried to steer toward players of character.

One player found that out in 1995. He was returning to his hotel room with a couple of ladies, neither of whom was his wife, and was on the elevator enjoying their professional talents when the elevator doors opened and Bears first family members Ed and Virginia McCaskey stepped into the elevator.

The player was a former Bear as of the next off season.

DISLIKED

Todd Sauerbrun was a second-round pick in the 1995 draft. He breezed into training camp with his "Hangtime" license plate and one of the strongest punting legs in the NFL, but one of the poorest attitudes from his teammates' perspective.

"I think Todd was the first person we put in a cold shower, took outside [naked] and tied up to the goal post in the snow," says tackle James Williams.

"Todd was an interesting character. He was a spoiled brat, still is. We were out at the Pro Bowl but nothing changed. A lot of times a guy will leave and go somewhere else, then figure out 'This is what I did wrong; I had a little personality glitch.' Todd will never figure that out."

THE WATCH

Frank Kmet was an All-American defensive tackle at Purdue after being the Illinois Player of the Year in 1988 at Hersey High School. But a broken leg in his senior season hurt his NFL chances after he was drafted by the Buffalo Bills in 1992. He eventually wound up with the Bears in 1993, where coach Dave Wannstedt and his staff decided that Kmet's NFL future lay on the other side of the ball.

Kmet went on the Bears' practice squad and eventually was put on the 53-man roster, in the vacancy created when the team released veteran guard Tom Thayer in midseason after Thayer returned from a back injury. A few days before the end of the season, Wannstedt went to Kmet and told him to start attending offensive line meetings now that he was an O-lineman.

Kmet went to his first meeting on Wednesday. On Friday, his third day as an offensive lineman, quarterback Jim Harbaugh came into the meeting room carrying 12 boxes. "Brought you guys a little something for Christmas," he said, passing out one box to each lineman.

The boxes were about the size and appearance of Kleenex boxes and "I thought, 'Geez, this guy's making a million bucks a year and he's giving out Kleenex? What a stiff.'"

Only they weren't Kleenex; they were Rolex watches, inscribed on the back with "Thanks. No. 4" and registered as official sports memorabilia.

"So here I am, on offense three days, and I'm getting this unbelievable watch," Kmet said. "I'm thinking, hey, this offense stuff is pretty cool."

A couple days later, Kmet's phone rang. It was Thayer, who'd blocked for Harbaugh.

"Hey, you got my f-ing watch," the caller growled.

"Tommy was always great to me," Kmet recalls. "So I want him to know that I'm taking good care of his watch."

MOTORMOUTH

The only thing more unstoppable than Minnesota Vikings John Randle's pass rush was John Randle's mouth.

A notorious trash talker with an outrageous sense of humor, Randle would study opponents' personal histories in their teams' media guides, and was rumored to occasionally have the book on the week's opponent on the bench during games. Sometimes against the Bears, though, he goofed.

Matched up against Bears guard Todd Burger, he harassed Burger about Burger's wife Jennifer, doing a little trash talking and taunting. Burger, normally a talker himself, didn't respond. After a few plays, Randle found out why.

"John," a teammate corrected, "Burger's wife is Denise. Jennifer is [left tackle] Andy Heck's wife." It was the only time the Bears remember Randle being at a loss for words.

REGGIE

James "Big Cat" Williams came to the Bears as a defensive tackle, then switched to offense in the early 1990s. By 1994 he had earned his way into the starting lineup at right tackle, which put him on an annual collision course with Green Bay defensive end Reggie White, among the greatest ever to play the game.

Williams would hold his own in their epic battles. But the meetings were not without their doses of sheer terror.

"He wasn't the fastest but just enough that he could give you problems, and then [he had] that underneath move, that 'club' move," Williams says. "I remember before my first start against Green Bay, the Packers had played Dallas on the Monday night before. We were over at Curtis Conway's house, where we'd meet for *Monday Night Football* to eat, drink, cook, and we were sitting there a little after halftime.

"All of a sudden Reggie hit Erik Williams with that club-hook move and dropped him on his shoulders. The whole room got quiet and everybody looked at me. Somebody said, 'Damn, that's going to be you next week.' And it was my first year starting.

"Reggie didn't talk much. But we played on Halloween in that rainstorm in '94 and I was this feisty young guy, gonna make my mark, and I started with the, 'Hey, Superman, whatcha got today? C'mon, you ready to play today?'

"He didn't say a thing. He just raised his head a little and looked at me, and his eyes were red, blood red. I don't think I said another word to him the entire game."

ATTENTION GETTER

Mid-'90s safety Anthony Marshall was miffed at not starting. Asked what he thought he needed to do to convince the Dave Wannstedt coaching staff, Marshall mused, "I think I gotta put a bug in their eye."

OOOH, THAT HURTS

Linebacker Barry Minter, upset at a season-ending loss at Tampa Bay to the Buccaneers, sadly predicted, "A loss like that really sticks in your crotch."

PERSPECTIVE

Chicago never quite seemed to embrace Jim Harbaugh completely, even though he guided the Bears to an 11-5 record and the playoffs in 1990 and 1991. Maybe it was because fans still savored the taste of Jim McMahon and Harbaugh replaced him as well as Mike Tomczak.

Whatever the reason, and whatever the perception outside of the huddle and locker room, Harbaugh was held in very high regard by teammates. He was tough, a leader, and took more batterings than outsiders knew.

"I thought the world of Harbaugh," says Tom Waddle. "I thought he was tougher and a better quarterback than people gave him credit for. He was negatively affected by Ditka, and I don't know if Mike was the right coach for him. But I know he was tough as nails and all the players admired him.

"We played two games back to back in '93 and he got sacked 18 times total, five times on three-step drops even. He was bruised, battered, bleeding, and came back and never once said anything against his O-line. We receivers probably didn't help him too much either. I know the system sure didn't help him. We were trying to run the Dallas Cowboys' vertical passing game and Wendell and I were 'horizontal' receivers."

'ZO

Defensive end Alonzo Spellman, talking about some bad breaks the Bears had been getting one season, observed, "We're 4-7 right now but we could just as easily be 5-3."

TOUGH TIMES

You knew things were bad and down to the bitter end when Spellman proclaimed, "It's time to circle the horses." Spellman was memorable on the field, when he wanted to be.

"He could not work out for months and still look like a Greek god," said tackle James "Big Cat" Williams. "Then I met his sister and she's built just like him: ripped. It was just genetic. When we first met him, everybody said, 'Oh, he's got to be on juice, or something.' Then we started meeting family members.

"Our thing was, if we could have made 'Zo mad every Sunday, he'd be in the Hall of Fame right now. He was the most incredible athlete ever. We were playing Buffalo in '94, and on one play alone, he took a tackle with his right arm, shoved him off; took a guard with his left arm, shoved him off; hit the fullback, knocked him flat, and made the tackle. We said, 'Dude, if you could do that every day, you would be awesome.'

"And he could have. He just did not have the right attitude. In New England in '97, he ran the running back Curtis Martin down from 70 yards. He could do that any time he wanted to. 'Zo was just not that kind of athlete."

WELCOME TO THE NFL

Curtis Enis' NFL career was short, generally unremarkable, and, well, colorful at times. His rookie year he was involved with the Champions for Christ group that included several teammates; his second year he arrived in training camp driving a black, chromed-up Hummer which he declared was just like him, "black and powerful," and after changing his number from 39 to 44, went several days with an extra 4 to become "444." His third year he was put at fullback and reduced to a minor role and wasn't re-signed after the 2000 season.

But his signature moment may have been his first day in '98 training camp. He had held out for 28 days in a convoluted negotiation between the Bears and his agent, and finally was in. Dave Wannstedt at that time had instituted a "bull-in-the-ring" contest before the afternoon practice, a one-on-one type of bout not seen in the NFL. Coaches brought the entire team together after calisthenics and before breaking up would call out one offensive and one defensive player, to meet in a circle formed by the assembled group. The two combatants went at

Curtis Enis   *AP/WWP*

each other on a snap count in a matchup that often served to put fire in the practice, at least for the winning-player's unit.

Enis came out for his first practice and was immediately called out. Against him: veteran linebacker Rico McDonald, a gentleman off the field but one of the most ferocious hitters and meanest members of the defense. Enis fancied himself a tough guy; the coaches yelled, "Go," and Enis was promptly on his back, looking out the earhole of his helmet.

He did pay the defense back the following year. Safety Ray Austin was angering offensive players with hits during camp, living up to his nickname "Advil" for the headaches he caused while with the New York Jets. On the last play of the last day of camp, Austin hit Enis, who'd had enough. He grabbed Austin, ripped off his helmet and head-butted him, leaving Austin with a huge knot on his forehead and in search of some Advil.

DANGEROUS MAN

Olin Kreutz became one of the best centers in the National Football League in a very short time. He established himself also as one of the toughest individuals in a sport of tough men.

"Olin doesn't give the impression, but he is one of the smartest players I've ever been associated with," says tackle James "Big Cat" Williams. "His bad-boy mentality, acting crazy, lot of fun—that's Olin, but he's probably one of the most studious guys I've played with. Olin is the most interesting guy I've played with.

"And Olin was not someone you mess with when he's upset. He has a little bit of a martial arts background, which makes him even more dangerous to go along with that attitude. He's into that kind of martial arts with some sort of grappling. So if Olin gets you on the ground, and doesn't like you, and gets hold of an arm, it's coming out. Separated."

BAD WELCOME

In 1994 the Bears were trying to get to the playoffs and eventually would behind Steve Walsh, and would upset the despised Minnesota Vikings in the first round of the playoffs. But some of their toughest battles were not on the field.

Coach Dave Wannstedt believed in physical practices; the approach had served him well in stints with Jimmy Johnson coaching the Miami Hurricanes and Dallas Cowboys. But the Bears were starting to wear down in '94 and wanted to scale back the constant hitting in practices.

"We elected Trace Armstrong to go up and talk to him, tell him that 'We're a veteran team, we're near the end of the season and you're kicking our asses. Please back off in practice, the guys could use it,'" says Tom Waddle.

"I came in on a Thursday morning and I could hear this loud conversation happening as I'm walking in from the parking lot. I see Wannie and Trace going at each other, and I hear Wannie at one point say, 'Listen, if you don't think you can play for 60 minutes, I'll play Al Fontenot in there.'

"And Trace said, 'That's not the issue, Dave. The issue is that we're a veteran team and we need to back off a little bit. Guys are beat up.' Dave wasn't having any of it, and Trace was sent packing the following year."

HATED GUY

Denver defensive end Neil Smith may have been one of the NFL's best in his prime, but don't sell his act to tackle James "Big Cat" Williams.

"I hated that guy," Williams says. "He tried to poke me in the eye and tried to spit on me, and from that point on I hated him. A couple years after that I did an appearance for Spellman, a softball game, and then Smith comes over, all smiley, 'Hey, how ya doin'?' And I just told him, 'Hey, I don't want to talk with you.'

"I remember thinking, 'I would like to hit that son of a bitch with a bat.'"

"ROOKS"

When Clarence Brooks arrived in 1993 as defensive line coach under coach Dave Wannstedt, his first position-group meeting included Trace Armstrong, Richard Dent, Steve McMichael, William Perry, guys with some time and experience. Brooks, in his first NFL job coming from the University of Arizona where he was an assistant, didn't make a great first impression when he opened by talking about the importance of hustle on defense.

Dent called him "Rooks," as in rookie. Brooks corrected him: "Brooks." "Right," said the Colonel. "OK, Rooks."

MORE RANDLE

The Bears went up to Minneapolis and John Randle, who always had a show ready for them. His prime target: guard Todd Burger, a converted college defensive tackle with a temper and the one whom Randle most often lined up over.

During one timeout, the Bears were coming out of their huddle, the Vikings out of theirs, and all of a sudden, as they near the line, the Bears hear Randle yell to his teammates:

"When I say 'Burger', you say 'Bitch,'" recalls James "Big Cat" Williams. "And off he went with the rest of the Minnesota huddle yelling, 'Burger,' 'Bitch,' 'Burger,' 'Bitch,' 'Burger,' 'Bitch.'

We lost it because it was something you never expected to hear. And he did it about five or six times. All we could do was laugh, and Burger was just pissed, red-faced, ready to kill somebody."

The Vikings in later seasons moved Randle out to defensive end. He was undersized at about 270 pounds and extremely quick, but the move to end wasn't easy. Williams and guard Chris Villarrial were the right side of the Bears' line and when Randle was out there, they got after him, cussin' him, punching him, cheap-shottin' him and getting in his face.

Then Randle jumped back inside to his more natural position of tackle and was over left guard Todd Perry. Perry came back to the huddle after Randle went to tackle, and muttered to Villarrial and Williams, "Hey, cut that crap out. Leave him alone. You don't have to play against him now."

MR. NEGATIVE

Troy Auzenne was the Bears' second-round draft choice in 1992 and eventually became a starting left tackle during the Dave Wannstedt years. He was an excellent pass blocker from his days at Cal. But it was not his pass protection that made him the most memorable Bear to someone who saw more than a decade's worth of them.

"Most memorable was without a doubt Troy Auzenne," says tackle James "Big Cat" Williams. "He was the most negative person I've ever met in my life. Troy could talk you into a stupor. His locker was next to mine, and I've never met a person who, every day, just found something wrong. From the weather to the people, there was always just something wrong. He was a good guy. But I don't know what it was. Everything, EVERYTHING was negative.

"Troy could get to Tony Wise. He could stand around for 10 minutes just talking, about nothing sometimes, and Tony would be red-faced and ready to explode."

Chapter 3

DITKA AFTER XX

Iron Mike Ditka is second only to George Halas in the Pantheon of Bears coaches. Fittingly perhaps, it was the Old Man himself, who'd let Ditka go to the Philadelphia Eagles in 1967, who brought Ditka back in 1982 to restore the roar in his beloved Bears. It worked; the Bears had their only Super Bowl four seasons later and were back among the elite teams in the NFL for the better part of a decade.

How it happened: Ditka was coaching special teams for the Dallas Cowboys and had been thinking for several years about becoming a head coach. The only place he wanted to coach was in Chicago, so he wrote Halas a letter in 1981 in which he said: "I just want you to know that if you ever make a change in the coaching end of the organization, I just wish you would give me some consideration."

Halas did more than that. He hired Ditka in a deal struck around Halas' kitchen table, and the turnaround began almost immediately. That turnaround would go through distinct phases: the makeover of the mind and personnel of the team; the 1985 season and Super Bowl XX; and the aftermath years.

Super Bowl XX was a defining moment in Bears history, in NFL history for that matter, just like the '63 and '40 title games and other landmarks. Since then, however, a lot has happened...

*   *   *   *

Mike Ditka's exit from Chicago traces to Oct. 4, 1992, in the House of Sound, the Hubert H. Humphrey Metrodome in Minneapolis and the home of the Minnesota Vikings. On that date, the 2-2 Bears were in complete control of the Vikings, leading 20-0 early in the fourth quarter, blessed with a first down near midfield due to a roughing penalty on the Vikings, who were demoralized and about to fold.

Then came the call that would change franchise history. Quarterback Jim Harbaugh came to the line with a pass called to running back Neal Anderson and flanked out to the left, hoping to create a mismatch against a linebacker on a surprise fly pattern down the field, a "Double-Seam" call with four receivers going deep.

But Harbaugh saw the Vikings' defensive alignment and decided to audible to a quick hitch pattern, with Anderson to drive off the line, stop and take the normally high-percentage short pass.

The trouble was, Harbaugh had been expressly ordered not to use audibles in the Metrodome because the din of the crowd made it virtually impossible to be sure all the players would hear the call, especially if they were away from the ball the way Anderson was.

"I don't think players were really listening for audibles," said offensive coordinator Greg Landry. "They might have heard but we really had stressed 'no audibles' to them so it may have been that they really weren't paying attention because we weren't calling audibles."

"It was the last thing we discussed [before Harbaugh went on the field]," Ditka said. "The very last thing. If it hadn't been discussed, I wouldn't have a problem."

Harbaugh yelled out the change, Anderson didn't hear it and broke down the field as Harbaugh made his quick drop and threw to where Anderson would have been on the hitch.

Instead, the ball was intercepted by Minnesota safety Todd Scott, who had no one in front of him and went untouched 35 yards for a touchdown. When Harbaugh returned to

Mike Ditka being carried off the field after Super Bowl XX.
AP/WWP

the sidelines, Ditka went berserk. He lambasted Harbaugh verbally, stalked away, then came back with another blast of rage.

The Vikings suddenly came alive, as did their fans, and rolled off two more scores for a 21-20 win. The loss fueled Ditka's fury. "Audibles are part of the game," he said. "But audibles are to get from a bad play to a better play, not from a good play to a worse play. We went backwards."

Most of the players indeed weren't expecting any audible, certainly not in that situation.

"We went into the game and Ditka had a mandate: no audibles," says Tom Waddle. "Because of the noise, we are not going to audible, regardless. If we send in a play that doesn't look like it's going to work, eat it. If it's a pass play, throw it out of bounds. Just hold onto the football. But we're not going to audible."

"The funny thing is that the audible was the right call, in another situation. But Neal wasn't looking for an audible because we'd been told we're not going to. Jim audibled to a 'hitch' and Neal kept running, Todd Scott picked it and ran it back for the touchdown. The irony was that it was a good audible, just not an approved audible."

The incident refused to go away. The Vikings game was followed by a bye week, so after a week of questions upon questions, Ditka and the Bears went into Monday getting ready to look ahead for the Oct. 18 game against Tampa Bay. But The Audible refused to die and it was about to take Ditka down even further.

At the Monday press conference, the first question was not about the Bucs, practice or anything else. It was about The Audible. Ditka blew up.

"We've had probably 400 plays this season," Ditka said, seething. "And all you sons of bitches can talk about is one damn play."

Phil Theobald, veteran columnist for the *Peoria Journal-Star*, wasn't in any better mood than Ditka. "Coach," Theobald said, standing up from his desk, gathering his papers and walking out right past Ditka and the podium, "I have been insulted by enough people in my time and I told myself the last time Bobby Knight did this kind of thing that I wasn't going to be called a son of a bitch ever again."

The room, and Ditka, were floored. Finally, Ditka stammered, "Fine." Theobald left, and less than three months later, so did Ditka.

NOT A HARBAUGH FAN

Mike Ditka's relationship with quarterback Jim Harbaugh ended on a national stage with that famous blowup in the Metrodome, Ditka in Harbaugh's face over changing a play call. But their association didn't get off to an especially great start either.

Ditka in fact argued strenuously against drafting Harbaugh in the first place. Ditka was never one to spend too much time scouting college players, but he was big watcher of college bowl games when he had time. He had seen Harbaugh not play especially well in a Michigan bowl appearance at the end of the 1986 season and concluded that Harbaugh was not a big-game player.

When draft day arrived, Ditka wanted defensive end/ linebacker Alex Gordon. Player personnel chief Bill Tobin wanted Harbaugh because of concerns, for good reason, over the health of Jim McMahon. Michael McCaskey cast the tiebreaking vote and Harbaugh became only the second quarterback drafted by the Bears in the first round in 36 years.

WHAT MIGHT HAVE BEEN

Players on the Super Bowl team savor the accomplishment but almost to a man believe they should have made it to more than one final game. Nowhere was that feeling stronger than in 1986 when the Bears went 14-2 and set an NFL record for fewest points allowed (187).

The problem was at quarterback. Jim McMahon couldn't stay healthy, Doug Flutie was brought in, and disaster followed in the form of a playoff upset loss to the Washington Redskins.

"All our people were hurt and they decide to bring Flutie in, that he'll be our starter," says Mike Hartenstine. "They couldn't just put Flutie back there in the pocket because he was too short, so they had to roll him [out] and now our offensive linemen have to learn all new blocking assignments and techniques for the game. For that one game.

"When I really knew we were in trouble was when [offensive coordinator] Ed Hughes was sitting in the locker room before the game. Ed is signaling Flutie the plays the way he would be in the game. He signals about 20 plays and Flutie got maybe two right out of 20. And I'm sitting there thinking, this is going to be our starting quarterback for the game?

"Granted our defense didn't do great, but I'm thinking I can't believe this, two out of 20 plays right."

WAR GAMES

The situation in the Middle East was deteriorating in '91 and several Bears were talking about it in the weight room. One was guard Mark Bortz, a serious student of warfare, and the question was put to Bortz: What do you think the percent chances are of us going to war in the Gulf?

"Probably 70-30," Bortz surmised.

William Perry saw it differently. "I think it's more like 75-35," Perry said.

"Fridge," one teammate pointed out, "that's 110 percent."

Fridge reflected, then emphatically declared, "Well, if you go to war, it SHOULD be 110 percent!"

COVERAGE SACKED

Donnell Wollford was one of the Bears' two first-round picks in the 1989 draft and he was an instant starter and eventual Pro Bowl cornerback, one of the Bears' better pass defenders in the 1990s. But his time with the Bears and coach Ditka got off to a very rocky start.

After a Bears loss late in Woolford's rookie season, Ditka announced publicly that Woolford "apparently can't cover anybody."

Harsh words for a young player on a team that was floundering for more reasons than his coverage. But Woody "took it more or less as a challenge," he said. "I didn't understand it at first because when you come up from college, people say things that maybe they don't mean. Ditka's comments really went in one ear and out the other, but it was shocking for a coach to say something like that about a player. Then I found out that's the way he is, so I don't even think about it.

"Except," Woolford said with a sly smile, "I knew it wasn't true. If it was, they wouldn't have drafted me."

IN AWE

Think that NFL players are used to seeing stars and aren't affected by what they see around them? Maybe. But not if it was Mike Ditka.

"I remember driving to Halas Hall and walking down the stairs to the meeting rooms and just being terrified because of all the stars who were there," says Tom Waddle. "It was like you died and went to football heaven, with Dent, Hampton, Singletary, that offensive line, and then Ditka walks in. You don't ever forget that."

Not that Ditka was without flaw in how he ran things. Indeed, one of his strengths—loyalty—arguably was one of his weaknesses, too.

"Mike was loyal to a fault and probably stayed with guys longer than he should have," Waddle says. "But that was just the way he knew. So what would happen is he would keep guys on maybe a little long and then say things about them when things didn't work out, which burned him anyway."

ALIENATION

Mike Ditka brought the players together after his arrival in 1982. He transformed the mood, the chemistry, the physical makeup of the team and fused it into a potent club to wield against the rest of the NFL.

But five years later, he lost many of them. The strike of 1987 sent players out on an informational picket line and the Bears brought in replacement players, the so-called "Spare Bears." While Buddy Ryan in Philadelphia was contemptuous of the replacement players with the Eagles, Ditka declared that the "real Bears" were the ones wearing the uniform on Sunday.

After the strike was resolved and went away, the residue of perceived betrayal did not.

"In '87, he alienated certain players," says Dan Hampton. "It's like in a marriage, if you find your wife is cheating on you; you can stay together but it'll never be the same again. It was never the same again. Even though we had the best record in football in '88, it wasn't the same. By 1989, we were getting to the point of being exposed, and by '90 we were old and beat up, just meaner than everybody else, so we won the division, but that was it."

HOW BIG CAT BECAME "BIG CAT"

"The first time I came up to the Bears after signing as a free agent in 1991, Dave McGinnis, who was our linebackers coach, and Ditka were standing out in front of Halas Hall," James Williams recalls. "When I got out of the limo, Dave said, 'Damn, that's the biggest cat I've ever seen in my life.'"

"Somehow that stuck and I became 'Big Cat.' Now I wouldn't be surprised if half the young guys on the team didn't know my real name."

"OVERACHIEVERS"

Mike Ditka was sometimes without equal as a motivator. Other times...

After the 1991 season, which ended with a 52-14 annihilation at the hands of the reviled 49ers, followed by an upset loss in the playoffs to Dallas, Ditka perhaps unwittingly alienated his players for what would prove to be a disastrous last time. He made a comment after the season that a lot of the players were "overachievers" and that he was "just playing the hand I was dealt," which many interpreted as a slap at team president Michael McCaskey and personnel chief Bill Tobin, with whom Ditka often feuded. Unfortunately the players were the ones who felt stung.

"If you have a coach saying, 'These guys are sending me a bunch of overachievers' and 'this is the hand I'm dealt,'" said quarterback Jim Harbaugh, "there's not a lot of harmony there, you know? There's no doubt about it. Guys talked about that a lot."

Not nicely either.

"It's kind of a slam," Harbaugh said. "Tom Waddle is a good player. How is he an overachiever? You're either good or you're not. It's tough to read that 'You guys aren't that good' or 'You're the hand that I'm dealt,' then turn around and tell us, 'Hey, you guys really are good. Let's go out and win this game'. It's a contradiction at the least. Why do you make those two different statements?"

"It's convenient," Harbaugh said. "If you lose, it's 'I didn't have the players.' And if you win, well, 'I motivated 'em.'"

Iron Mike didn't earn himself locker-room points either with a scathing comment in the Halas Hall hallway during Pro Bowl voting earlier that season.

"Nobody here can [urinate] in the direction of the Pro Bowl," Ditka growled.

SHOUTING MATCHES

Mike Ditka got into his players' faces. And they occasionally got into his. Ditka the ex-player didn't have a problem with that.

"I don't know how many times I was in the middle of a fight between 'Horne and Ditka," says Tom Waddle. "Those guys would have to be pulled apart on the sideline. They would be screaming and m-f'ing each other and afterwards 'Horne would go back to him and say, 'Coach, I didn't mean anything by that.'

"And Ditka would say, 'Hey, what happens on the field stays on the field.' And how refreshing was that?"

SEEING IS DISBELIEVING

The 1988 playoff meeting between the Philadelphia Eagles of Buddy Ryan and the Mike Ditka Bears was memorable for many reasons, but the main one was that no one actually "saw" the entire game.

The game, won by the Bears, has come to be known in NFL lore as the Fog Bowl, for the lakefront fog that rolled in during the game and obscured most of the action from the fans and even the players in some instances.

"The Fog Bowl was unbelievable," says Dave McGinnis, now coach of the Arizona Cardinals, then the Bears' linebackers coach. "You couldn't see anything. It was such a surreal feeling. Plus it was a big game, and you had Buddy coming back. There were so many elements to it and then for the fog to come rolling in over the south end, it was an unbelievable feeling.

"The further and further you get away from it....We've got Louis Zendajas on our staff in Arizona, and he kicked those four field goals for Philadelphia. He and I laugh about that game a lot. He's got a huge picture of him kicking a field goal into 'the white.' You can't see anything."

HANGING ON

Wide receiver Tom Waddle is a classic Bears success story. He was an undrafted free agent out of Boston College, discovered and signed by scout Rod Graves, who would go on to head personnel for the Bears and eventually become general manager of the Arizona Cardinals. But it wasn't a straight line into the NFL once Waddle started out.

"I had three really strong camps in '89-90-91," Waddle says. "But when you make it to the last cut, Ditka would tell you, 'This is the hardest time, but when you come the next day, bring your playbooks because not all of you are going to make it.'

"When you'd drive down Washington Rd., you learned quickly that if your position coach was standing out there on cut day, you were in trouble. In '89 I pulled in and kind of expected to see my guy there. In '90 I didn't know if he was

going to be there, and he was. In '91 I was sure he wasn't going to be there, and he was.

"I would go up the steps, and there's this L turn in the stairs. And I had this irrational fear that not only was Ditka going to cut me, but he was going to jump across the desk and beat the shit out of me. So I would go into the office prepared not only to

*Former Bears
Mickey Pruit
(52) and Maurice
Douglass (37)
celebrate in the fog
during the famed
Fog Bowl, a 1988
playoff matchup
in which the
Bears defeated the
Eagles at Soldier
Field.
AP/WWP*

get cut, but also to get beaten up by the coach, for some strange reason. I have no idea what that was all about; I just remember going into his office shaking.

"The third year he cut me after being the leading receiver in camp and I went up there ready to whip his ass, because I knew he was going to cut me. Obviously that wasn't possible physically and a good move for my job. He cut me but told me I was going to be back on the roster because Wendell Davis is going to go on IR.

But in Waddle's first game ('91) he was on the sidelines, admiring the game, and admiring himelf in uniform as the game was going on. He was waving to his brother halfway through the second quarter when it happened.

"WADDLE!" Ditka roared.

Startled, Waddle ran over and got the word: "You gotta go in," Ditka commanded.

"WHY?! WHAT'S WRONG?" Waddle yelled in disbelief.

"Anthony Morgan is hurt and we don't have anyone else," Ditka said, ending the discussion."

"That was an inauspicious beginning to my career," Waddle says.

LIFE SAVERS

After Mike Ditka had his heart attack, Hampton and Steve McMichael got into his best cigars and liquor cabinet. The two went through a number of vintage vices over a period of time. Finally Ditka came back. But that didn't deter the two miscreants.

"What are you two doing?!" Ditka challenged when he came back and found the two in his office puffing on two of his best stogies.

After a long pull on the Cubans: "We're saving your life," they answered.

JIMMY, WHAT WERE YOU THINKING?

By mid-1988, quarterback Jim Harbaugh was getting restless. He was the Bears' No. 1 draft choice the year before but wasn't getting on the field much behind Jim McMahon and Mike Tomczak. So he came up with another idea.

He began badgering special teams coach Steve Kazor, insisting that he wanted to get out on the field and cover kicks.

"That idiot," says Glen Kozlowski. "He's got the gloves on, getting all psyched up and ready to be the tough guy. I was out for a play after hurting my knee on the previous punt, so I isolated on Harbs.

"He's going down the field yelling like a madman, and he gets just jacked. I mean, jacked. Somebody blindsides him and he goes flying through the air all the way out of bounds. His helmet's turned around and he's looking out the earhole.

"Ya' know, Harbs never chirped about covering kicks again."

McMICHAEL-WEIRD, OR...?

"The most eccentric teammate by far—and I'm sure he's going to get all the votes—is Steve McMichael," says receiver Tom Waddle. "Cap [Boso] was a space cadet, just kind of out there, a great player who worked his ass off. But you'd be in the middle of a deep conversation with him and all of a sudden he'd look at you and say, 'Do you find me sexy?' Just whacked out stuff like that. 'Absolutely, Cap.'

"But I didn't speak to McMichael for two years out of fear and respect. I got there in '89 and don't think I talked to any of the veterans until I stepped on the field. I just stayed out of their way, kept my head down and walked past guys as fast as I could. It was truly an era when you didn't speak unless you were spoken to. You remember the days when McMichael recognized you and said, 'Hey, kid, how are ya?' Of course, there were some expletives thrown in.

"He was eccentric in a good way. As strange as it sounds, he was kind of a stabilizing force for our team. He was someone everyone looked to in a tight situation to make a big play. The greatest example of that was stripping Blair Thomas of the football against the Jets on Monday night. They were running out the clock, Pat Leahy missed a short kick, and with a minute and a half left, Thomas went through the line, McMichael just reached around and ripped the ball out."

MING

Steve McMichael was one of the most colorful Bears of the 1980s and early '90s. He'd been cut by the New England Patriots and picked up by the Bears and Ditka, eventually having the last laugh on the Pats by helping destroy them in Super Bowl XX.

"Ming," a hardscrabble Texan, was great on camera and a really intelligent guy. When he got on camera he understood that for notoriety, he had to push the envelope a little bit and he did. So he really developed a schtick and a persona that was signature.

But Steve was "the best football player that I ever played with," says Trace Armstrong. "Steve had great ability, but he didn't have dominant ability, yet he was a dominant player for a long time. He did it by working at it.

"I played with Steve for five years and he never missed a practice. They would drain 60 cc. of fluid off his knee Wednesday morning and he'd be out there practicing Wednesday afternoon."

McMichael enjoyed some off-field celebrity as part of the media he so richly despised, culminating with his installation as a color(ful) commentator on Channel 5, the NBC affiliate. That gig ended after a series of hijinks that included the on-camera snipping of host Mark Giangreco's tie with a pair of scissors.

"Steve was probably one of the toughest guys I ever played with," Armstrong says. "But he had this Hollywood style, too. He bought a Rolls-Royce convertible, red with a white interior and a white top. I'm going in to work one morning and here comes this red convertible, big guy driving with long hair flapping in the breeze, and this little chihuahua he's holding as he's driving.

"And the chihuahua's got some kind of outfit on. That was vintage Ming."

MORE MING

"We've got leaders," cornerback Lemuel Stinson said during a difficult stretch of 1992. "Steve McMichael is a leader in his own way. Violent, but a good leader."

TURNCOAT

Jim McMahon left the Bears and wound up with the San Diego Chargers when they faced the Bears in a 1989 preseason game. In the second half, Bears quarterback Jim Harbaugh noticed that signal-caller Mike Tomczak was signaling Bears offensive plays. But he wasn't signaling them to the Bears' offense on the field.

Harbaugh looked across the field and saw McMahon standing next to the Chargers' defensive coordinator and he blew up.

"I said, 'Hey! What are you doing?'" Harbaugh says. "Tomczak just sort of blustered and flustered, saying, 'Hey, it was only for one play. Big deal.' But I could never figure out what he was doing that for or why. I still don't know."

FIRST IMPRESSIONS

James "Big Cat" Williams was a Bears fixture for more than a decade, an undrafted free agent who came in as a defensive tackle

Jim Mcmahon   *AP/WWP*

and left as one of the all-time great offensive linemen despite playing on poor teams. But he had to overcome some tough first impressions of teammates.

"I hated McMichael when I first got there, but he kind of grew on me," Cat says. "He and Mark Bortz I thought were just the biggest rednecks."

"It took me a while to realize what kind of guy Bortz really was. He was smart. He was a lot smarter than I thought he was at first, and when I first got there, I thought he was just the dumbest country redneck I'd ever met in my life. I think I was just waiting for him to slip up and say 'nigger' one day.

"Bortz knew how to push the little buttons. He never overstepped the bounds but he knew how to push you and get on your nerves. He didn't mean anything by it; it was just him. And once I got to know Bortz, Bortz was all right.

"McMichael was a little different. I never knew where he was coming from. He was old-school, said what he wanted, did what he wanted, and I found it interesting as well as obnoxious. He thought he was a little smarter than everybody else, 'You can't tell me anything. I can do everything.'

"He just walked around with his chest puffed out with that little ugly damn dog. He'd unzip his jacket and that stupid dog's head would poke out. I just wanted to crush that stupid dog. I didn't hate the dog; I hated him with the dog."

TIGHT FIT

Tight end Jim Thornton earned the nickname "Robocop" for his physique, which he didn't mind showing off. But it sometimes required some creative wardrobe management.

Robo found out that he needed a collared shirt for a function when he arrived at Glen Kozlowski's house. Koz told him to go up and help himself to anything in his closet that fit.

"Robo came back down with a shirt that I must have worn when I was in 10th grade when I was probably 110 pounds," Koz said. "I mean, it was like that shirt was painted on."

Jim Harbaugh offered a suggestion. "Robo, you were supposed to go in Koz's closet, not his kid's."

Remembers Koz: "And my oldest was six or seven at the time."

"OPEN THE DAMN DOOR!"

Ron Rivera and Glen Kozlowski were roommates in Platteville. One night Dan Hampton was among those coming back well after curfew, when the doors were locked and you'd probably get fined for coming in late. Hampton started tossing pebbles at the window to get them to come down and open the door for him.

The pebble tapping finally woke the two up. They looked down and saw Hampton. "[Screw] you," they said. "We're sleeping."

They went back to bed and a minute later the window shattered as a huge rock came flying in, glass everywhere.

"Get down here right now and open the g— d— door!" Hampton roared.

"We went down and opened the door for him," Kozlowski says. "Right away.

"And the beauty of the whole thing is that he wasn't going to practice then. He'd just sit around in those stupid football pants cut off like shorts and T-shirt that he cut the sleeves and waist out of and wore the shorts really high."

TOUGH CROWD

It wasn't especially easy to break in with the Bears of the 1980s and even when you did, it could be rough. Tom Waddle was trying to make the team as an undrafted free agent rookie, and during one wide receivers meeting, Waddle spoke up and asked a question about what coaches were explaining.

"What do you care, rookie?" veteran Dennis McKinnon challenged. "Your ass is gone in a week anyway."

Waddle did more than survive the week. He came back from being cut more than once and went on to be one of the most productive receivers in Bears history, with 173 catches.

McKinnon would finish with 182.

MEDICAL MARVEL

Cap Boso was running a really bad fever one night and got dehydrated. So he hit upon the idea of filling a bathtub with ice and water to try to break the fever. He jumped in and immediately became one giant cramp. The cramping caused him to hunch forward so that suddenly his nose and mouth were under water and he was about to drown. Fortunately he got out of the tub and into a hospital.

HAMP KNOWS HE'S DONE

Dan Hampton had a long and distinguished Bears career, beginning as the fourth overall pick of the 1979 draft and finishing in 1990. When the end came, he knew it.

"Alan Page would say everybody's a beanbag. Every time you go out and lay it on the line, you take out one bean. Sooner or later, you're out. That's how I was at the end of my career. At the end of it, I could not have played one more quarter. That was the way I wanted it. I was out of beans."

The beans ran out against the Raiders in 1990.

"They kept pitching the ball and going left, and I'd never been hooked in my entire life, and [guard Steve] Wisniewski kept hooking me. He got to the shoulder about four times and drove me off the ball two or three yards, which I'd seen other people have happen, but I'd never had that before. That was like sticking a knife in me. I thought, I'm done.

"I remembered back when I came in and Tommy Hart, a great speed rusher, was through and people saying 'the old gray mare ain't what she used to be.' Well, I was the old gray mare. I could not believe I could be hooked."

CELEBRITY STATUS

Tight end James Thornton was among the more recognizable Bears, if not for his facial features, certainly for his biceps and forearms, exceptional even in a world of large limbs. Such were they that they earned him the nickname "Robocop." And he didn't shrink from displaying them, in a manner of speaking.

Robo was driving with a few teammates in the car one evening when a car full of fans pulled alongside. "Robo, Robo," they called out, trying to get Thornton's attention. Finally Robo rolled up the window of the car, muttering, "I hate all this attention they start paying to you," Thorton complained.

"Well," chided receiver Glen Kozlowski, "maybe if you didn't have 'Robo 80' as your license plate..."

The boys were at a hockey game and fans kept coming over to Robo for autographs. "I wish they'd stop asking for autographs," Robo complained.

"And he was wearing a jacket with 'Robocop 80' on the back! I looked at him and said, 'Are you going to make me say it again?'" Koz said.

NOT-SO-OFFENSIVE LINEMAN

The Bears' offensive line of tackles Jim Covert and Keith Van Home, guards Tom Thayer and Mark Bortz, and center Jay Hilgenberg was arguably the greatest in franchise history. Bortz, Covert and Hilgenberg went to Pro Bowls and were the core of the NFL's dominant power rushing offense of the 1980s and into the early 1990s. And each had his own personality.

"I used to stand in the huddle next to 'Home and he'd get tired and lean on me," recalls Tom Waddle. "So you've got this six-foot-eight behemoth leaning on my little six-foot, 180-pound ass and it looked crazy. I thought I had a great rapport with those offensive linemen because I was the same kind of athlete as a lot of them, which wasn't great. So we had this mutual respect level.

"I never wanted to leave the field because there was someone like Mark Bortz there who played with a muscle completely pulled off the pelvis in his groin. Most people would have had to be sedated and spend time in the hospital. He's out there grinding it out. I get hit and who am I not to come back to the huddle when you've got this guy doing that?

"He would never acknowledge that he was hurt. He had too much pride and was too tough a guy. He didn't say a whole lot. He just kind of grunted."

"They all were tough in their own way. Bortz didn't really want to fight you. He just wanted to beat you up from whistle to whistle, and he did a great job of that. 'Home was someone who wouldn't take any grief from anybody.

"Jay was kind of the quarterback of the line. Bortz and 'Horne were the enforcers."

GAME MISPLANS

Da Coach and offensive coordinator Greg Landry sometimes bickered over playcalling. But they weren't the only ones.

"It seemed like a lot of people weren't on the same page—Greg and Mike, Greg and [receivers coach] Vic Rapp, Greg and Johnny [Roland, running backs coach]," Harbaugh says. "It seemed like it was different things all the time. Everybody had different ideas how they wanted things to work. I don't think everybody agreed on the right way to do things. It created problems.

"During the week, you'd practice three different ideas or whatever, then come Sunday, Greg would be calling the plays he wanted, and you weren't always doing the same thing in the game that you were doing during the week. There seemed to be conflict within the coaching staff, with the front office. The players felt at the time like they weren't the players the coaches wanted."

CHEATING

Golf at the Midlane Country Club in north suburban Wadsworth has been a Bears standard for years. And it has seen its share of hijinks.

A lot of the players took up golf and started playing at Midlane, which also meant that they weren't always very good. That didn't stop them from competing and doing anything within the rules—and beyond—to win.

In fact, creative cheating was sometimes in order and a goal in itself; what can you get away with? And with the stakes sometimes reaching into the hundreds of dollars per hole as the rounds wore on, players pushed the limits.

Glen Kozlowski was caught in the act once. Playing with Neal Anderson and Cap Boso, Koz hit one into the rough near a green. He was in amid some small trees and out of sight—or so he thought.

A member of the foursome, who shall remain anonymous, remembers: "I'm watching a ways off, waiting for Koz before I hit, and all I can see are his feet. All of a sudden a hand comes down, picks up the ball, then the club swoops down like a swing, and a little later the ball flips up onto the green.

"Koz comes out of the bushes: 'I couldn't see where it went; where'd it go?' Somebody said, 'Wow, it's up by the pin. Great shot.' I couldn't let Cap lose the hole on a hand mashie, so I told Cap and he goes flying across the green, Koz takes off laughing, and Cap catches him and they go wrestling all over the place, yelling. I don't know if we even finished the round, but that was golf with Koz."

Complete lie, says Koz.

"That's total bull!" Kozlowski rebuts. "He made that up. Harbs did that, not me!"

"See, what I did, I was in a place where I had no shot and yeah, I threw it out. Cap's yellin', 'You can't do that!' I said, 'Hey, I didn't have a shot. What was I supposed to do? And yeah, I threw it. But it was a great throw!'"

SPEAK UP

Cornerback Lemuel Stinson, asked if he intended to discuss his situation with the coaches, said, "We'll get together and conversate on things."

THE WHITE GUY

Tom Waddle took his share of knocks. Some had to do with the color of his skin. So did some of the compliments.

"Defensive backs all saw me as this slow little white guy and for some reason thought the way to play me was to beat the stuffing out of me at the line of scrimmage. So I probably saw more bump-and-run coverage than most guys.

"There were some overtly racist things, more in the early years until you earn people's respect. There were some things that weren't politically correct today. I can honestly say that I did not stoop to that level, although I did try to bite Benny Blades' finger off.

"I unfortunately crossed his path and Joey Browner's. Joey was six three, 235 and brought the hammer. Wasn't the friendliest guy. And Blades was just out there to hurt you.

"I was playing Deion Sanders, who was a great guy, in '91 or '92 and had five catches, 70-some yards and a touchdown on the day. After the game I'm feeling good about myself and here comes Deion Sanders up to me. He wasn't a mouthy guy, a classy guy who worked hard out there. He says, 'Waddle.'

"I said, 'Yes, Mr. Sanders?'

"'Waddle, you're the best white wide receiver I've ever played against,' Sanders said."

Waddle was flying high. But not for long.

"I go into the locker room feeling good, walk over to John Mangum, probably my best friend on the team, and he says, 'Great game. You had some catches, yards, you scored, and we got the win,'" Waddle recalls.

"I said, 'John, that's not even the best part.' I told him Deion had come up to me and told me I was the best white wide receiver he's played against.

"He kind of looked at me, laughed, and in that Southern drawl of his, says, 'Well, let's see. There's you, Eddie McCaffrey and Ricky Proehl. Shoot, there's only three of you in the league.'"

JUST A LITTLE MORE MING

McMichael provided his own form of rookie orientation for young Bears in 1986. The rookies were in a small room next to the locker room, away from the veterans. McMichael blasted open the door, stalked into the room and began pounding his head with his helmet.

Blood was coming down and McMichael was beating himself, bellowing, "You better be ready!" Then he stalked back out of the room.

No one spoke at first. The rooks looked around nervously at each other, until finally No. 1 pick Neal Anderson, in his Florida drawl, observed what they were all thinking: "Ah don' know what the hay-ell that means," Anderson said, "but that boy's a fool."

PLAYERS "STRIKE"

The Bears were affected like everyone else by the labor problems that cut into the 1982 and 1987 seasons, shortening them to nine and 15 games respectively. But the Bears staged a work stoppage of their own in 1991 as well.

The players were fed up with not having a decent indoor practice facility. When the weather was intolerable outside, they were forced to get on buses and ride to an area high school and use the gymnasium there, practicing in basketball shoes with full pads and on a basketball court.

When "practice" was over, it sometimes took two hours to bus back to Halas Hall in rush-hour traffic. That meant arriving occasionally as late as 7 p.m., still in pads, sweaty and still needing to shower and dress before going home at the end of a 13- to 14-hour day during the season.

"It really whether they want to admit it, wore our team out," says defensive end Trace Armstrong.

So the players staged their "strike." They went out to practice fully dressed and ready to play. They went through stretching exercises, then as a group turned and walked off

Neal Anderson
AP/WWP

the field and back into the locker room at Halas Hall in Lake Forest.

Ditka, who had alienated himself from much of the team in 1987 by declaring that the strike-breaking players were "the real Bears," was furious. He and the other coaches tried to get into the locker room while the players were taking their

stuff off, yelling that they needed to practice and get some work done.

Mike Singletary got up and stood outside the door and didn't move. "You guys," Singletary told the coaches, holding his ground, "shouldn't come in here right now."

They didn't.

ROOMIES

Guard Kurt Becker and receiver Glen Kozlowki were assigned as roommates. Bad pairing, for the room's sake.

Kozlowski was rehabbing an injured knee in 1986, had his leg in a cast and was talking to his wife on the phone. All of a sudden Becker jumped on his back and started pulling Koz's head back, demanding that Koz tell his wife "Who's your daddy? Who's your daddy? Tell her who's your daddy"

Koz escaped, but the first stone had been cast. That night, while Becker slept, Koz wrapped blankets around Becker's feet and set them on fire. "Oh man," Koz marvels. "Those things went up like nothing I've ever seen. He's running around the room yellin' and screamin' and I thought he was going to die."

The next day, Becker snuck up behind his roomie and put him in a wrestler's sleeper hold and rendered Koz completely unconscious. But again, Becker had to sleep sometime, so Koz waited.

That night, after Becker'd finished the contents of a number of beverage bottles, Koz began firing the bottles against the cinderblock wall, just above Becker's head. Becker was comatose so he never woke up, until the next morning when he had to crawl out of bed over a bunch of broken glass and cut himself all up.

"Then [trainer] Freddie Caito comes around and makes us shake hands and promise to stop it," Koz says. "Too bad. We were having fun together. And hey, we were just getting started."

CLUELESS

Quarterback Jim Harbaugh lost his wallet in Glen Kozlowski's car. What was remarkable was that it had $1,200 in it. What was more remarkable was that Harbaugh didn't miss it for three weeks.

Mike Singletary   *AP/WWP*

"I think I lost my wallet," Harbaugh told Kozlowski one day after practice.

"It wasn't that Harbs didn't miss $1,200," Koz says. "It was that he never went into his wallet so he didn't miss it. That's how clueless Harbs was."

FAREWELL

Pro football is a business. Players know it. Coaches know it. Fans know it. But when Mike Ditka left the Bears, "that was hard for me," recalls Tom Waddle. "When he left, for a lot of us, the wind kind of came out of the sails. The game had not become such a transient business and guys were still with their teams. So it was the passing of an era.

"And we weren't that bad a team. We weren't that bad. We just couldn't come through at the right times sometimes."

HAMPS CHRONOLOGY

For most of the 1980s the Bears seemed invincible, and for much of it they were. But more went out of the team in the early successful seasons than many recognized.

"Every year's team's chemistry is different," Hall of Fame defensive lineman Dan Hampton says. "Into '84, we were still bulletproof and young. But by the time we'd won the Super Bowl, we'd shown a lot of age in two years. McMahon was more beat up, Walter was going from a guy averaging five a carry to three and a half, Covert's back was starting to go out, my legs, McMichael's knees...

"Going into the '86 season I told the guys on defense, 'We are going to have to be the ones that do it. Buddy's gone; we can't cry. And if we come in fourth or 10th or whatever on defense, everybody'll say it was Buddy Ryan.' So I wanted to make sure we all understood where we stood.

"In '87 we still had the nucleus of a good team, but it wasn't the same due to the fact that we practiced at such a clip, that we had such egos and pride, that we played every day hammer and tong. We didn't want to go 10-6 and just be good enough for the playoffs. In '86 we went 14-2. You do that and you're burning a lot of gas.

"By the '88 season, Otis was hurt and Wilbur was gone and we were playing with Rivera and Morrissey. Good solid players, but they didn't give us that great ability of Otis and Wilbur. Todd Bell wasn't the same, and Fridge had gained about 100 pounds and wasn't the same player.

"And Vince Tobin was not the same type of factor Buddy was. With Vince's ideology of more bend-don't-break, our defense wasn't as dangerous. In '84, '85, we were an 'offensive' defense. I always remember Bill Parcells and Chuck Noll telling me they had huge problems preparing for us.

"But by '87 we had slowed down enough to where we were almost blockable on occasion. In the 49er game, in the '88 championship, they were running one- and two-man patterns on us and staying in 'max-protection.' And you get two helmets on me and McMichael, with Richard out of the game, even with Singletary, we didn't have great players doing things. So our window of opportunity was shot.

"When Buddy left, Fridge went to 400 and became a nonfactor after about '86. Certain players, if you don't challenge them, will take what they can get. I'm not dogging Fridge; I love Fridge. But by the middle of the '87 season he was nowhere near the player he was his rookie year. He had been a real solid player but now was getting knocked off the ball."

In 1987 the Bears were preparing to face the Raiders. Perry had not been playing especially well for a while, and the coaches made a change.

Tobin came in the meeting room and said, "Hampton, you're starting at right tackle."

McMichael and Hampton, who were more mobile than Perry and loved running stunts and games together, looked at each other.

"We had a good game, beat the Raiders 6-3, from that point on, it was me at defensive tackle, which really made for a better overall defense inside, with guys like Al Harris at left end and then Tyrone Keys. People don't always remember that in the '88 [NFC] championship game, the Niners just had Jerry Rice and John Taylor out on two-man patterns and the eight other guys in blocking for Montana.

"It was a great era, but like all good things, it started decaying from inside. It was a good run but kind of sad how it ended."

Chapter 4

1985

The 1985 Bears rank among the greatest teams, not only in franchise history, but also in the annals of NFL legend. The confluence of coaches, players and every other factor was like few others anywhere anytime, and there are untold events and stories behind the headlines.

DALLAS WHO?

The Dallas Cowboys were just so much road kill for the 1985 Bears, 44-0 losers to the Bears in a game that proved beyond any doubt that this was a team, if not for the ages, then certainly for the 1985 season.

Unfortunately, the Cowboys brought some of their fate on themselves.

"The first game of the year, we had to come from behind to win [against Tampa Bay]," says Dan Hampton. "Then we kind of got in synch and got going.

"But I will never forget getting ready for Dallas. Ditka was from Dallas and we'd played them a couple times and lost. We thought that if we don't do anything else, we need to win this game for Ditka. By then he had gotten to where we loved him. It took a year or two for us to understand. He's got a lot of bark on him and you have to figure him out.

"And by then we were ready to kick Dallas' ass. We're 11-0 and they're 8-3, and all week, Everson Walls is saying crap like, 'Yeah, the Bears are playing teams like Detroit and all these people. They haven't played anybody.' People pointed out that we're 11-0 and he's still, 'They haven't played anybody.'

"After we finish up with them and it's 44-0, a bunch of writers are around the locker, and I said, 'I have to give Everson Walls credit. He was right. We're 12-0 and we still ain't played nobody.'"

PRIORITIES

Mike Tomczak had injured his right arm during a game and left Soldier Field with it in a sling, which was a problem when trying to navigate his truck. He was parked near the Mercedes Benz belonging to Steve McMichael and wife Debi. Not a good place to be with an injured arm.

McMichael had lined up a case of beers on his car trunk for some refreshment after the game. Tomczak, however, in trying to exit, bumped McMichael's Mercedes, sending the beers tumbling and rolling all over the parking lot.

McMichael immediately started trying to run down the rolling brew. Debi had a different worry, namely what had happened to the car.

"What are you doing?!" she screamed at McMichael.

The ever-pragmatic Texan kept gathering up the beers. "Baby," he drawled, "You can ALWAYS get another Mercedes."

SETTLE THIS

It was a fourth-and-one situation, a critical game moment, when linebacker Ron Rivera ran onto the field as a rookie in 1984. Up ahead of him were Dan Hampton and Steve McMichael in an intense discussion. Rivera hustled over to get in on the expertise the two veterans were obviously dispensing.

"Hey, Rivera, settle this," Hampton demanded. "Who's better: the blonde in section 22, row 7, or the brunette in 24, third row? I got $100 says the blonde."

"What do you say, rookie?" McMichael snarled.

Rivera knew enough to understand that he was in a world of hurt with either choice. Then came a flash of inspiration: "Hey, I like 'em both."

One answer, two enemies. On the way off the field after the defensive stop, he took shots from both, with the same line: "You idiot, you cost me $100."

TOUGH CHANGE

Mike Hartenstine had been a successful defensive end for almost a decade when William Perry arrived as a draft choice. The defense was dominant, but Ditka wanted Perry to play, and Hartenstine lost his job even though he was outplaying Perry at the time.

"Ditka made him a media hero letting him run the ball and catch the ball," Hartenstine says. "I'm sitting there getting older. The media's loving Fridge and I'm outplaying the guy, but they had to play him, almost because of the media. Plus, they didn't want to look bad blowing a No. 1 pick.

"Ultimately Fridge was a good player and I liked him; it wasn't anything personal. I just hated that I lost my job in a situation where I shouldn't lose it. If I'm not out-producing somebody, then I should lose it.

"I played anywhere at that time, tackle or end. And we had that '46' where I'd always be that weak-side end because you had Wilbur and Otis flying in, so all you needed was back-side pickup. I was mostly on the right then."

Having been relegated to reserve status after laboring so many years to help his team get to the top made the Super Bowl just a little tainted.

"It was pretty bittersweet," Hartenstine says. "I felt a lot like Walter did. He didn't get a chance to score and I didn't get a chance to play against New England. We'd played them earlier when I was starting and beat 'em. I could've played the whole game and I wouldn't have hurt our defense. Richard got hurt one game and I played against Minnesota, which had one of the best offenses, and we shut them out. I knew I could play. Ditka did it, I'm sure, but Buddy was the one who told me."

Hampton remembers: "Halfway through the '85 season, Fridge had gotten in shape and was doing the offensive thing. And that was partly because Ditka didn't want to look like an idiot and Buddy's saying he's not good enough to play our defense.

"Hartenstine had been playing 11 years and was starting to slow down, so they decided, we're better with Fridge at tackle and Hampton at end because then we've got four young guys who can go."

KICKING: THE ROUGH LIFE

"I didn't mind the kickers like Kevin Butler wearing the little shoulder pads and going around in the short-shorts," says linebacker Jim Morrissey.

"But what really got me was that when we went out to practice, Kevin and the kickers were putting on suntan lotion. I thought, yep, they're on a different schedule than we are."

DESTROYING THE GIANTS

The game against the New York Giants in the '85 postseason was a signature game in a season full of them.

"The Giant game was big because we thought they were the second best team in football, and they would win it next year," says Dan Hampton. "We went with a real pass-defense type deal. They had a good offensive line, good back, good quarterback, and Buddy felt we had to be able to pressure Simms."

"He put me on the nose and basically just went with a five-man rush. Then we had all our games inside and they couldn't block us. The next deal was that we had played a good game the year before against Washington to get to the championship game, but then we stepped on our dicks. That was a big game. The Super Bowl was anticlimactic."

SHUFFLING

Not every player was on board for the legendary Super Bowl Shuffle.

"The biggest problem I had with the Super Bowl Shuffle was that they did it the day after the day we lost to the Dolphins," said Mike Hartenstine. "We're on the plane coming home from Miami and everybody's talking about going down to do the Super Bowl Shuffle. I was like, 'Screw you guys, we just lost a goddamn game and we're going to do a video about the Super Bowl after we got our asses handed to us. I'm not going down there.'

"To me it was just wrong. I probably would have done it if it was a different set of circumstances because it was a team kind of thing and I'm about the team. Actually I don't think Walter or McMahon did it that day. Hampton didn't do it, or McMichael. We were pissed."

CENTERS OF ATTENTION

The 1980s saw two of the best centers in NFL history playing at the same time: the Bears' Jay Hilgenberg and Miami's Dwight Stephenson.

"What Hilgy was so good at was letting you go the way you wanted, getting you off balance, and then dumping you," Dan Hampton remembers. "He was hardly ever on the ground.

"That's how Stephenson was. He took Fridge down a number of times in that Monday night game and everybody was thinking, 'Wow.' Fridge would go into him and Stephenson would just get that weight going and just throwing him on the ground. After the game Buddy said, 'Here you are, 400 pounds, and the guy's throwing you around like a bag of shit.'"

CORE OF THE 46

Few defenses in NFL history have terrorized the league the way the "46" defense of Buddy Ryan and the Bears did. But if the number-name of the defense recalled safety Doug Plank, the true flowering of the 46 came in '85, after Plank was gone.

"The whole thing was predicated on me," says Dan Hampton. "I could not get hooked either way and if I was just single-blocked, I had to hit the quarterback within two seconds. I don't mean to beat my drum, but it was the fact that I was un-blockable with a single block.

"It wasn't a lot of moves, more like a surge rush and hit the quarterback. It was predicated on us having three world-class pass rushers. It's just how are you going to handle it."

BUDDY VS. VINCE

The Bears' great defense of the 1980s arrived with Buddy Ryan, who was brought in from Minnesota by Neill Armstrong to be defensive coordinator. But Buddy wasn't the only defensive guru to direct that legendary defense.

Vince Tobin arrived in 1986 after Ryan left for the head-coaching job at Philadelphia. There were obvious differences from Ryan to Tobin, although the statistics actually improved under Tobin.

"Buddy had a great defensive philosophy and he wasn't afraid to use it," says Mike Hartenstine. "It was funny, because when Tobin came, he had as good a defense as Buddy did as far as what he could throw at you, but he would never use it.

"We could go in at halftime and Buddy would pull some defense that we hadn't run since the first day of training camp and we'd use it. Tobin'd say, 'Oh, they probably won't get it right.' If it wasn't in the game plan, he'd hesitate to use it. Buddy wouldn't."

The image that Tobin ran a taut ship and Ryan was the loose leader of a band of brigands wasn't completely accurate. Tobin was strict, sometimes to a fault, but Ryan had his lines of conduct and you'd better not cross them.

"Buddy was actually a real disciplinarian," said Hartenstine, who played for Jack Pardee, then Buddy, then Vince. "It seemed like he was real easy-going, but if you didn't do it exactly the way it was supposed to be done, you caught hell for it.

"We'd be out there running 'gassers' where you run goal line to the 20 and back, to the 30 and back, and everybody had to touch the line. We might be all the way from the goal line to the 50 and somebody's missed a line and he'd say, 'You're all doing it over.' So you didn't want to be the guy who missed the line, or the guy who let everybody else down. He was very smart, too.

"We'd argue and fight over tackles and sacks and finally Buddy'd say 'OK, that's enough, let's get to work.' But when

Tobin came in, you couldn't say a word in the meeting, you just had to sit there and listen to what he had to say. It was more of a team with Buddy. And we worked and knew when to work."

Dan Hampton remembers the first meeting with Tobin and the change from Ryan.

"Buddy had a very dominant personality," Hampton says. "The best players in the world could be belittled by Buddy and I wouldn't bat an eye. You would never back-talk him. Then Vince comes in and he doesn't have the credentials to tell us to get our feet off the chairs.

Buddy had an unorthodox way of doing things. Players would lie on the floor, watch film, and if they fell asleep, they fell asleep. As long as they got done what they needed for Sunday.

Ditka once happened by a meeting of the defensive unit and saw bodies on the floor.

"What are you doing, letting these guys lie on the floor, sleeping?" he demanded of Ryan.

"Yeah, and I hear 'em snoring sometimes too," Ryan shot back.

HIS BIG BREAK

Linebacker Jim Morrissey was an 11th-round draft choice in 1985, another of those late-round draft choices that Jim Finks and the scouting staff seemed to find that were part of the unsung foundation of a dynasty. But for Morrissey, it took a little help in the form of holdouts by Al Harris and Todd Bell in the Super Bowl season.

"I came in in 1985 but was released on the last cut of training camp and went back to my hometown of Flint, Mich.," Morrissey says. "I got a call from Bill Tobin the next week, after the Bears had beaten Tampa Bay in the opener. Brian Cabral was a linebacker for the Bears and hurt his knee on a kickoff, so the Bears called me back and signed me for a week-to-week situation.

"At that time Todd Bell and Al Harris were sitting out the '85 season, and Coach Ditka, who was always fair, said, 'I don't care how big you are; I don't care how fast you are or slow, or what you look like in the shower. If you're a football player, you can play on my football team,' and that's what I wanted to hear as an 11th-round draft pick.

"When I came in he said, 'I need you for special teams; I don't need you for playing linebacker. You're week to week, so enjoy yourself. If either Todd or Al come back, you're the odd man out, unfortunately.' So I went week to week living with my grandparents in Northbrook and had a great time."

"What he doesn't tell you," guard Tom Thayer joked at the 2003 Fan Convention, "is that he disconnected the phones of both Todd Bell and Al Harris the whole year."

"Don't tell Todd or Al that," Morrissey said.

BUDDY ON MOTIVATION

Mike Ditka may have been cast as the master motivator, but few did it with the style of Buddy Ryan.

"We're watching film one week and there's O. J. Anderson running over somebody," Dan Hampton remembers. "Ryan says to Otis, 'Ooh, you better get hurt in practice this week. I don't want him running over you like that.'

"That's all he had to say. Otis was ready to go, muttering 'I'll show that *#*$&%&%.' And he was talking about showing Buddy, not just Anderson.

"He'd tell McMichael, 'McMichael, I don't care if you go out and get drunk. Just don't take any of the 'real' players with you.' And he'd say it in a way that would have McMichael just fuming.

"Vince didn't have the personality to do that. Vince was more of just telling you when to show up, what to do and you did it."

Ryan had an impact on the offense. "He'd see that McMahon was our best chance, so rather than yell at him because he wasn't like Terry Bradshaw, Buddy would be looking at him, finding ways to pump him up," Hampton says. "And he did that to the whole team.

"He'd say to the offensive line, 'You fat asses can't block anybody in practice; how you going to do it in a game?' And Covert, Bortz and those guys would turn into animals."

A CASE OF RESPECT

For the Ditka Bears, there was no half-speed in practice. It was all or nothing. But there was a bond even between combatants.

"There was a great respect," says Dan Hampton. "Our defensive line could all go in and pick up 300 pounds, do reps with it and power-clean. The reason we were so good was because we had explosion. And those offensive guys were the same. Covert was a badass. Bortz, you'd have to kill him if you got in a fight with him."

MEAL TICKET

As a group, the defensive linemen were always different. They came in and as a unit decided they wanted to have hot lunches. They spread it around and a couple times a week somebody bought hot lunches. Pretty soon the offensive guys were sitting there eating their baloney sandwiches and the defense was having hot lunches, and the offensive guys started grousing about it. Management got upset at the whining and got hot lunches for everybody.

Chapter 5

Early Da Coach

MAKING CHANGES

After George Halas hired Mike Ditka to coach the Bears, changes followed immediately. Some in fact seemed even sooner.

When Ditka took over the Bears, it was with the idea that he would make changes. Part of that would include weeding out players he didn't think fit with the program.

"It was brutal for everybody," said Mike Hartenstine. "He came in and we met up at a bar called Me and Mrs. P's. Ditka's up there with his wife, me and my wife, Hamp and his wife, Steve and his wife.

"Ditka buys every bottle of champagne in the place and we drink it all, the eight of us. Ditka's getting all looped up and starting to go, 'I'm getting rid of this guy, he ain't shit' and 'This guy's no good' and these are guys we've played with for years, our buddies, and we didn't want to hear this. 'This guy's worthless.' And this is before we even had a practice together!

"I'm sitting there thinking, man, I don't know if I want to know all this stuff. I might be on the list too."

NICKNAMING

How did Steve McMichael get his other nickname of Mongo? From the character played by Alex Karras in the film *Blazing Saddles*, in which Karras gave his signature performance, knocking a horse unconscious with a roundhouse right.

And when did James Thornton become "Robocop?" Television commentator John Madden observed that Thornton had the same physique as the half-man, half-robot character in the movie *Robocop*.

STILL MORE MING

In 1983 the Washington Redskins put a 24-7 thrashing on the Bears, after which coach Mike Ditka was in a foul mood in the locker room. But no one could find McMichael.

All of a sudden the door burst open and in came Ming the Merciless, who reduced the room to laughter.

"Quick, lock the doors," he roared. "The Redskins are coming in here after us to kick our asses some more."

FIRST IMPRESSIONS

Hall of Fame defender Dan Hampton had arrived in 1979, the fourth overall pick of the draft, and liked previous coach

Neill Armstrong. But the team was slipping in the wrong direction.

"In 1981 we're getting ready to play the final game of the season," Hampton says. "Ricky Watts was drinking Drambuie before the game to warm up. Dan Neal came to me and said, 'Guys are drinking over here, go say something to them.'

"I said, 'Go tell the damn coaches.' They went and told the coaches and one of the coaches came to me and said, 'Go tell them to stop.' The inmates were running the asylum. That's something we never had a problem with with Ditka. We didn't have a good team at first for a year or two, but we knew we were pointed in the right direction.

"He showed up with a Bible and George Halas and had this competitive fire inside him. Buddy had a condescending attitude toward him. Buddy was an old-school guy who said you became a coordinator first, had success and then become a head coach. He thought Ditka had kind of back-doored the thing. It took a while for Mike to earn respect.

"Buddy told him to put Mark Bortz on offense. By '84, it wasn't the same garden-variety offensive player. Ditka was getting guys who had something.

"It's one of those deals where he wasn't happy and was going to make changes. That made us ecstatic. We liked the guys on the team, but we wanted to win, and if we had to get new players to do it, so be it. He thought like we did, that we had to get to where we could whip Pittsburgh's ass, or match up with Dallas. He said, 'My goal is to win a Super Bowl. I won a championship as a player, as an assistant coach, and I know what we have to do to win one.' That was like pie in the sky to us because we'd always been middle of the pack.

"In 1983 we went up to Minnesota and beat the Vikings. Ozzie [Jim Osborne] had tears in his eyes after the game and I said, 'What's the matter?' He said, 'I've been here 11 years and we've never beaten Minnesota up here.' I said to myself, 'Shit, it's changing. We're not doormats any more.'"

NICE GUYS DON'T FINISH

Bob Thomas finished his Chicago career about the time Ditka's coaching reign was beginning. It didn't take long for Da Coach to make an impression on the veteran kicker.

"At the end of my career I was playing for Ditka and we were playing the Detroit Lions," Thomas says. "Eddie Murray was the kicker for the Lions then and Ditka sent Dave Duerson after Eddie towards the end of the game, and of course he killed Eddie.

"I never thought it was a good idea to do that, by the way. Teams had a tendency to remember that sort of thing and retaliate the next time they saw you.

"So Eddie's down on the field, the game was stopped and after the game, Gary Fencik and I, who had played golf with Eddie and he was somewhat of a friend, went over into the tunnel to see how he was doing. He thought he'd separated his shoulder, so it was bad.

"The next day, Monday, WGN radio always used to have a call-in show with Ditka and Wally Phillips. And we would all listen religiously Monday morning. Ditka says, 'You know what's wrong with this team? It's not like the old days. We have a bunch of wussies on this team that go over and apologize to people on the other sideline.'

"And I'm thinking, 'Oh no, holy crap.' So I pick up the *Tribune* and it says a couple of players apologized to Eddie Murray and I'm thinking, OK, at least I'm not named. Then I remembered that there was another paper in town, so I pick up the *Sun-Times* and there it is: Bob Thomas and Gary Fencik 'apologizing' to Eddie Murray.

"So I walk into the locker room and Fencik is sitting there in his locker. I say, 'Hey, did you listen to Wally Phillips this morning?' He said, 'Yeah, at least it's not in the *Trib.*' I said, 'You wanna see the *Sun-Times?*'

"He turns white as a sheet and I, being a lawyer, say we're going to go up there and we are going to cop a plea and do whatever we can to get out of this. We go up to the office and Iron Mike is sitting there, smoking a cigar, and we say to him, 'Mike, it really wasn't an apology. We really just wanted to see how the guy was. We play golf with him in the off season, he's been a friend,' and so forth. Fine.

"We leave and we're relieved, thinking, 'OK, he took that pretty well.' So we head down to the team meeting, and in comes Ditka. He goes off: 'You know why we're losing? We have wussie players like Thomas and Fencik.'

"So I guess things weren't completely fine."

GETTING OFFENSIVE

"The thing I loved about Ditka," says Mike Hartenstine, "was that I'd been with two defensive-minded coaches in Pardee and Neill, and Ditka was the first offensive-minded coach for me. And that's what I always thought we needed, because our defense never seemed to be the problem. It wasn't just his presentation that 'I'm here, we're going to win the Super Bowl.' Just that he came in and said, 'This is my offense.'

"Trouble was, he came in with the Dallas offense, all that motion and crap. And we couldn't do it. So he said, OK, now THIS is my offense. And he came up with something else. I thought that was great. Just put points on the board."

Chapter 6

THE "BETWEEN YEARS"

After George Halas stepped down following his fourth stint as head coach, the franchise slumped at first, then had some up-and-down times under coaches Jim Dooley, Abe Gibron, Jack Pardee and Neill Armstrong. There were a couple of trips to the playoffs, but it was mostly a time of winning battles (the Bears were a team few wanted to play despite Chicago being among the NFL doormats) and losing wars. These were the Between Years, between Halas and Ditka, and they have their own stories and tales.

JUMPING SHIP

The Bears struggled through the early 1970s before Jack Pardee arrived and the Bears made the playoffs in 1977 with the coming of age of the '75 draft that included Bob Avellini, Walter Payton, Roland Harper, Mike Hartenstine, Tom Hicks, Virgil Livers, Doug Plank and Revie Sorey. But the satisfaction was short-lived when Pardee abruptly left to coach the Washington Redskins after giving his Bears short shrift before meeting the Dallas Cowboys in the playoffs.

"Pardee kind of jumped ship on us bad and I never appreciated that, ever," defensive end Hartenstine says. "It came down to the understanding that he was going to get the Washington job if he got us into the playoffs, and he got us into the playoffs in '77. We were getting ready to play Dallas in the wild card game and it's something like 60-below here, and Pardee says, 'No, I want you guys here, in Chicago, because the holidays are coming up and I want you to be with your families.'

"Well, that was all bullshit. Pardee was packing his house up, getting ready to move, so he didn't want to take us anywhere because he was trying to get packed up, get his kids into schools, and get the move going. So he kept us here instead of going somewhere warm to prepare for Dallas, like you normally would for a playoff game. Everybody did after that.

"It was so cold that you couldn't be outside for more than 45 minutes at a time. You couldn't work on anything offensively timing-wise because everything was ice and frozen and you couldn't win. I was disappointed because he never gave us a shot in that game.

"We ended up getting blown out in Dallas and I hated that he wanted us here just because he wanted to take care of his house. And we knew it at the time. He was offering [Doug] Buffone the house if he wanted to buy it, so we all knew he was going."

BLASTED

"You think kickers never get hit, but teams always send some big guy after the kicker almost every play," says Bob Thomas. "Usually you can get around them, but one time against Green

Bay I'm running down, feeling happy about the kickoff, and one of these linemen was a little irritated that I'd faked him out.

"As the back started down the sideline, I turned, never saw this guy and got hit. I really looked on film like a crash dummy in one of those seat-belt commercials. Jack Pardee was our coach and showed that play in slow motion about 20 times. After that he gave me a bottle of wine for coming of age as a football player.

"I went to the sideline and wailed, 'Does that happen to people on every play?'"

STICKING TO BASICS

Bears coaches have long been criticized for conservatism, which might have stemmed from having a long history of being supplied with great running backs. Whatever the reason, there was definitely some resistance to change.

"I came into the league in '75 and we really weren't a very potent team but we had a lot of good people," Mike Hartenstine says. "And we played people hard, really got after people. Teams didn't usually win the week after they played us. In those days you could really grow a team too. I loved playing with those guys. Even though we were 4-10 my rookie year, we were almost never out of games.

"We had Pardee as our head coach and he was obviously a great defensive coach, but offensively he was a lot of five yards and a cloud of dust. When Walter ran for 275 yards, we won 10-7, which was ridiculous. Sid Gillman came in and tried to help the offense out, but Pardee wouldn't listen to anything he would say, so Sid left after one year, 1977.

"Bob Avellini was totally a Sid freak, loved Sid and wanted to throw the ball because he knew that when you had a great runner you could throw the ball because everybody was going to be up there to stop Walter. Pardee said no, we were going to run the ball."

HEAVY LIFTING

"I used to love working out with Plank," Mike Hartenstine says. "He was a great guy to lift weights with, coming up with new ideas to do things and tax ourselves. One time, though, we were lifting weights and all of a sudden, Plank's finger just exploded. Exploded. Blood all over the place."

GET OUT OF THE WAY!

Bob Thomas was the Bears' place-kicker for many years, but he almost didn't survive his rookie preseason.

"I was drafted by the Rams, cut in the last cut, and re-signed by the Rams," Thomas says. "I had to go through procedural waivers, and the Redskins and Bears picked me up. Because the Bears were lower in the standings, I ended up with Chicago.

"My roommate was a guy named Doug Plank. When I walked in, I knew he was the right guy to ask. I asked him, 'Doug, what happens if I have to make a tackle?' I don't want you to think I didn't make any tackles at Notre Dame, but we were playing Northwestern at the time.

"Doug said, 'Bob, they're going to see you're a little guy, see that No. 16 and that you're wearing black shoes where everybody else is wearing white. So just plant your feet and when they try to run around you, make the tackle and you'll be a hero.

"I had no cause to use that information my rookie year until the last game. We were playing the New Orleans Saints and winning. I kick off the last time of the year and here comes this running back, six-two, 235 pounds, down the sidelines, and there is nobody between him and the goal line except me.

"A lot of things went through my mind, like my Mom would be crying at the funeral. But I thought I had to at least make an attempt at what Plank had said. So I planted my feet firmly in front of that back, and when it was all done, I had cleat marks up one side of me and down the other.

"The only reason he didn't score was that he tripped over my goofy facemask when he stepped on my face. Plank was laughing and said, 'Bob, that's the one guy I wasn't counting on.'"

THE SACK

Mike Hartenstine's sack of Philadelphia Eagles quarterback Ron Jaworski in 1980 was one of the highlight-film hits in Bears history. What happened after the hit, though, was as much a tale as the sack itself.

"Jaworski just held the ball too long," Hartenstine says. "I was blocked on the play going against Stan Walters and took a big outside rush, and I'm rushing, rushing, rushing, and I get around Walters, and Jaworski's a little ways away. He's holding the ball, holding the ball, holding the ball, and I'm running at him and figured I'd never get there.

"Well, I whacked him. There was no penalty on the play. He went out of the game for a couple plays but he came back.

"I got in the locker room and all the reporters are asking, 'What do you think about Vermeil wanting the league to fine you for that?' I said, 'Fine me for what?' 'He said you speared Jaworski, tried to kill his quarterback.' I didn't know how he could say that because there wasn't even a flag on it.

"A week later I get a letter from the NFL that I'm being fined $1,000 for spearing. So my agent and I go to New York to appeal it. I'm sitting there with Rozelle and we're looking at the thing from every angle, all over the place, and he's got all his henchmen there and they're cringing every time they show the hit. Everybody keeps saying, 'You speared him, you speared him.'

"Finally I said, 'You know, we've got Cs on our helmet. If I speared him with my head down, that C would be facing down pointing at the ground. When I hit him, you could see the C still up. My head's not down.

"Then Rozelle says, 'Yeah, you're right, you didn't spear him. But you hit him too vigorously, so we're keeping your money.' So I won the appeal but I still lost my money. I didn't win anything except to know that I was right and I didn't spear him.

"The thing was, the next time we played them, I speared him right in the sternum. Definitely with my head down. He drops the ball, goes down, and McMichael picks it up, runs it to the 10 and we eventually score the touchdown.

"As I'm coming off the field, Fencik's looking at me, just patting the top of his helmet and smiling. I just smiled back and said, 'Yep, speared him that time, so I got my money's worth.'"

WHEN THE LIGHT CAME ON

Every NFL player was good in college. But most don't have the talent, mind or some ingredient to make it at the next level. And even for the greatest, there was that moment of breakthrough when they start to figure it out.

"When I got here, everybody up here was physically as good as you are," says Dan Hampton. "I didn't have any technique. At Arkansas we were in pretty much a 'run' conference. I was terrific against the run but on pass rushes, I'd just run into the guy and try to rassle him and try to get off him. I wasn't getting to the quarterback.

"We were getting ready to play Tampa Bay in the fourth game of the season. Wednesday we were in meetings and Jerry Eckwood, who was with me at Arkansas, was running and was a great talent. They'd pitch the ball to him and he'd sweep, outrun everybody and gain 20 yards.

"Buddy says to me, 'Big Rook, this kid from Arkansas, has he got great speed?' I said something like, 'Supposedly he ran a 4.3 in the combine.' Gary Fencik was in the back of the room and said, 'Yeah, and supposedly you was a great pass rusher.' Everybody laughed, but boy, that pissed me off.

"Later that day I was downstairs watching film and heard someone in another room, and I stuck my head in. It was Ted Albrecht. He was watching film on Leroy Selmon. He was always a big film guy. I asked him if that was Leroy, and he said, 'Yeah, he's the best I play against.' So I came in, sat down and started watching.

"I noticed that everything he did was keeping someone off balance. That's basically it. When you're playing basketball and you're trying to get to the basket, you're keeping the defensive guy off balance. It's the same thing, getting people off balance and getting rid of them.

"That game I had two sacks. It was just like the light went on watching Leroy and emulating what he did. It was incredible. All this was possible. At the end of my rookie year, Buddy Ryan told me I was playing as well as any defensive lineman in the game. The next year I made All-Pro."

The light had come on.

POINT OF PRIDE

Mike Hartenstine rarely missed a play in his career, let alone a game. Sometimes that required some creativity as well as a high tolerance for pain.

"I enjoyed that I never missed a game," Hartenstine says. "I missed one game in my career. I missed a high school game. None in junior high, one in high school, none in college, none in the pros through 11 years. I had two separated shoulders at the same time and once sprained both feet and that was hard. But you just do it.

"When I broke my thumb I had two pins sticking out of my thumb and it was pretty painful. The doc just taped it up and I think I had one of my better games, against Minnesota.

"But after it was fixed, the pins were sticking out and they put a cast right over the pins. So every time I would hit somebody, it would drive the pins in. I said, this isn't going to work, and had the doc cut a hole in the cast right over the pins, and I concocted this plastic bubble over it and that made it a lot easier."

BRIAN'S TUNE

Ed McCaskey took care of the family of Brian Piccolo when Brian was fighting his losing battle with cancer. He went to see Piccolo one last time and broke down when he saw how ravaged Piccolo was by the disease.

Piccolo saw Ed's tears and reassured him. "Don't worry, Big Ed," Piccolo said. "I'm not afraid of anything—only Nitschke."

Piccolo died the next day.

GOOD-HANDS GUY

Kickers never had it too rough in training camp. Sometimes, though, there was a little pain to be endured.

"It was always tough for me in training camp because the toughest thing we had to do was play catch with the quarterbacks," says Bob Thomas. "There were usually three quarterbacks. My first year was Bobby Douglass' last year, and I noticed that the other two quarterbacks paired up really quick, and told me I was going to warm up Bobby Douglass. And he threw the ball about 150 miles an hour, knocked me down a few times.

"I wasn't happy to see Bobby go, but at least I wouldn't have to play catch with him. And then they drafted Vince Evans."

TOUGH GUYS

Wally Chambers, a first-round draft choice of the Bears, was one of the dominant defensive linemen of his day. But few knew the whole story about how tough he really was.

"Wally was really awesome," says Mike Hartenstine. "The funny thing about Wally was that he had such great ability, strong and quick, but we'd be at practice and Wally would never practice. I'd wonder what was up with Wally because I had to do my stuff and then do some of his stuff, which was twice the work.

"I asked what the deal was and they said, 'Oh, Wally's got gout.' I couldn't understand that. Then later in my life I started getting gout attacks and I don't know how the guy could even play. I couldn't imagine playing with it. But he would play games and be effective in games. It was so painful.

"But Wally did and played well. That made him even more amazing."

Playing alongside Chambers and others who followed was Jim Osborne, a character in his own right. "Ozzie was a funny guy. We were playing down in Atlanta and running down a play, and Hamp just pushes Ozzie so Hamp could get to the play. Ozzie goes down and all of a sudden you hear this shriek and screaming. He'd hit a sprinkler head, cut his knee open and he's bleeding all over the place, screaming like a banshee."

HALAS LINGUISTICS

"When I arrived," Bobby Douglass remembers, "Mr. Halas had just quit coaching and Jim Dooley was my coach. But

Mr. Halas was ever-present. We'd have quarterback meetings every day and he would bring me into his office and we'd get into a cussing match pretty much every day.

"I learned more words from him than I did in any of the training camps."

WITH FRIENDS LIKE THAT, WHO NEEDS ENEMIES?

Mike Hartenstine came into the NFL when linebacker Doug Buffone was an established veteran. Buffone helped Hartenstine learn the NFL, including when to duck.

"Douggie taught me so much," Hartenstine says. "I hear him on the radio sometimes saying that I helped him stay on, but he really helped me. I was pretty good at two-gapping and keeping guys off Doug, and he knew I would be going where I had to go. I think we didn't give up two yards a run to our side, more like 1.6 yards or something like that.

"But I remember that he knocked me out in the Astrodome against Houston. He was swinging around the quarterback and kicked me right in the head. I was out. I was out twice in my career and that was a pretty good one."

Chapter 7

'63 Champions
and the Sixties

The sixties were among the most tumultuous times in American history, so it's only fitting perhaps that they rank among the most turbulent in Bears history as well. From the peak of the 1963 NFL championship to the valley of the 1-13 season of 1969, it was a time of extremes: Dick Butkus, Gale Sayers, Doug Atkins and dozens of others who were as colorful as the time in which they lived and played.

THE PICK

The winning touchdown in the championship game was set up by an interception from defensive end Ed O'Bradovich, who sniffed out a pass headed for the Giants' right flat.

"We had it nailed down," O'Bradovich says. "Joe Fortunato knew exactly where and when they were going to do it. On that particular play, Joe called it, 'Watch out for the screen,' just to remind me. Stroud was the offensive tackle and he starts dropping back, but he was too good. I wasn't going to suck in on it.

"So I went just so far in, then broke out into the flat, and next damn thing I know, the ball's coming and I put my left hand up and brought it in. I went a few yards and it turned out to be the winning points in the world championship game.

"The goofy part was, Y. A. Tittle after that game was on the front page of *Sports Illustrated*, all messed up, blood on his uniform, and that uniform winds up in the Hall of Fame. And we won the damn game."

GETTING ALONG

Offensive and defensive players don't necessarily dislike each other, but sometimes there's tension when one unit isn't holding up its end of things. The '63 Bears were a legendary defensive unit, but offense was another matter.

During one dry spell for the offense, as the two units passed each other with the defense leaving the field after getting the ball on a turnover, expectations were spelled out.

"Just hold 'em," defensive end Ed O'Bradovich snarled at the offensive players. "Just give us a rest, get a first down or two, and we'll come back and get you six. Don't fuck it up."

The guys on offense had their own perspective on that rift.

"That stuff was mostly from the defensive team," said quarterback Bill Wade. "The offense never paid much attention to all that. The defensive team just seemed to need something to gear itself up. We were out there just to do the job. We gave people a lot of fits offensively. Even though we averaged 14 points a game, our turnover ratio was the smallest in the league.

"Offensively we thought we did our part and they did their part. They were more colorful, you might say."

VIOLENT WORLD

New York Gaints middle linebacker Sam Huff became a national celebrity when he was wired for sound and filmed during a game. The show, "The Violent World of Sam Huff," was an eye-opener to the NFL game, letting people see inside the game as never before.

But Huff wasn't necessarily the legend around the NFL that the publicity factory of the New York media made him. Huff would go on to make the Hall of Fame, but don't sell "Sam Huff the Legend" to the Bears. They regularly faced true Hall of Fame middle linebackers like Green Bay's Ray Nitschke and Detroit's Joe Schmidt, besides having the originator of the middle linebacker, Hall of Famer Bill George.

Sports Illustrated came to George, who was one of the premier middle linebackers himself, and interviewed George about what he thought of the notion of wiring up Huff for a TV special. George thought for a second and suggested a casting change.

"If they're really going to do it right," George muttered, "they oughtta get Joe Schmidt to play the part of Huff."

I'LL GET YOU

Ed O'Bradovich was one of the toughest members of a tough defense. He didn't ask any quarter, nor did he give any. But there was a code among warriors, and woe to the enemy who violated that. New York Giants running back Phil King found that out when he hit Eddie O. from behind after a play in the Bears-Giants game in 1962.

"We're playing in Wrigley Field and a play is over with and I'm standing there," O'Bradovich recalled. "All of a sudden something hits me, BAM, from behind, and I'm flying through the air. I get my senses, turn around, and I see this No. 24, who turns out to be King, and he starts running.

"I take out after him and he runs behind a bunch of Giants and I'm trying to grab him, swinging at everything, which is stupid because all you do is break your hand. There was no flag and nobody knew, so everybody's screaming at me, 'What are you doin'?! You're losing the game for us!' So Don Chandler kicks a field goal and they beat us. Man, I was feeling bad, young guy playing with all those great veterans.

"I was thrown out of the game, but in those days you didn't have to leave the sidelines. So I was looking at him and pointing at him, 'You son of a bitch, I'm going to get you.' It's getting down toward the end of the game, and he's got his eye on me, I got my eye on him.

"Bang, the gun goes off, and he takes off running for the dugout. I take off from our bench sprinting after the guy. Down in the dugout all the Giants are there waiting for him and it was an ugly scene. I went down into the dugout and finally I said, 'You tell that son of a bitch, he's gotta come out of Wrigley Field sooner or later and I'm going to be waiting by the bus for him.' But he dodged me and I never got him back.

"That was Sunday and we had Monday off. Tuesday I get there, get dressed, waiting to have our meeting, and somebody walks down and says, 'The Old Man wants to see you.' I'm thinking, 'Oh brother, here we go.' I went upstairs and Halas says, 'Sit down, kid.' Here I am, starting as a rookie and he says to me, 'Kid, I don't want you to ever forget this. You lost the game for us. They fined you $100. So you know what I'm going to do? I'm going to fine you another $100. So have a nice day.' That was Halas.

"Then I ran into Phil King at the Muelbach Hotel. We're touring with the Harlem Globetrotters all over the country, and we're in Kansas City. King was at the hotel and somebody comes up and says, 'He knows you're here and he's hiding.' I couldn't find the son of a bitch."

"BIG MAN"

Doug Atkins in his prime, and probably for a while after that, was the most feared man in the National Football League. There have been others who were feared but few as colorful to that point that everywhere players meet, there are Doug stories.

Atkins was huge, six foot eight, 260 pounds, and athletic. He played in the era before sacks were counted, but he and Deacon Jones, the man who coined and popularized the term "sack," were the greatest of their day.

Big Man, as Atkins' teammates addressed him, was just as interested in running up impressive totals off the field. He and defensive tackle Fred Williams both loved martinis, so one day Fred challenged Atkins to a contest.

They went out after practice to see who could drink the most, last man standing wins. The players knew the two were holding their drink-off and came in the next morning to find Atkins and Williams present, mostly, but looking like road kill. They asked Williams what had happened.

"Well, Doug had 21 and I had 21," Williams reported.

"So it was a tie?" Ed O'Bradovich quizzed.

"No," Williams said, "I figure Doug won because he threw me over his shoulder and carried me home."

EQUIPMENT GAMES

The Bears were in training camp at St. Joe's in Renssalaer, Ind., and everyone went out for a few pops the night before the start of practices. The next morning, about 9 a.m., the players were dressing, going to their meetings and starting to do warmup exercises. No Doug.

Halas gave his welcome-to-camp speech and went to his golf cart as players headed for their drills. Still no Doug.

Mike Dikka as a Player   *AP/WWP*

Then out from the locker room came Atkins. Just dressed in shorts, a helmet with no facemask, no shirt. He ran slowly past the Old Man in his golf cart without either of them uttering a word. The players were all watching as Atkins jogged along the Christmas tree line by the field, then walked along a road, then trotted around the whole perimeter of the field as Halas just watched, not saying a word.

Doug ran right past Halas again and headed straight into the clubhouse. No practice. After practice the players headed into the lunch room and there was Atkins going through the lunch line.

"Hey, Big Man, what the hell was that?" he was asked.

"I's just breaking in my new helmet," Atkins drawled and went back to eating his lunch.

OK, Doug. No further questions.

WELCOME TO THE NFL, ROOK

During Mike Ditka's rookie season, he went against Baltimore linebacker Bill Pellington, a renowned tough guy with a reputation. On the game's first play. Pellington punched Ditka squarely in the mouth. Not to be outdone, Ditka did exactly the same thing to Pellington on the next play.

Things went on like that for a while. Finally Ditka felt something land on his arm: a piece of cloth with a lead ball tied up in it. Ditka thought Pellington was now trying to get him with a blackjack and went to the referee with his complaint.

"Give me that damn thing," the official barked. "That's my flag!"

OUTTA CHICAGO

Halas and the Bears were the first team to lose a player to the rival American Football League when end Willard Dewveall played out his option in 1960 and signed with the Houston Oilers. They also could have lost Ditka.

In May, 1966 Ditka was offered a $50,000 bonus, $300,000 for three years and a home on a golf course to sign and play for Houston in 1967, when his Bears contract would be expired. It looked pretty good to someone making $25,000.

Ditka never played for the Oilers. The NFL and AFL worked out a merger plan that ended personnel raids. Still, Halas knew Ditka had signed with the rival league and the Bears exercised their option of cutting Ditka's salary 10 percent. Ditka exercised his right of free speech, more or less, and commented that Halas threw nickels around like manhole covers.

Ditka was traded to Philadelphia for quarterback Jack Concannon.

NO DARTS

Riley Matson and Ed O'Bradovich went out drinking one night in Renssalaer, came back in, and went to see if Doug Atkins was in, which wasn't likely. Atkins was in his room playing darts. O'Bradovich wanted to play.

"Let me play darts," O'Bradovich announced and grabbed the darts.

"No, you're not playing with my darts," Atkins declared, whereupon Big Man picked O'Bradovich up completely overhead and threw him down on the floor like a sack of potatoes.

"That was it for the darts," O'Bradovich recalls. "I learned damn quick right there. Don't interrupt the Big Fella when he's playing his darts."

KNOW WHAT YOU'RE IN FOR

"When you came to play the Bears it was very simple," said safety Davey Whitsell. "When you had to go up against guys like Doug Atkins, Stan Jones, Ed O'Bradovich, Bill George, Rich Petitbon, Larry Morris, you have some of those gorillas looking at you, come hell or high water, the Bears were going to put a physical beating on you.

"I don't care whether you won or lost. You were going to know you were in the damnedest game you were ever in in your whole life."

SMART GUY

Bill George invented the middle linebacker position when, as a nose tackle in a five-man line, he stood upright and a little back off the ball. Johnny Unitas once said that the only man he feared defensively was Bill George. Not for George's physical skills, which were enormous. But for his savvy.

"I'd be playing left defensive end and we might be on the goal line and I'd have outside containment," Ed O'Bradovich said. "Unitas would be calling an audible and George'd be yelling, 'O'B, O'B, jump inside, jump inside, they're coming inside.'

"Sure as shit, I'd jump inside the tackle or tight end and make the tackle and look great. He did that all the time. He could think right with Unitas."

GOOD AND THEY KNEW IT

"We were completely loose in '63," said Doug Atkins. "We were loose the whole year. We laughed at everybody, and how we won, I don't know. We got every break going. We held the opposition to about 10 points."

DRINKING BUDDIES

Defensive linemen Fred Williams and Doug Atkins had their share of epic drinking contests that usually ended with Atkins the winner. But not always.

"We got into a martini-drinking contest one night and I think it was 21 when I left it," Williams said. "He had to drive me home and how we made it I'll never know. My wife was in our apartment in Chicago, and when I got into the apartment, I fell into the bathtub and I couldn't get out.

"So she called Doug, who was living in the same apartment hotel. Doug comes down and she hands him the baby and says, 'You hold the baby, Doug,' but then she looks at him and says, 'Hell, you're as drunk as he is.'"

THERE'LL NEVER BE ANOTHER SAYERS

Gale Sayers came to the Bears one pick after Dick Butkus in the 1965 draft and became one of the greatest runners in NFL history in just 68 games. His career was shortened by a disastrous knee injury against the San Francisco 49ers in 1968, but his legend is vivid in the minds of those who tried to stop him, usually unsuccessfully.

"He was the only guy I think who could be running full speed, stop on a dime, tell you whether it's heads or tails, and not even break stride," said Hall of Fame Green Bay defensive back Herb Adderley.

Philadelphia Eagles defensive tackle Floyd Peters got credit for a tackle that he had very little to do with, all a credit to Sayers.

"He gave me a [shaking] fake and my body went one way, my mind went the other way and something happens to your motor when that happens," Peters said. "It's hard to explain. But my legs just went limp and I had nothing left.

"The only problem was, Gale made one too many fakes and came back into me. I hit him and knocked him down and he said, 'Nice tackle, Floyd.' I told him, 'I didn't tackle you. You ran into me.'"

Sayers didn't just seem to have eyes in the back of his head; he actually might have had them.

"I had great peripheral vision, there's no doubt about that," Sayers said. "I could see everybody on the field. So I knew where to run or cut. I had a feel for where people were. I know that many times, many runs, I would watch the film and there'd be a fellow coming from my blind side. No way I could see him but I could feel him."

After the knee injury, Sayers returned the following season to rush for more than 1,000 yards, a further testament to his greatness. But the magic was gone and so was he a short time later, but not before he'd made his statement.

"They say that once you get a knee injury, you should think about quitting," Sayers said. "A running back very rarely comes back from the type of knee injury I had.

"But I wanted to prove that one could come back from a serious injury within a year. So many times they say it takes two years, three, but I wanted to prove that you could come back. And I had one of the worst knee injuries ever."

WEIGHTY MATTERS

Rick Casares, one of the top running backs in Bears history, came to the Bears from Florida by way of the U.S. Army.

Gale Sayers   *AP/WWP*

The result was some exceptional conditioning, but it still didn't save him from Halas.

"In the off season, guys had to work other jobs so it was hard to get all the way in shape," Casares said. "When we came in you had to run the mile the first day in camp and there was a specific time that the linemen had to make and one for the backs. You had to run before you got to camp, otherwise you ran that mile every day until you made your time.

"Practices were two-and-a-half-hour sessions in 90-plus degree weather and we hit all the time. We had the leanest team in the league. Coach Halas believed that a player performed his best at a lighter weight. Our heaviest lineman was Doug at 280, and Halas wanted him at 260. At that he was really sculpted.

"We had to be exactly what they wanted us to be. Some of our linemen would be coming in for weigh-ins with bags of food in their hands so they could eat right after they were done. Halas had me down at 220 pounds. I came in and for some reason I got on the scale and only weighed 218 and thought, oh my. I drank some water, got back on the scale but it barely budged.

"I scrounged through the locker room and I found a wrench. I stuck it inside my shorts and taped it on my stomach and came back in. Halas says, 'OK, get on the scale.' Well, now I'm 221. He says, 'That'll cost you $25 for being a pound over.'"

Chapter 8

THE ORIGINAL MONSTERS

The Bears dominated much of professional football from its earliest days. But that dominance reached legendary levels in the 1940s with the arrival of Sid Luckman, Bulldog Turner, George McAfee and others who took the foundation that George Halas had built and put something atop it that still is the stuff of legend.

73-0

This game defined the Bears for decades and was perhaps the embodiment of all that came to be known as "The Monsters of the Midway." On Dec. 8, 1940 the Bears of George Halas played a game for the football ages, destroying the Washington Redskins of George Marshall 73-0.

Ten different Bears scored touchdowns, and by the end of the game, the officials asked the Bears to stop kicking the extra points because, with the kicks sailing up into the stands and staying there, they were about out of footballs. The defense intercepted eight passes and ran three back for touchdowns. The Bears rushed for 372 yards to three for the 'Skins.

When the final gun sounded, someone remarked, "Marshall just shot himself."

The stage had been set, however, three weeks earlier.

"We were in Washington and they'd beat us [7-3] but we had a play there in the latter part of the game where we thought they held Bill Osmanski on a pass that would have been the winning touchdown," said Hall of Fame halfback George McAfee. "We were frustrated about not getting the call, and Mr. Marshall said after the game that we were crybabies." Bad idea.

"When we left Washington, we were one mad bunch of Bears."

Halas, being a master psychologist, fueled the rage by putting the press clippings on the clubhouse wall the Monday before the championship game.

"That was really the big buildup for that game," halfback Ray Nolting said, laughing. "I don't think a more determined bunch of football players ever existed."

They took it out on the Redskins. In a big, big hurry.

On the first play of the game, from the Bears' 24, quarterback Sid Luckman sent Nolting in motion and gave the ball to McAfee, who picked up eight yards between guard and tackle. But Luckman had seen what he wanted: the Washington linebacker followed Nolting.

Luckman sent McAfee in motion on the second play, took Turner's snap and reverse-pivoted, handing the ball to Osmanski. "Bill was really driving when I handed that ball to him," Luckman recalled afterwards. "I knew he was going someplace in a big hurry."

Osmanski started off tackle, dipped inside, then swung wide behind George Musso, pulling from his right guard spot, and was off. Near the Washington 35, Redskins Jimmy Johnson and Ed "Chug" Justice closed in for the tackle, but Bears right end George Wilson hurled himself into both would-be tacklers, obliterating them in one of the most famous blocks in NFL history.

Osmanski went the rest of the way to complete the 68-yard TD run.

Newspaper columnist and 1960s Bears announcer Irv Kupcinet was a referee in that game. "Irv said he made a key block on one of the Redskins for us too," McAfee said, laughing.

The Redskins weren't laughing. Washington quarterback Slingin' Sammy Baugh found end Charlie Malone all alone deep in the Chicago secondary and laid the ball right in Malone's hands. But Malone dropped the sure score and the Redskins were headed for a shutout.

Asked later if Malone making that catch would have changed the outcome of the game, Baugh reflected. "Sure," he replied. "The score would have been 73-7."

At one point Halas considered not running up the score. But he'd reminded his boys at halftime that Marshall also had called them "strictly a first-half ball club." Another bad idea by Marshall.

"When we got around 40 points, George [Halas] tried to pull off the dogs and not run the score up," Nolting said. "But when it got near 60 he was all for it again and said just go ahead. And we did."

"It was such a big surprise the way it went, we didn't quite realize everything that was going on until the next day or two, even a couple years later," remembered Clyde "Bulldog" Turner, the big center and linebacker who would go into the Hall of Fame along with five other teammates from that game. "Not only were we looking good that day, they were looking bad, too."

Luckman remembered that "George Preston Marshall, owner of the Redskins, came out with these blaring headlines, 'The Bears are front runners, the Bears are crybabies, that Washington was going to destroy them.'

"He said, 'Here it is; this is what the Redskins think of you. My opinion of you is that you're the greatest football team in America. But you've got to prove it to yourself and you've got to prove it to your families and to the fans of America.'

"And we devastated them."

WARTIME

Many Bears, including George Halas, spent time in the service during World War II. Don't tell them that "football is like war." No Packer on his meanest day compared to a German or Japanese soldier with a rifle.

Defensive lineman Jack Karwales, who played for the Bears and then for the world champion Chicago Cardinals in 1947, was stationed in the Pacific, on the island of Tinian, when the first atomic bomb arrived, as did the B-29 bomber Enola Gay under Paul Tibbets.

"The bomb came over by ship and we unloaded it at the dock," Karwales said. "All of a sudden we had all these guys in khaki with no insignia, no medals, no rank. We wondered what the hell they were doing there.

"Leo Balarini was the head chef on the island and he was from Chicago. He came over to my tent and says, 'Jack, c'mon over. We're feeding the guys who are flying the Enola Gay, Tibbets and his guys.' So I went over to be there just to be part of it.

"It was an early flight to get out of there and boy, were they loaded down. They were overweight with ammunition and the bomb and I saw them take off and come back. We were all tuned into Tokyo Rose and we knew about when they'd probably drop the bomb. All of a sudden she went berserk and the radio went out of whack and we knew that was it.

"We knew we were part of something big, but nobody knew it was going to be that big."

ORIENTATION

Hall of Fame tackle and linebacker George Connor was a rookie in 1948 and was on the sideline for his first game. Starting tackle Fred Davis told Connor to watch him and whenever Davis put up his hand, Connor was to get his helmet and come in on the next play and give Davis a break.

Davis finally raised his right hand and in went Connor. The defensive lineman opposite him proceeded to punch him square in the mouth on the first play. Connor dismissed the gesture as a consequence of not wearing a facemask and as an effort at intimidation.

In the second half, Davis again raised his hand, Connor went in and a different defender smacked him in the mouth. Connor thought afterwards that it might be some anti-Notre Dame bias. He found out otherwise the next Sunday.

Instead of going for his helmet when Davis signaled, Connor watched the next play. What he saw was Davis reach out and punch his opposite number in the mouth as soon as the ball was snapped, then trot off the field, leaving Connor to deal with the incensed opponent.

HEALTH RISK

Defensive lineman Jack Karwales had to overcome an unusual surgical problem in order to get on the field against NFL players.

Karwales, then in the military, was circumsised in 1943. "They'd line you up and if you needed it, they'd chop ya'," Karwales said. "So I'm lying in bed and I get this offer to go to the All-Star Game and I'm real weak. And then the base commander wouldn't let me go. When I got out of the hospital,

I went into his office and closed the door so hard I knocked all the glass out of the door. He froze and I said, 'You son of a bitch!' And he was a major and I was a PFC. I was so hot."

A Carmelite priest from Chicago who was assigned to Key Field in Meridian, Miss., where Karwales was stationed, got Karwales out of that predicament and he came up to Chicago. But when Karwales got to Northwestern he came a day late and wasn't in the best of shape after his "procedure."

"I am weaker than hell but I check in and get my uniform, my sweatsuits and all that, and go on out to practice," Karwales said. "Harry Stuhldreher, who's coaching at Wisconsin, has everybody in session, talking to the whole group and I barely made it out onto the field. He yells, 'Kavallas'—he had this funny way of talking—'start running around the field and don't stop 'til I tell you to.'

"I start circling and circling and they're doing a scrimmage and he calls me into the group. I had shin splints so bad I couldn't walk up the stairs after practice at Dyche Stadium, where we were sleeping. 'What's the matter, Kavallas, don'tcha want to play?' Stuhldreher demanded."

"Coach," Karwales said, "don't give me that shit. Why am I here? I just got circumcised and I was in the hospital."

"Why didn't you tell me?" Stuhldreher asked.

"I didn't think that would matter," Karwales said simply.

So they "shot me with a preparation of snake oil or venom or some damn thing in both of my shins," Karwales said, "and that relieved the pressure."

MOMMA LUCKMAN

On Nov. 14, 1943, in what would be another NFL championship season for the Monsters of the Midway, Sid Luckman threw a record-tying seven touchdown passes in the Bears' 56-7 victory. But his mother wasn't impressed.

"That's one of the few games my mother ever went to," Luckman said. "She was always afraid I would play and get hurt. I was running with the ball and she was sitting with my brother and sister, and yelling, 'Please, Sid, please, Sid, give them the ball. Let them run with the ball.'"

STAT MAN

The NFL didn't start keeping track of sacks as a statistic until 1982, although the term was coined by Hall of Fame defensive end David "Deacon" Jones in the 1960s. The sack totals of bygone eras are fun to imagine, although there would have been fewer sacks if for no other reason than the offenses of the pre-1960 NFL were run-based.

Still...

"As a defensive end, they didn't keep track of sacks as a statistic," said Ed Sprinkle, a Bears defensive end from 1944-55. "They didn't have them. They were just another tackle. Bulldog [Turner] and I always knew that the opportunity was not always there for you to make a lot of tackles, too. If you were right defensive end and they ran to their right all the time, you might not get the opportunity to make a tackle.

"But in one game against Baltimore I made five sacks. Back then, though, they were just counted as tackles. There were a lot of things written about me over the years, but I do know that if they had kept track of sacks then the way they do now, I'd have been right up at the head of the class.

"But I looked at it as just going out there to play a game and try to win. I get a kick out of guys now, when the quarterback falls down and they run over and tap him on the ground, then turn around and point to themselves, like 'That's *my* sack.'"

BRONK

Bronco Nagurski was the standard of rugged for the era in which the Bears formed their "Monsters of the Midway" persona. At 230 pounds, he could deliver a blow like few others in his time.

He could take one like few others too.

In 1930, his rookie season, Nagurski was being hit hard in a rough game at Wrigley Field, a venue notable for its being a little short for a football field. The line defining the back of one end zone in fact went up onto the bricks of the outfield wall in one corner.

With the Bears in possession at the opposing two-yard line, Nagurski took the handoff and blasted head-down into the line. He smashed through one tackler, then a second, then hit the goal post, in those days sitting at the goal line. Bronk didn't stop, just kept churning off the post and powered through the end zone and into the brick wall, which finally brought him to a dazed stop.

Coming over to the Bears bench on the sideline he was asked if he was OK.

"Yeah, I am," he said, shaking his head, "but that last guy really hit me."

TOUGH GUY

Hall of Fame center Clyde "Bulldog" Turner is supposed to have fallen out of a third-story window of a hotel and was saved when he hit an awning that broke his fall. A policeman came running up as Turner was collecting himself and asked, "What happened here?"

"I don't know," Turner answered. "I just got here myself."

Teammate Ed Sprinkle remembers Turner. "There was a lot of camaraderie back then with your teammates," Sprinkle says. "It was just fun to be a Bear and play in the NFL. Bulldog Turner was

Bronco Nagurski   *AP/WWP*

one of my better friends; we went to the same school, Hardin-Simmons, and we roomed together on the road for eight years. He was a kind of guy who loved to drink and I tried to take care of him a lot. We'd get into some funny situations.

"He was one of those guys who wakes up all beat up and bandaged up and says, 'How'd I get here?' You tell him, 'You bet people you could go out the window and walk around the building.' He'd say, 'Why didn't you stop me?' I'd tell him, 'Stop ya? I bet you could do it!'"

SALESMAN

Playing for George Halas probably meant needing a second source of income besides football, as it did for a lot of pro football players before the money of television. Players got a couple of tickets to give away, but tackle Lee Artoe had other ideas.

Artoe wouldn't give his tickets away; he'd go out in front of the stadium and sell the tickets. Then he'd come in late and Halas would chew him out. "You out there again selling the damn tickets?"

BOYS, BOYS

Being teammates was no assurance of being accorded anything close to civil courtesy. Sometimes just the opposite.

"My first scrimmage, you're a newcomer and getting established, and I'm playing against Ed Sprinkle," said Jack Karwales. "We were having a charity game to raise money for the school system in Renssalaer. And he gives me a shot in the head. We lined up and as I go by him he gives me an elbow right in the side of the head.

"I grabbed him, we went down and I stepped all over him with my cleats. Walked right on. I missed his face but I got him in the chest. Sprinkle would clothesline guys, hit them in the neck and he'd do it to his own guys in practice. He was a dirty son of a bitch.

"Sprinkle and I were running a golf tournament together and he got some people to donate equipment. And then he kept it all! Everything. His garage was packed full of the stuff. So I go to Ed and says, 'Ed, when are we going to give this out and give it to the players?' He says, 'I'll take care of it, Jack.' The son of a bitch never did."

THE CLAW

Sprinkle's clothesline had a name: The Claw. "I'd come in on the quarterback and have a blocker on me. And there'd come the halfback going out for a pass. So I'd jump or reach out and hook 'em.

"When you got into the pros, the coaches don't have time to teach you how to play football. So nobody ever told me how to play defensive end, do this or that. They would tell you in the defenses where to play or what to do, but how you played was more or less something you developed on your own.

"I played in a 'down' stance, a three-point stance, but a lot of defensive ends then didn't. I'd always key off the guard. If the guard pulled out and was coming down the line to hit me, I could see him and would go in and hit him instead. If the ball carrier went wide, then I used the momentum off him to take myself wide and keep the ball carrier from going wide. But stuff like that I more or less learned myself."

Sprinkle doesn't like to be reminded of his reputation as one of the league's dirtiest players. He also vehemently disagrees with that assessment of him as a player.

"I get very agitated about that because I don't think I was a dirty football player," Sprinkle says. "I didn't deserve that. Somebody who never saw you play will say, 'Oh, you were a dirty player.' It rankles you a little bit. I played hard and I played mean and what the hell, if they call that dirty, then so be it. That's not how I thought about it.

"If I was rushing a quarterback and had a chance to hit him, if he's running, I'd hit him. That's part of the job."

Much is made of the toughness and crustiness of past-era players toward each other, and many don't like the shows of friendship among players on the field before and after games. But truth be told, it wasn't all animosity among combatants back then, even among the toughest.

"Lou Creekmur [Hall of Fame guard for the Detroit Lions] would be blocking on me and he weighed 260-270. He'd be coming at me, and I weighed 210 and had to beat the guy some way. Well, we'd always meet down at The Cottage on Sunday night and Lou was in there laughing, and said, 'Well, you got me on that one today.' I asked him what he meant and he said, 'You knocked my tooth out.'

"But it wasn't animosity or anything like that. We left it all on the field. He once said he came out blocking me, raised his head up and all he could see was two feet coming right in his face. That was a really outstanding Lions line. Dick Stanfel was the other guard and he was the MVP of a championship game. Dick was an All-Pro player and I think he was even better than Lou. Lou was good, but Stanfel was outstanding.

"I had guards coming out at 250 with a couple of steps first and I knocked guards on their backs. It was just the way I played. Abe Gibron was a heck of a blocker and Marion Motley was maybe 250 and blocking on me, so I had to really work to get around them to get to Otto Graham. One time Abe came out at me and I just hurdled him, over top of him. Graham was rolling out my way and I was able to get a sack of Graham, but there weren't too many against him because he had a pretty good line.

"Abe and Lou Groza were the left side of their line and Lou was blocking on me. But then he told Abe to switch after a while, that he didn't want to block on me. So he switched and had Abe pull and block me.

"We'd play Philadelphia and Steve Van Buren, who had some great days and great games. But most of the time he wasn't running my way. He'd run the other way. But he was big and he was a tough one to tackle.

"The Cardinals had that so-called 'Dream Backfield,' with Paul Christman, and he didn't like getting hit. One time supposedly he said he fired the ball in my face and knocked me out. It never happened. If it had, I would have tried to kill him."

WHAT MIGHT HAVE BEEN?

World War II took many of the great Bears and members of other NFL team into the horrors of battle and far, far from football. Sid Luckman was on a tanker in the North Atlantic where he dodged German U-boats and mines. George McAfee went into the navy in 1942, as did Halas. Bill Osmanski, who'd scored the first touchdown in the 73-0 game, served as a navy dentist with the Marines on Okinawa.

"I remember asking Mr. Halas once, that had the war not come along, just how good could that [1940s] team have been?" McAfee mused. "He thought about it a minute and said, 'There's no telling.' And I believe he was right."

SPRINKLE'S DAY

Ed Sprinkle was one of the most feared players in the game during his 1944-55 career. He was out of tiny Hardin-Simmons in Texas, the same school that produced Clyde "Bulldog" Turner, and played the game never asking nor giving any quarter.

He would go to the Pro Bowl (then just the NFL All-Star Game) the first three years of its existence (1951–53) and again in 1955. But his breakthrough came in the best of all possible venues, the NFL championship game of 1946, won by the Bears 24-14. Sprinkle provided the game's violent turning point.

"We played against the Giants in the championship game in 1946 and that was one of the best-remembered games I ever played in," Sprinkle says. "They had switched me to right defensive end in that game. We'd had an All-Pro defensive end, George Wilson, who played right end, and they wanted to put me at left end. I said, no, I played right end. I'd played some defensive end in college and at the Naval Academy, so they moved him to left end and put me at right end."

Unfortunately for the Giants. They were without fullback Merle Hapes, who was suspended for failing to report a bribe attempt, and Giants quarterback Frank Filchock could have used Hapes' pass protection. In the first quarter, Filchock dropped to pass and Sprinkle came in right over a blocker and hit him with a blow that broke his nose. It also caused the ball to sputter out of his hands and up in the air where it was grabbed by defensive back Dante Margnani, who returned it 19 yards to give the Bears a 14-0 lead.

"Dante almost walked in for the touchdown," Sprinkle said. "I had a really good game and that was the game that really set my career off."

Chapter 9

THE OLD MAN

George Halas isn't part of NFL history; he is NFL history. He was there to start the whole thing; he nurtured it, defined it and helped create an American institution. And why not? He's one himself.

Halas may have helped found the National Football League, but that didn't always get him special consideration once the games started. Halas was ranting and raging on the sideline during one 1920s contest when referee Jim Durfee suddenly marched off a five-yard penalty.

"What the hell's that for?" Halas bellowed.

"Coaching from the sidelines," Durfee hollered back, citing what was then against the rules.

"Well, that's how stupid you are," Halas roared. "It's a 15-yard penalty, not five!"

"George," Durfee said, ending the discussion, "your coaching's only worth five."

TOUGH GUY-TOUGH COACH

Hall of Famer George Connor was kicked in the head by a Packer and needed stitches in his chin at halftime. He went into the boiler room of Lambeau Field, then called City Stadium, to have the cut stitched up.

When he was finished, he was a little late for the second half and the stadium gates were padlocked. Connor yelled to some Bears fans in the stadium, who came down and got into a fight with stadium people to get the gate open.

Connor ran into the stadium, but the Bears were on the other side of the field, play was going on, and he had to wait for a timeout to run across to their side.

"Where have you been?" Halas yelled. "You're late. That'll cost you $50."

CASH CRUNCH AND A MOTHER'S LOVE

Halas would come to be the cornerstone on which the National Football League was built. But very early in its history, the Bears were within minutes of being taken from Halas.

It almost happened in 1933. Profits were thin in the early years. Halas sold cars to make a living; co-owner Dutch Sternaman pumped gas. In 1932 Sternaman needed money to pay the mortgages on an apartment house and gas station, so he offered to sell Halas his share of the Bears for $38,000. Halas went for it.

Halas agreed to make his final payment in 1933, with the deal being that if he could not come up with the full amount, everything would revert to Sternaman. Halas would be out. The Bears in fact won the NFL championship in 1932 too.

But they lost money, a deficit of $18,000. So when the final payment on the buyout of the Bears was due, Halas was short.

Fortunately, Halas had a friend in Charlie Bidwill, who would eventually buy the rival Chicago Cardinals. Bidwill put up $5,000 to buy Bears stock from Halas. Bidwill also helped set up a bank loan from a bank that was closed because of the Depression.

Halas got $5,000 from his mother, Barbara, a widow who lived on the income from a grocery store she'd opened after Halas' father suffered a stroke. Her Bohemian duck was Halas' favorite dish growing up, and now she was serving him something even more important.

Halas faced a noon deadline. If the final money wasn't in the office of Sternaman's attorney by noon on Aug. 9, 1933, the Bears would belong to Sternaman, who would put the franchise up for sale. By 11 a.m. that day, Halas was still $5,000 short.

Then C. K. Anderson, president of First National Bank in Antioch, phoned Halas to say he'd learned Halas desperately needed funds. He agreed to lend Halas the money and Halas ran over to the bank's office in Chicago to get the check. Halas picked up the money and ran to the office of Sternaman's lawyer, getting the money to him at 10 minutes before noon, just before the fire sale would have started.

Halas had his Bears.

NEGOTIATING WITH HALAS

Winning the '63 world championship didn't loosen Halas' legendarily tight purse strings. Mike Ditka once remarked that the Old Man threw nickels around like they were manhole covers, and few of his players would disagree.

The Bears had just won the world championship, and the players were waiting to see what they'd get as a bonus, knowing that Packers players got things from Lombardi and other teams gave things to the players. Bears players instead got a paperweight, not from Halas and the Bears, but from Mayor Richard Daley. "That's all we got, from the mayor, not the team," fumed Ed O'Bradovich.

"Everybody wanted out or more money," O'Bradovich said. "So I waited to find the time to make my move. It was about 9 or 10 o' clock at night and Halas said, 'Sure kid, c'mon in.' I was making about $11,000 a year. I said I wanted a $5,000 raise."

"No," Halas said.

"What do you mean by 'no'?" O'Bradovich asked.

"Just what I told you—no."

O'Bradovich reminded Halas that they'd won the world championship and that in the title game against the New York Giants he'd intercepted the Y.A. Tittle pass to set up the winning touchdown.

"Anybody could've done that," Halas barked.

"Nobody did it but me and that pass led to the winning touchdown," O'Bradovich countered. "I want my $5,000 raise, bonus or whatever you want to call it, or get rid of me."

"No, you're not getting the $5,000, and we're not getting rid of you," Halas declared.

O'Bradovich continued to make his case until Halas ordered him out of the room. As he got to the door, Halas got in the last word, as always.

"Normally when a player leaves camp, it's $100 a day," Halas said. "But for you, I'll make it $200. Have a nice night, kid."

O'Bradovich was a veteran in more ways than one. "I think in my years I held out four times," he said, "and lost every time."

THE BOOK

Halas taught O'Bradovich the NFL meaning of "creative book-keeping." Going into one negotiation, O'Bradovich had what he thought was one of his better years. But what Halas did was keep The Book, the grading book he'd pull out when it came time to discuss how someone had played, and to "show" the player how bad he'd really been.

O'Bradovich went to see him again about a raise, because he was getting interest from the Dallas Cowboys. He wanted $10,000 from Halas. He walked in and said, "Before we start the conversation, pull the book out."

"All right, kid," Halas said, pulling out the book.

O'Bradovich had been through this before with the Old Man, with Halas going game by game in his ledger and "documenting" missed tackles and other sundry misdeeds, concluding, "according to this, you're one of the worst defensive linemen we've got. I can't give you the raise."

"He'd do that to everybody," O'Bradovich says. "No one knew where the grades came from and everyone suspected the Old Man had more than one set of so-called books."

O'Bradovich told Halas to go right to No. 87 and he pointed out to Halas game by game what he'd done. "According to this," O'Bradovich concluded, "I was the best defensive lineman you had."

Halas looked up from the book at O'Bradovich. "You know what you can do with these grades?" Halas announced. "You can take 'em and stick 'em up your ass. Thank you very much and don't let the door hit you in the ass."

HALAS AND "BIG MAN"

Halas met his equal in defensive end Doug Atkins. The two went at each other constantly, with Atkins knowing how to get under Halas' skin and being good enough on the field that Halas wasn't going to put his foot down too hard. Besides, he couldn't always be sure exactly what Big Man would do anyway.

Playing the Minnesota Vikings, Atkins had been out the night before and had a few too many and wasn't feeling too well. The Vikings were doing a number on the Bears and Atkins was throwing up in the huddle, sick as a dog.

At halftime the players had orange slices and Cokes. Halas always had two Coke bottles prepared for him for halftime, special Cokes with Early Times whiskey mixed in. Atkins was heaving in the huddle and still killing Vikings left tackle Grady Alderman, throwing him through the air like a clown jumping off a board.

At halftime, Atkins came in and grabbed one of Halas' bottles of Coke and liquor. He downed it without missing a beat as the trainer started yelling. Then Halas walked in and saw the one bottle left, and it was in Atkins' massive paw.

So, with the Bears getting pummeled on the scoreboard, the main thing at that halftime was not some adjustment, but rather that little bottle. Perhaps the greatest defensive end in NFL history and the founder of the league (and one of its genuine legends) started arguing. Halas grabbed Atkins' hand with the bottle in it and started tugging. Atkins tugged back, and the two tugged away until finally Atkins muttered, "Oh, take it, ya' old fuck."

ON THE RUN

Halas in his autobiography *Halas on Halas* put some of the finances and emotions of the early game in perspective in his team's first-ever season. Fans became emotional about their local team then not so much out of allegiance (the league hadn't been around that long, and there was no TV or radio in the beginning) as out of betting results.

His Staleys had beaten the Rock Island Independents 7-0 in a game that had been attended by a legion of Staley fans who'd chartered a train, and those fans had cleaned up in an upset over a strong team. When the Bears returned for another game three weeks later, Halas figured feelings were running high, so he lodged the team at the Hotel Davenport, across the river from Rock Island.

Word from a number of gamblers was that Bears tough guy George Trafton, whose career at Notre Dame ended when Knute Rockne caught him playing semipro ball, would be knocked out of the game as early as the first quarter. It didn't quite work that way.

Trafton proceeded to knock four Rockford players out of the game in the first 12 plays, the last being Independents fullback Fred Chicken, initially deemed the one most likely to do in Trafton. The Rock Island doctor returned Chicken to consciousness but with 19 stitches in Chickens scalp and a cast on his broken wrist.

This scarcely improved the mood of the Rock Island fans. So as the 0-0 game wound down to its last play Halas devised a play with Trafton carrying the ball through an exit to get him out of the stadium. The gun went off (presumably not one fired by a Rock Island fan,) and Trafton was through the exit, quickly donning a sweatshirt that was provided underneath the stands to disguise his number. Trafton jumped into a car and got across the bridge and the state line to Iowa.

The Bears' share of the gate receipts from that game has been pegged at different amounts, sometimes $3,000, other times $7,000. Whatever the amount, it was in cash, so at the Hotel Davenport, Halas gave the money to Trafton to bring to the team's train. His reasoning: "I knew if we did encounter obstreperous Rock Island fans, I would run for the money but Trafton would run for his life."

GOOD IDEA

Halas was an innovator of epic proportions and also of little creations if they offered an advantage. He got an idea that it would be possible to install tiny radio receivers in players' helmets and met with Motorola founder Bob Galvin and others, coming up with a concept far ahead of its time.

Halas had a wire buried around the football field to act as a transmitter and put receivers in the helmets of the quarterback and the defensive captain. For three games he was able to radio in instructions. Then the league got wind of his breakthrough and banned its operation.

Today every NFL quarterback has a receiver in his helmet that allows him to get his plays and instructions from coaches on the bench.

MONEY MATTERS

Ed O'Bradovich thought he'd had a pretty good season one year and decided he needed a $4,000 raise from Halas to sign his next contract. They sat down, O'Bradovich made his pitch, and Halas answered that, well, O'Bradovich really hadn't played all that well, and besides, the Bears were losing money. O'Bradovich, ever the team player, dropped his demand to $3,000.

Halas declared, though, that O'Bradovich had been skirt-chasing, running with riff-raff, and not doing his workouts and calisthenics the way he was supposed to. OK, O'Bradovich figured, make it $2,000.

The haggling went on and O'Bradovich said $1,000 would do it. Halas hemmed and hawed and poor-mouthed until O'Bradovich stood up and threw in the towel.

"Hey, Coach," O'Bradovich concluded, "let me give you a check for $500."

SNEAKING UP

Halas would tell the story on himself during his playing days of a painful encounter with Joe Guyon, a full-blooded Native

American then playing for the New York Giants. Guyon in 1927 was quarterbacking the Giants and faded back to pass as Halas bore in from his spot at right defensive end.

Halas had visions of a blind-side hit (the term "sack" wasn't invented yet; that would be coined by Los Angeles Rams Hall of Fame end David "Deacon" Jones in the 1960s) and maybe a fumble.

Guyon got off the pass at the last second, then spun to greet Halas with a knee that broke several of Halas' ribs. Guyon, who'd played with the Carlisle Indians and other teams with the great Jim Thorpe, took a look at the writhing Halas on the ground and shook his head.

"C'mon, Halas," Guyon admonished. "You should know better than to try to sneak up on an Indian."

Chapter 10

WALTER

Walter Payton set records and defined the Bears for more than a decade. He was the symbol of a team and eventually of a city. He was beyond description, except perhaps for the simplest:

"He was the greatest Bear of all."—Mike Ditka.

Walter Payton played for the Bears from 1975, when he was the fourth pick of the first round out of Jackson State, until 1987. When he died in 1999, more than just the football world cried.

The Bears and the city of Chicago held a moving tribute to Walter on the Saturday following his death. Former teammates, team officials and current players all said what was on their minds and hearts, and the crowd of more than 20,000 in Soldier Field shared some of the sadness of the moment as well as the magic of Walter.

The most poignant moment came not from a coach or member of the Bears' offense. Defensive end Dan Hampton, himself voted to Pro Football's Hall of Fame in 2002, was one of the toughest of a tough bunch of players, but the memory of Walter was more than he could bear up to as his comments came to a close.

His voice choked with emotion, Hampton looked both back and ahead as he recalled teammate Walter Payton.

"I remember this guy playing on this field and leaving it on this field time after time," Hampton said, struggling for control as his hands shook and his voice broke slightly as he spoke to the crowd at Soldier Field.

He paused as tears came to his eyes. Then he finished: "I have a little girl [who's] four years old. Ten years from now, when she asks me about the Chicago Bears, I'll tell her about a championship and I'll tell her about great teams, great teammates and great coaches, and how great it was to be a part of it.

"But the first thing I'll tell her about is Walter Payton."

*   *   *   *

Walter took fun seriously. Once, after sprinkling powdered sugar in his moustache, Walter burst into a meeting on drugs being conducted by an NFL official. "Ain't no cocaine on this team!" Walter yelled.

*   *   *   *

Defensive end Clyde Simmons, who finished his career as a Bear in 2000, had the rare distinction among his Chicago teammates of being the only one who played on the same field with Walter. Simmons was a rookie with the Philadelphia Eagles in 1986, and his second NFL game was against the Bears, when the Eagles came to Soldier Field. The game was a hard-fought, 13-10 contest that was settled in overtime by a Kevin Butler field goal.

Simmons, a backup at the time who ultimately would go on to become one of the NFL's all-time great pass rushers, got in the Bears game briefly and made his first career tackle: a stop of the Bears' Hall of Fame.

Later the tackle came up in conversation, "and the first thing that came to Payton's mind was, 'Did you hit me hard?'" Simmons said. "I said, 'No, I was just happy to hold on.'"

"You have to understand how special it is to be a Chicago Bear, and Walter Payton always did," Hampton said, recalling Payton's simple order to teammates every week: "'Play your [butt] off.' That's all he ever wanted from us."

*   *   *   *

Safety Dave Duerson was voted to his first Pro Bowl in Hawaii after the Bears' Super Bowl victory. He went out for his first practice, enjoying the warmth, but was beset by a different kind of warmth, courtesy of Walter.

"Walter had put some unscented liquid heat in my [athletic supporter]," Duerson says, shaking his head. "Let's just say, it was a very hot afternoon in warm, sunny Hawaii."

*   *   *   *

Training camp was prime time for the legendary Payton mischief.

Defensive tackle Jim Osborne recalled the fatigue and exhaustion from two-a-day practices in camp that left tired players in a deep sleep at night. Payton, though, was not above dipping into his endless supply of fireworks and detonating a large firecracker in the dorm, jolting his teammates out of whatever sleep they were enjoying.

Yet Walter "never missed practice, was always the first one there ready to go," Osborne said. "He was the guy you knew you could count on. That's what inspired the rest of the team."

*   *   *   *

Tackle James "Big Cat" Williams did not join the Bears until 1991. One of his only career regrets: that he never got to block for Walter. But that doesn't mean he never shared a Payton moment.

"He's probably one of the greatest men I've ever met," Williams says. "Not because of what he did on the field, but because of how he made you feel off it."

Payton once took Williams with him to a north suburban mall for an interview that was supposed to take perhaps 15 minutes. They were there nearly two hours and at one point were in a jewelry store.

"Walter pulled two people aside and tried to sell them wedding bands," Williams recalls, laughing. "For the rest of [the 1999] season I played for Walter, his family and his ex-teammates. I keep them all in my heart and in my head."

*   *   *   *

Walter inspired even Packers fans. Defensive tackle Jim Flanigan, who was drafted by the Bears in the third round of the 1994 draft and had seven seasons in Chicago, grew up in Wisconsin, in the middle of Packers country.

One day Flanigan, then in high school, learned of Payton's legendary workout regimen that included grueling runs up a steep hill in Barrington. Flanigan's father played for the Packers, and Flanigan would play for Green Bay himself after the Bears released him in 2000. There was a ski hill near Flanigan's boyhood home and he went there to run to try to emulate Payton.

*   *   *   *

Walter, who was a mixture of power and grace matched only by Jim Brown, once explained one of his training techniques to Don Pierson of the *Chicago Tribune*.

Walter did extensive running in sand as part of his training, explaining that "if you have to come under control to make a cut, the pursuit will catch you. In the sand, you have to move one leg before the other is planted. It makes all your muscles work. Sometimes when I'm done even my neck will be aching."

Because of the ways he trained, Walter sometimes had everyone else's neck aching.

*   *   *   *

Walter was a race car driver, amateur and professional. He owned a restaurant and was an entrepreneur. He invested in forest land and nursing homes. He leased heavy equipment and made up to $1 million a year giving motivational speeches. But there was more to Walter.

"People see what they want to see," Walter said. "They look at me and say 'He's a black man. He's a football player. He's a running back. He's a Chicago Bear.' But I'm more than all that. I'm a father. I'm a husband. I'm a citizen. I'm a person who is willing to give his all. That's how I want to be remembered."

*   *   *   *

How great were Walter's accomplishments? Twelve years after Walter retired, he still held or shared eight NFL records, including the all-time rushing record of 16,726 yards. (This record was finally broken by Dallas' Emmitt Smith in 2002.)

*   *   *   *

Mike Ditka inherited Walter when he came to coach the Bears in 1982. He knew what he had, and at Walter's memorial service said it as well as anyone in attendance. Ditka called Walter "the best runner, blocker, teammate and friend I've ever seen. Truly the best football player I've ever seen. Coach [George] Halas is saying, 'Hey, I've finally got the greatest Bear of all.'"

*   *   *   *

NFL television analyst John Madden offered to end all arguments about who was the greatest.

"Walter Payton was the greatest," he said. "If you wanted yards, you'd want Walter Payton. Who do you want to block? Walter Payton. If you wanted someone to catch, Walter Payton. He played on some bad teams. How about if you want somebody to make a tackle after an interception? One year he had 18."

*   *   *   *

Walter's older brother Eddie, himself a kick returner for four NFL teams, recalled a Mississippi gas station attendant mistaking him for Walter and giving him a free tank. In a high-pitched voice imitating Walter, Eddie told the man, "If you're ever in Chicago, look me up."

*   *   *   *

Despite the increased emphasis on passing, football's rushing record has always been something extra special, like the home-run record of first Babe Ruth, then Henry Aaron, or the consecutive-game streak of Lou Gehrig and now Cal Ripken. When Walter broke Jim Brown's record, he got a call from President Ronald Reagan in the locker room afterwards.

"The check's in the mail," Payton joked.

*   *   *   *

Walter took whatever edge he could and he'd do whatever he could to stretch things a little, but usually with a warrior's sense of humor. Most of his runs ended with his hand darting out of the pile and placing the ball a foot or two farther down the field. He was said to have kidded that he'd added 100 yards to his career total with those sneaky inches.

Most of the time he'd be caught and the ball placed where it belonged. Once he joked to a vigilant official who was spotting the ball, "How do you expect me to catch Jim Brown if you do that?"

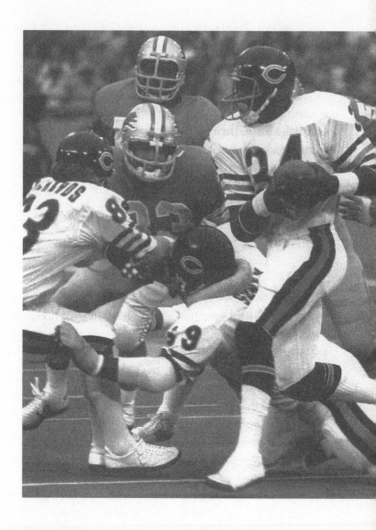

*   *   *   *

Walter and his financial advisors managed his money and investments very well, but not all financial matters were easy. After Walter gained 1,395 yards in the first 16-game season, he

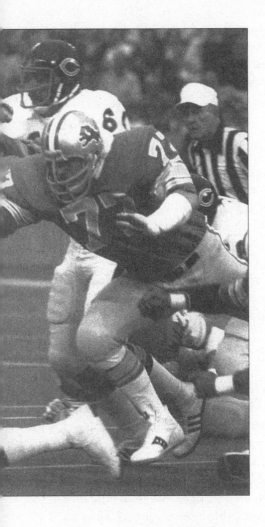

*Walter Payton
picks his spot
against the Lions.
AP/WWP*

sought $513,000 in salary from the Bears, which was 70 percent
of O. J. Simpsons pay envelope of $733,000, tops in the NFL.
The Bears offered $391,000 a year. Eventually Walter agreed to a
three-year deal averaging $425,000 a year plus some incentives,
but he understandably wasn't particularly pleased.

"The thing is, people want me to beat all O. J.'s records," Walter said. "'Beat this, beat that.' Why don't they want me to beat his salary? Tell me that. It's like telling a little kid in baseball, 'I want you to catch every ball and when this guy comes up, let him go.' I can't do that."

*   *   *   *

Walter set the NFL single-game rushing record with 275 yards against the Minnesota Vikings on Nov. 20, 1977, a record since broken by Corey Dillon of the Cincinnati Bengals. Of Hall of Fame tight end John Mackey it was often said, "the lucky ones fell off," and there were those who felt the same about trying to tackle Walter, certainly that day.

"It's similar to trying to rope a calf," said Vikings cornerback Bobby Bryant. "It's hard enough to get your hands on him, and once you do, you wonder if you should have."

*   *   *   *

Gale Sayers was without question one of the NFL's most dangerous and electrifying kick returners off his era and all time, with a peak of 37.7 yards per kickoff return in 1967 (which was second in NFL history but remarkably, didn't lead the league that season; Green Bay Packer (of course) Travis Williams ran 18 kicks back an average of 41.1 yards that same year).

But Walter was a force in his own right with what little time he was given. Walter led the NFL by returning 14 kicks an average of 31.7 yards in 1975, but coach Jack Pardee took him off that duty after he got knocked out against the Rams.

*   *   *   *

In his NFL career Walter missed exactly one game because of an injury. Or did he?

In Walter's rookie season, facing the Pittsburgh Steelers, Jack Pardee and running backs coach Fred O'Connor chose to play former Northwestern star Mike Adamle and gave Walter the day off to rest a sore ankle. That was not how Walter saw it.

"Excuse me; an ankle?" Walter later said. "I played once after getting my ankle taped three times. Taped the skin without prewrap because they said it would hold better. Put on my sock and taped it again. Then I put on my shoe and had it spatted. Gained 100-something yards, scored a couple of touchdowns.

"If you're ready to play and the coach won't let you, is that a missed game?"

*   *   *   *

When Payton broke the all-time rushing mark of Jim Brown, not surprisingly his thoughts at the press conference afterwards were not about himself or Brown:

"The motivating drive for me has been for the athletes who tried but still failed to reach that certain achievement, and also the athlete that didn't get an opportunity to, like the [James] Overstreets, the [Joe] Delaneys and Brian Piccolos. They simplified what the game is made of and what I did out there is a reflection of those guys, because they made the sacrifices as well, and it's a tribute to be able to bestow that honor for them."

Chapter 11

BUTKUS

By acclamation in and out of the NFL, Butkus was the greatest linebacker ever to play pro football. He was a Chicago native who lived and played by a code of violence that few could match, not so much for his much-chronicled malevolence, but for his sheer excellence and force of will. If you played against him, or even with him for that matter, you never forgot it.

THE GREATEST OF ALL TIME

Dick Butkus, who roomed with Ed O'Bradovich, was a dead-serious kid. "He wouldn't know if the sun was out or anything, always had his head down, real serious," O'Bradovich remembered. But he made an impression in a hurry.

About halfway through Butkus' first training camp as a rookie in 1965, defensive back Richie Pettitbon was among a group of Bears veterans talking about players. Out of nowhere, Pettitbon

Dick Butkus   *AP/WWP*

offered a prediction: "This guy is going to rewrite the record books," Pettitbon forecast. "He's going to be the greatest of all time."

LOST SOUL

The Bears of Butkus' reign may not always have won, but Butkus made a lasting, devastating impression on those who faced him.

"He knocked out L. C. Greenwood on a punt and he knocked out Warren Bankston, who was a fullback and a good special teams player," said Pittsburgh Steelers center Ray Mansfield. "I remember Warren coming over and crying, 'I don't know who I am.'"

CARNIVORE

"Before you tried to block on Dick, you had to overcome the mystique," said Baltimore Colts center Bill Curry. "It was almost like an odor. He exuded a kind of presence. He dominated a game the way no other player has. He intimidated officials. He'd take the ball away from somebody after the play and shake it in the official's face, and the official pointed their way and gave them the ball. It was awesome."

In the lobby of Halas Hall, the Bears have a display of their Hall of Fame players, including a "description" of Butkus. Minnesota Vikings running back Dave Osborne had been annihilated by Butkus on a sweep against the Bears, and Osborne was asked after the game what had happened to his blocker on the play.

"I don't know," Osborne reflected. "Maybe Butkus ate him."

BRAIN POWER

Butkus was incensed at a call made by official Norm Schacter and raged in the face of the veteran striped shirt. He was shaking his finger and yelling until finally Schacter had had enough.

"Butkus," Schacter warned, "if you don't get your finger out of my face, I'm going to bite your head off."

Butkus stomped off but not before getting the last word. "If you do," Butkus snarled, "you'll have more brains in your stomach than you do in your head."

ROSTER MANAGEMENT

At one point in the dismal 1-13 campaign of 1969, most of the special teams were staffed with starters. Butkus went to coach Abe Gibron and demanded to know why he, Doug Buffone, Ed O'Bradovich and other front-line players were on first-team special teams when there were guys in uniform who never got on the field.

"We can't trust them," Gibron said simply.

"Then what the hell are they doing on the team?" Butkus bellowed and stormed out.

THE TOUGHEST

One day at practice Gale Sayers was asked who the toughest guy he ever played against was. Sayers didn't say a word, just pointed out toward the field: at No. 51.

Sayers had faced Butkus in two college games. "Wherever I went, there he was," Sayers marveled. "I went left. There he was. To my right. There was Butkus."

Los Angeles Rams coach Chuck Knox offered this assessment of Butkus. "He was the kind of linebacker that, when he hit our backs, the back would go back to the huddle and be talking out his earhole and want to know who was supposed to block that crazy sucker..."

INTIMIDATOR

"He tried to hurt you," said Dallas Cowboy Dan Reeves. "He was so competitive. Not only did he not want you to gain a yard, he didn't want you to gain an inch. As soon as you had that football, you were the enemy."

"Dick was not satisfied with an ordinary tackle," said New Orleans Saints receiver and eventual Bears special teams coach Dan Abramowicz. He had to hit you, pick you up, drive you, grind you into the ground."

"It was horrifying playing against him because he literally could intimidate an entire offensive team, and I mean good teams," said Atlanta Falcons running back Alex Hawkins.

"We had a rookie center who was playing against him for the first time," said Dallas Cowboys coach Tom Landry. "And Butkus grunted a lot and growled a lot when he was back there. The first time that rookie center came off his eyes were open wide all the way, he couldn't believe what he was hearing from Butkus. Butkus had him intimidated and he hadn't even blocked him."

SIMPLE MISSION

"Dick was an animal," said Hall of Fame defensive end Deacon Jones. "I called him a maniac. A stone maniac. He was a well-conditioned animal and every time he hit you, he tried to put you in the cemetery, not the hospital."

Chapter 12

THE PACK

The Bears would not have become the Bears without the Green Bay Packers. Halas would not have been what he was without Lombardi, Ditka without Forrest Gregg (for better or worse). They live in a rarified place that few can understand who haven't been there themselves. But they can be enjoyed by friends and enemies alike.

THE PEN

Agent Steve Zucker was fond of the Bears pen that the Bears had given him to mark the signing of Jim McMahon's first big contract with the team. The pen had worked perfectly for many years for Zucker, through quite a few important deals.

But that changed when defensive tackle Steve McMichael, cut by the Bears in April 1994, was about to sign the contract Zucker negotiated with the Green Bay Packers.

Zucker handed McMichael the pen and Ming initialed a few things, then prepared to sign formally.

"All of a sudden, the pen just stopped writing," Zucker recalls. "It had never done that before, ever. I think a Bears pen just couldn't bring itself to see Steve McMichael become a Green Bay Packer."

HIT LISTS

The Packers added a mean note to the storied rivalry when a number of their players came out for a 1986 game wearing white towels from their belts, with various Bears players' numbers listed on the towels. The message: This is a hit list.

The Bears had their own answer for that.

"They came out wearing those towels, hit lists, with our players' number on them, for each guy they were going to 'get,'" says linebacker Jim Morrissey. "Ditka says to us, 'Whoever gets one of those towels, I'll give him a hundred bucks. Bring it to me on the sideline and I'll give you a hundred bucks.'

"So we're running on after special teams and Glen Kozlowski comes running over to Ditka waving towels: 'Hey, coach, I got a couple towels for ya.' I think he went into the Packers' huddle and just started ripping towels off everybody."

"THE PAYTON GAME"

In 1999, the day after a Soldier Field memorial service for Walter Payton, the Bears appeared headed for yet another loss to the Green Bay Packers. But Walter had other ideas.

Bears kicker Chris Boniol pushed a 32-yard field-goal try wide left with five minutes, 56 seconds remaining. But some things are

Walter Payton   ***AP/WWP***

simply meant to be, and after an emotional week following Payton's death Monday from liver cancer, Bears players believed a victory was somehow waiting for them.

They had no idea that Walter himself may have had a hand in making that dream happen.

"I don't want to say that we came out and dedicated the game to Walter," said receiver Bobby Engram. "But we did feel his presence."

So did the Packers. They trailed the Bears 14-13 when Brett Favre drove the team down inside the Chicago 20 and Ryan Longwell prepared to kick a 28-yard field goal that would give Green Bay a 16-14 victory that would have been the 11th straight in a storied rivalry.

The ball was snapped and placed down. Longwell approached and delivered the kick. It started on its trip toward the uprights in the north end zone. It was up to the heavens at that point.

Defensive lineman Bryan Robinson jumped up and got a hand on the ball, deflecting it far short of the goal line where it was recovered by safety Tony Parrish. Afterwards, Robinson was not about to claim sole credit for his game-saving play.

"I think Walter Payton actually picked me up," Robinson said, "because I know I can't jump that high."

Robinson wasn't the only Bear stunned by what he saw and experienced that day. "I have just one word," said running back James Allen. "It's sweet. 'Sweetness.'"

Said coach Dick Jauron: "We've got to believe Walter Payton had a hand in the final play."

A LITTLE RESPECT, PLEASE?

Bears and Packers players didn't always especially care for each other. But it wasn't enough that many Packers and Bears players haven't always been the best of friends. Sometimes that pent-up emotion from both teams erupted into occasional extracurricular activity.

"The lack of respect is what got to me," said tackle Mike Wells. "It just seemed like we had everybody against us today. There was even a cop on the sideline yelling at us and I said, 'Get out of our bench.' And he was like, 'Oh no, this is my area.'

"I couldn't believe the audacity some of the people had. Even their water boys didn't respect us."

Says guard Tom Thayer: "There is nothing worse than driving away from Green Bay after losing a game. Everybody is giving you the finger and you just have to accept that.

"And there is nothing more gratifying than pulling away from Green Bay after you've beaten the Packers, because the finger they give you just doesn't mean as much."

FAVRE STOPPER

Maybe it was the thought of facing Brett Favre in another Bears-Packer game. "We're at a big disadvantage," said defensive coordinator Greg Blache. "They got Brett Favre and Ahman Green and we just got us and that's not a fair fight. We're a little bit out-manned right here."

What would make it a fair fight, Greg?

"A restraining order."

KEEP YOUR HEAD DOWN

There is no place in the world where the football experience is what it is at Green Bay's Lambeau Field. But keep your helmet on at all times and don't let your guard, or linebacker, down.

"I loved playing the Pack," says Mike Hartenstine. "That was my favorite field of all time. I loved coming out of the locker room, you'd be underneath the stands and they'd wheel those fences out to stop the people. They'd be throwing beer, pop, hot dogs, batteries on you, and you had to keep your helmet on and your head straight ahead. Then you got in the stadium and you felt like you were in the arena.

"It got real vicious when Forrest Gregg got up there because he and Ditka hated each other. You had to have your head on a swivel at all times because you knew people were coming. He coached it that way and probably more against the Bears."

DITKA-GREGG

Many believe that the Bears-Packers hatred was at its worst during the Mike Ditka-Forrest Gregg years. The two were fierce competitors and rivals from their days as players under Halas and Lombardi, but this went deeper and had none of the respect that usually comes between two individuals who were, as players, equals.

An incident in Gregg's first year as Packers coach, 1984, killed any chance of respect.

The Packers were leading 14-3 nearing halftime of the Aug. 11 exhibition between the two teams, which were at opposite ends of the NFL world. The Bears were on the brink of their epic run through the NFC Central and the Packers were down, which was why Gregg was hired—to restore the roar.

With 1:12 remaining, Gregg called a timeout, which was a violation of the "code" during preseason, but Gregg wanted to send a message to his own players that the Packers were now out to bury people. Normally coaches would let the time run out and get their players in the locker room healthy.

Ditka was outraged. He yelled at Gregg, who said his guys needed to work on their passing game. The rhetoric worsened and the two had to be restrained from going at each other. During the second half, Ditka's mood worsened and he had sideline shouting matches with defensive coordinator Buddy Ryan, too—all in a preseason game!

The Packers would win 17-10 and the era of bad feelings was in motion. The teams have never played each other in preseason since.

SHUTOUT

Both the Bears and Packers had their times of dominating each other. "One year up in Green Bay, in 1949, against Tobin Rote, we didn't let them complete a pass," said Ed Sprinkle. "That was quite a feat to keep a team from completing one pass.

"The events surrounding the games were something. We played in the old City Stadium and the fans were right behind your bench, so I never took my helmet off. You might get a bottle.

"We stayed in the Northland Hotel downtown and then took a bus out to the stadium. They'd honk horns all night and try to keep you awake, but once I went to sleep, I was out."

THE "OTHER" BEARS-PACKERS RIVALRY

George Halas and Curly Lambeau may have been among sports' greatest rivals—they faced each other in the first Bears-Packers game in 1920—but there was much, much more than a feud between them. There was also a special bond.

When a retired Lambeau came to Chicago without a ticket to the 1961 Bears-Packers game in Chicago, Halas told the *Chicago Tribune* that Lambeau was guaranteed a seat at that game, even if it had to be on the Bears' bench.

Halas served as an honorary pallbearer at Lambeau's funeral in 1965. Halas was among the strongest advocates behind the Packers getting a new stadium, urging Green Bay citizens in

1956 to build what would be named Lambeau Field. Lambeau had accepted Halas' IOU in 1932 when, at the peak of the Great Depression, the Bears couldn't cover the $2,500 guarantee to the visiting team for a game.

And it was Halas who helped push through the league's policy of sharing television revenue, without which small-market teams like the Packers might never have survived.

Chapter 13

AFTERTHOUGHTS

ONCE A BEAR, ALWAYS A BEAR

Even when members of the Bears family leave Chicago, they never really leave. "It was so much fun to come to work every day," says Dave McGinnis, who came in 1986 as the linebackers coach, left to become defensive coordinator and eventually head coach of the Arizona Cardinals and nearly returned as the Bears' coach.

"You had a talented group of players that had a mission and that had a huge amount of personality. And the city was embracing that whole team. It was electric every day.

"We had so many personalities in every corner you looked. On Saturdays the players would bring their kids and their dogs and whatever up to practice for the workout and they'd take the kids up and throw them in the dryer or the whirlpool and the kids having a greattime. It was a great feeling around there, it really was."

*   *   *   *

"I loved playing with those guys because everybody came to play," says Mike Hartenstine. "The first time I met Jauron and his coaching staff at the fan convention, I told them, you don't even have to win in Chicago for people to love and appreciate you. Just beat the shit out of people when you play them. They'll embrace you here. That's how itwas. That's how it still is and probably always will be."

*   *   *   *

"I had an opportunity to go play in the USFL with the Chicago Blitz and George Allen," says guard and Joliet native Tom Thayer. "The reason I signed with the USFL was to stay in Chicago, because you never know where you're going to go in the NFL. Then two days later they have the NFL draft and I find out I'm drafted by the Chicago Bears.

"It was a great experience playing for George Allen and with some of the teammates that I played with in the USFL played in the NFL. But there's nothing like playing for the Bears. Nothing like it."

*   *   *   *

"I'll stay in Chicago," tackle James "Big Cat" Williams said after his release by the Bears. "This is where my wife is from, where my son was born, and where so many good things happened for me. This is home now."

PART II

PART II

Chapter 14

THE EARLY YEARS

DOME, SWEET DOME

Before I was a football player, I was a jumper. I liked to jump off of things. I still have a scar under my chin from tying a towel around my neck and jumping off the sewing machine to see if I could fly.

Now these are just flashes I can remember. You ought to remember I've used my head for a living, and I've killed a lot of brain cells.

My natural father left when I was two. After he left, my mom, Betty, was living and working up in Pasadena, a suburb that's now part of Houston, and met the man I consider my real father, E.V. McMichael. He never liked his natural name, didn't cotton to Eurie, Eurie Vance, so he just had folks call him E.V. His nickname was Mac, and that's what I called him to the day he was killed.

Anyway, they moved to a house in Pasadena, just down from the Astrodome. I was about four years old. I crawled up on the house—got a ladder, put it on the side of the roof and crawled up it—with an umbrella to see if I could float down.

But when I got up there, I saw they were putting up the big girders for the Astrodome. They were just starting to build it. I asked, "What is that?" They said, "They're building a football stadium."

That was my first recollection that there was such a thing as football.

EVERYBODY'S ALL-STATER

When I was five years old, Mac got a job in the oil fields in Freer, Texas, so we all moved down there—me, Mom, Mac, my older brother Richard and my two new little sisters, Kathy and Sharon. Freer had a Class 2A school, 2,800 people in the whole town. And I say there was an oil field—*was*. Mac eventually sucked it dry.

They didn't have peewee football. Had to wait until the seventh grade, junior high, until I could put pads on.

I was playing running back. In seventh grade, our quarterback had such a weak arm, he'd pitch the ball and I would throw it. Never got under center, though. I think quarterback was the only position I never played.

I have a reel of our last football team, and man, I never came off the field. I kicked, I was the tight end on offense, I played middle linebacker. I'm one of the few guys in America who, in my senior year, made All-State three ways, and I'm in the Texas High School Hall of Fame for football.

Hell, my senior year, I had six letters—football, basketball, baseball, track, tennis and golf. Track, I threw the shotput and discus. Tennis, I was the only guy in town who played the singles. There were a couple of doubles players and I practiced with them. It was usually just to get on the coed bus. You'd go to the tennis meet and get beat, but then it's all day with the girls.

Other bus rides weren't so much fun.

Football down in Texas, baby, there's a fever about it. We only lost one regular-season game my whole high school career, so there was some animosity. We'd know to get on the floor

An early action shot of me on the gridiron.

of the bus, because there were going to be rocks thrown in the windows leaving town.

Worse, playing offense for the Freer Buckaroos, you were a marked man. The little towns in the district we were from, we were like archenemies. One of the teams, San Diego, it was the closest town to us, about 30 miles away—I told you it was in the middle of the oil fields.

Our quarterback was Jim Acker, who ended up playing pro baseball for about 15 years, and I played football at the University of Texas with his older brother, Bill. The San Diego Vaqueros were the team that got Jim's knee—and they were going after it. They were going after mine, too.

It was my senior year; both towns were at the game. Everybody saw them going after our knees, and when they got him, both stands emptied. There was the big thing in the middle of the field, both teams, the people from town, all fighting. I knew who was responsible for it, so I started heading for the head coach. Well, he saw me coming and hauled ass down the sideline.

I still have a calcium deposit on my right leg from playing fullback—a deep hematoma. Going through the line, one kid grabbed my thigh pad trying to tackle me and moved it over. The next one, boom, into my thigh.

Still have that calcium deposit. That kind of influenced my decision on college. I wanted to be the one giving the hematoma.

TO READ OR TO THE REDS?

I really liked playing baseball more than football, to tell you the truth. I was the catcher on the baseball team at Freer, and I was better at baseball than football.

The Cincinnati Reds and the St. Louis Cardinals came to see me, but my parents wanted me to go to college and get a

With my parents Betty and E.V. McMichael behind me,
I signed to play at the University of Texas.
(Photo by Alice Echo—News Journal)

degree. When they came to see me, I had already signed to play
college football.

SAYING NO TO A BEAR

I had about 75 recruiting letters of intent from major colleges.
Bear Bryant, the legend at Alabama, called me on the phone.

My high school team ran the veer, just two backs. I was the tight end in that. In the wishbone, I was the fullback.

Bear told me, "I'll make you an All-American at tight end." I told him, "Bear, I want to be the hitter, not the hittee." It was that hematoma talking.

Darrell Royal, who was at Texas, told me, "We're going to play you at defensive end." Defensive end was really more like an outside linebacker. Back then, with the option, it was like a linebacker playing contain.

So I went to Texas.

It broke E.V.'s heart, because he was a cajun from Louisiana and he wanted me to go to LSU. But Texas was the bright, shining star where I was from. Darrell Royal was there, Earl Campbell was there, and my buddy from Freer, Bill Acker, was already there. He ended up calling us the Fear from Freer.

The last two years we ended up starting right beside each other, the two defensive tackles. That's pretty amazing, a 2A school having two defensive tackles at the University of Texas.

So Darrell Royal tells me he's going to play me on defense. What do you think happens the first day, right out of the box, at practice? The coach says, "Uh, Steve, are you a team player? Because we need you to play tight end."

I loved the guy. Everybody who knows him loves him. It's like what everybody says when they meet a president, "Man, he made me feel like I was the only one in the room." He had that. That's why he had good teams. People come to play for people like that.

A few games later, one of Earl Campbell's twin brothers, Tim, was playing defensive end and he got hurt. Then it's, "OK, Steve, we want you to play defensive end now." So I moved over there.

ON THE JOB

There was a change in college. I realized right away, when I first stepped on the campus, that football was different. In high school, it was a game. At the University of Texas, it was a business—that football factory thing. But I didn't want to be a factory worker. My degree plan was pre-dentistry.

At every stage of my career—it happened in high school, happened in college, happened in New England when I got to the pros—I was told that I'd never be successful on the next level.

So I had a plan.

That whole area down there, where I'm from, Duvall County, no dentists. I'd have had all the business.

I've always had a plan. Until somebody fucks with me. Then I get immediate.

BECOMING IMMEDIATE

The first game they started me my freshman year was at Texas Tech, Lubbock. That's the night Mac was killed.

He'd been to all my games. There was a guy down in Freer who had a private plane and he offered to fly Mac to the game that weekend, but for some reason Mac said no.

My mother didn't call me. She sent my father's foreman, who worked under him in the oil fields, and Jim Acker, my old quarterback. They both came up to Austin to get me, knocked on my door the next morning, and told me.

I don't want to get into what happened, but the bottom line is, he's gone. What came out of that, for me, as it pertained to my football playing, it was like a rage. An immediate rage. Here, something was taken from me, and I was playing a game that was all about the offense wanting to take.

I became immediate.

What I mean is, when the shit hits the fan in a street fight, you've got two choices looking at the person in front of you. One is to whip his ass. The other is to make allowances and walk away.

After that happened, I wasn't making any allowances.

LIKE A MOTH TO A FLAME

Another thing changed. I became a wild child. After what happened, in my mind, you better grab life by the throat because it can be taken from you real fast, before you want it to be over. That's when I started having an affinity for the neon lights. Before, I was the big-headed jock. All I did was go to school and play sports.

Down in Freer, everybody knows where you are every minute of the day. Even when you've got a girl out, they know where your car is, they know where it's passed by. E.V. McMichael wouldn't have put up with me being a wild child. I had a curfew, and at all times my mother was about enforcing the curfew. But in college, as a moth to flame, old Mongo was to the neon lights—even before they started calling me Mongo.

Actually, I was a bouncer for a time, in a strip club. You know how every college kid has a side job for a little extra money? Mine was bouncing. I'm telling you, it was a dream job. I've always been a bully's bully. But don't take that to mean I was the best bully. I bullied the bullies. Even in elementary school, I'd see a bigger kid bullying a smaller one, and I'd take up for the little kid.

Or the stripper.

They'd come into the club from time to time beat up, and most of the time it would be the man they were living with doing the beating.

I'd say, "Just tell me who he is when he comes here to pick you up tonight." There was a side exit door, and I'd go wait for them in the dark.

Those girls never got hit again.

Back when I was immediate, I used to do that in bars with total strangers.

A guy would be dominating a woman, and I'd step in front of him. My phrase was, "Son, I'm going to teach you what it's like to get out of your weight class."

There were two avenues he could take. He could stand there and be apologetic; then allowances were made. If he was a smartass, I'd begin the process of beating him down.

But when I'd get him beat down, who do you think jumped on my back the majority of the time? The woman. I'd tell 'em, "That's why he's beating your ass."

OVERLOOKED, UNDERAPPRECIATED

I've always sucked hind tit when it comes to awards. Most of those college All-Star games, the MVP gets the keys to a car. Well, at the Hula Bowl my senior year, I was told I was MVP before the game was over, so I'm thinking, "Man, I'm getting a new car."

I knew I was the best defensive player on the field. We ended up losing the game, but the opposing coach was Bo Schembechler. They interviewed him on the sideline and he said, "If it wasn't for McMichael, we'd be killing these guys."

At the end of the game, I walked out there on the field with the governor of Hawaii, and he handed me a wooden monkey bowl. For some reason, that's what they called it—a wooden bowl with a little plaque on it.

It was just something else to fuel me, like my sophomore year at college.

Playing with Earl Campbell, we were 11-0 going to the Cotton Bowl. Every year before that, both teams that went to the game got a Rolex commemorative Cotton Bowl watch.

We got a Seiko.

Another thing that happened that sophomore year, I played against the pox on my career for the rest of my football life—Joe Montana. He beat the hell out of us—and me in particular. Then he did it in pro football. But I consider him the best quarterback of all time.

Why me in particular? I was there, and it's all about me, isn't it?

The bowl is nice and all, but where's my car?

That's the immediate I'm talking about. What about me? Why is this happening to me?

HONEST TO A FAULT

In the three years I played defensive tackle—my sophomore year they moved me to tackle because I was in the weight room and getting a little bigger—I had 358 tackles and 30 sacks. That's why I made All-America two times, my junior and senior year, and All-Conference three times.

Actually, my college defensive line coach, Mike Parker, is a big reason for all of those honors and my pro career. He's the one who taught me the technique that helped make me a pro.

Anyway, my sophomore spring, just like in Freer, I was picked out for injury—and this time my own roommate did it to me on purpose.

I was going through the Texas offense like shit through a goose, and my roommate, the starting center, got fed up with it. He set me up. The guard hit me high and he dove across the back of my legs.

Tore a bucket-handle tear in my meniscus, my cartilage.

I didn't get it operated on. Played my junior and senior year with it. Nobody knew. After my senior year, I went to the Hula Bowl—shoot, I wanted to go to Hawaii. I scheduled an operation before going into pro ball.

Pro teams were coming down there scouting. The Steelers' Chuck Knoll actually came to Texas, working me out as Mike Webster's replacement snapping the ball.

I had a chance to go in the first round until I started telling all these people, "You know, I have a hurt knee and I'm getting it operated on."

Boom. Third round.

Still, it worked out OK. I ended up being the defensive MVP of the game—14 tackles, a sack—and that's the main reason the Bears brought me to Chicago. The general manager at the time, Jim Finks, told me, "The way you played in the Hula Bowl is the reason we're giving you a chance, kid."

Of course, that was almost two years later.

Hook 'em, Horns!

Chapter 15

THE CRIMINAL
ELEMENT

BIG MONEY

The New England Patriots ended up taking me in the third round of the 1980 draft—No. 72 overall. For a third-round defensive tackle, I got the most money ever paid at the time—a $45,000 signing bonus and a three-year contract, $45,000, $55,000 and $75,000. Big money, ain't it?

I bought a Cadillac, and I bought my mother one, too. Hers was a new Fleetwood Brougham, and mine was a used Coupe de Ville.

My college career ended with me as a Bob Hope
All-American and a third-round draft pick.

NEW ENGLAND, OLD STORY

I was still immediate. The way I was in a rage in practice, I think
those coaches up in New England took it for arrogance, a negative they didn't want on their team. In a way, I guess I never
really was on their team. But I tried.

As soon as I stepped on the field, who was there? John "Hog" Hannah. He was just on the cover of *Sports Illustrated*, "The Best Offensive Lineman of All Time." First thing out of the box, there was a drill called the nutcracker—my kind of game, brother.

It's a one-on-one confrontation with a running back coming through, like an offensive play is being run at you. Single-team block, you against him, and if the running back gets through, he wins. If you get rid of him and tackle the running back, you win. They put the little dummy bags about five yards apart—that's a gap.

When it starts out, there's a line and you wait your turn to go. Rookies are in the back. John Hannah's at the front. When he walked up to get in between the bags, I walked up to the front and told the veteran, Tony "Mack the Sack" McGee, "Excuse me, Mack the Sack, I think it's my turn."

He was only too happy to let me go. The coaches, they're like, "This little smartass, arrogant kid."

I got up there, stuffed him and made the tackle. He got up and said, "You embarrassed me that time, kid."

The next time up, Hannah taught me that pro football is not going to be fair. He taught me it wasn't going to measure up to the rulebook. I mean, you know holding, clipping, it goes on all the time. But the punching... He came off the ball with an uppercut to my gut with one of his fists. I was trying to hit his shoulder pads with my hands—and you know, that leaves your gut open, baby. He actually lifted my feet off the ground with this uppercut, and the running back went through. I told him, "Thanks. Thanks for the lesson."

When they released me, John was one of the guys who came down when I was cleaning out my locker and said, "Don't listen to them, kid. You've got a pro football career. They made a mistake releasing you."

Those guys aren't fake. The guys who are considered the greatest didn't win a popularity contest. They're good. They know what's going on and how to play the game.

STANDING PAT

New England is like any other NFL team. They procrastinate. They don't want to admit their mistakes. Look at the Bears with Cade McNown.

But they weren't going to play me. I never got on the field my rookie year. They actually put me on injured reserve, saying I had a back injury, just so they wouldn't have to release me. I stuck around to practice against the offense, at least until camp was almost over in '81.

They've got a name for it in football—"The Turk." They send a guy down there to say, "The head coach wants to see you, and bring your playbook."

They had a name for me, too. The head coach, Ron Erhardt, told me one of the reasons they were releasing me was that "we believe you're part of the criminal element in the league."

They knew I was running around, they'd have nosy rat fans writing in saying, "I've seen this guy running around all hours of the night."

Back in Boston in those days, the Combat Zone was still open. You better believe there were some practices they knew I didn't have any sleep before. It's that area like any city has, the bar row, like Rush Street in Chicago. Because it was called the Combat Zone is why it was eventually shut down. But that's what drew me—the Combat Zone? That sounds pretty interesting.

So there was that, plus the fact that this immediate fucker was fighting in practice all the time. A guy'd hold me, I'd fire up. Nothing really. Even most street fights don't last a minute.

Anyway, I knew what they meant. The criminal element. I was thinking, "Time to go to work."

*I broke in with the Patriots before I was identified
as part of "the criminal element."*

THE HALAS HAUL

I was still in New England the next day. The Bears called me on the phone; they wanted to give me a tryout. That's another thing New England did—it was the end of camp, the year was fixing to start, there were no openings.

The Bears wanted to give me a tryout to be the backup center behind Dan Neal. They had Jay Hilgenberg, but he was a free agent that year and he didn't know his way around how to play center in pro football. Me and Dan Hampton eventually taught him, though.

So the Bears asked, "When can you be here?" I told them, "Tomorrow morning." I got into Chicago late that night, in my Cadillac. That's just over 1,000 miles, Boston to Lake Forest.

The next morning, they tried me out at center. What they were really looking for was a center who could deep-snap, and I wasn't that. When they found out I couldn't do that, they sent me home. A "Don't call us, we'll call you" deal.

So in a couple of days, two teams cut me, and I drove back to Austin.

HULA OR HALAS?

In October, the Bears called me back. One of the guys I played college ball with, Brad Shearer, was a backup defensive tackle for the Bears. But he had a bad knee, and every time the cold weather would hit the couple years he was there, he was no use to them. Seven weeks into the season, he hurt his knee again, and that was the end of his career.

Jim Finks called me up and said, "Because of the way you played in the Hula Bowl, and the fact that we need a backup defensive tackle, we're going to give you a contract."

Yeah, Finks called me, but really I think it was George Halas who wanted me on that team. You know the collusion these owners are in, and I was the black sheep in the NFL. The Sullivans owned the Patriots at the time, and if I was the criminal element to them, you don't think they put the word out?

But Halas, he was all about violence. The way he played football, it wasn't a patty-cake. How do you think they got the moniker "Monsters of the Midway?" It was because everybody knew they played against those fuckers the next day.

BUDDY AND THE DOG

Up to the point the Bears called me, in my mind, when the season was over, I was going to go try out somewhere. So I was staying in shape. I was jogging and lifting in my spare time, but it wasn't my job any more—my job was selling tax shelters, but that's another story.

Old Buddy Ryan, the mean old sergeant he was, a sarcastic guy—my kind of guy, really, and he found that out—he disrespected players until they proved something to him. He'd call you by your number, "Hey 76."

After a while he started calling me "Tex," so I knew I'd impressed him.

But in that first practice, I was definitely "76." Before the practice, he asked me, "You been working out?" I said, "Yeah, I got a big black Great Dane, and me and him been jogging."

They worked my ass off in practice. I was taking every rep, especially since Alan Page was there, the last year of his career, and he never practiced.

Even the best shape I've ever been in, if I take every rep in practice, I'm going to be gassed. So I was gassed after practice. Buddy Ryan walks past me going into the locker room. You know what he says?

"Shit, 76, we shoulda hired the dog."

BAD NEWS BEARS

The first game after that practice that week, we played *Monday Night Football* against the Detroit Lions, and they weren't that good a team, either.

They ended up killing us, 48-17, and I didn't get to step on the field that night. So the game was over, and I ain't even played in this game, against a bad team that killed my team. In my mind, we're the worst team in the league—and I can't even play for this fucker? I might as well go home.

But I didn't.

I still remember one of the defensive ends from the Detroit Lions, Bubba Baker, and he's going against our offensive lineman Dan Jiggetts. Baker was killing him so bad that Neill Armstrong, our coach, pulled him. The backup was going to do worse, but to be a smartass Bubba came by the sideline yelling, "Come on, Armstrong, put Jiggetts back in."

STAYING AND PLAYING ARE TWO DIFFERENT THINGS

In my youthful arrogance, I thought I was better than everybody.

That helps. Sometimes arrogance is a good thing in sports. Every good starting quarterback has got that confident arrogance—I'm better than everybody. The bad ones don't have it. McNown just acted like he did.

I wasn't really playing, just special teams. The tackles in front of me, Jim Osborne, who had a 13-year career, and Alan Page, who had a 16-year career, were pretty durable. But I did get in the game the week after we lost to Detroit.

We played the San Diego Chargers in Chicago, and Page threw a shoe. I went in, and on my first play for the Bears, it was a running play and I tackled Chuck Muncie.

That's not too bad. But in New England, in an exhibition game, my first sack was against Jim Plunkett. At least I learned some things while I was watching. Alan Page told me something that mattered to me at the end of my career. He saw in practice how I was just full bore, and he said, "Young man, you're going to learn to look at your knees like retreaded tires. The less miles you put on 'em, the longer they last."

As the years rolled on, the immediacy kind of faded and I became the guy making concessions. My knees were having to get drained every week. The old immediate me would've kept playing and practicing and getting the knee drained. I figured out I could practice less, get the knee drained and be healthier for the game. The immediate Mongo didn't give a shit about that—I just wanted to eat.

THE CURB WARRIOR

Up at old Halas Hall, we had a janitor, Richard McMurrin, who used to draw this sarcastic little cartoon for the team to enjoy when we walked into the complex. It was one panel about whatever went on that week, and it was a good thing I could take a joke.

Once I got up there and my antics started getting infamous, most every week it'd be one of me.

Since I'd been out of work for six weeks, money was kind of tight. I'd been paying on my Cadillac, on my mother's, and on my house in Austin and trying to help the family, but after New England cut me there were no more checks coming in.

So I was still paying on my mother's Cadillac, but not mine. When I got to Chicago, the car dealer found out that's where I was, so he sent the repo guy to come get it. My Caddy actually got repossessed in the Halas Hall parking lot.

Richard loved to draw me and my dog hanging around.
(Cartoon by Richard McMurrin)

They got it while I was in practice, took all the bags in it and put them in the Halas Hall hallway.

Richard couldn't let that go. This was about the time *Road Warrior* was out—Mel Gibson in one of those post-apocalyptic movies—so McMurrin's comic strip the next week was the Curb Warrior. He draws me in that *Road Warrior* outfit with my foot up on the curb, hitching a ride, with all the bags they left in the hallway behind me.

Richard even got my Great Dane in one of his comics. He drew me and the dog sitting in the Lantern, a bar in Lake Forest. The dog's sitting next to me like my best friend, cigarette hanging out of his mouth and a beer in front of him, and I'm like an old drunk retired guy, extolling the virtues of how I used to play. The thought balloon's over my head and I'm saying, "There I was in St. Louis, kicking ass the way I'd been taught..."

THE COACH BEFORE DA COACH

Neill was a lot like another Bears coach, Dick Jauron. He was laid back, he wasn't a volatile guy, and all the guys liked him because he let them loaf and get away with shit.

That's where the phrase "brother-in-law" first came into my mind. They expected everybody in practice to "brother-in-law," that's half-ass it, so they look good. If you're on the defensive practice team going against the offense during their period, you were expected to brother-in-law.

It didn't make Dan Neal happy when he broke his neck firing off and I didn't give. That's when Jay Hilgenberg started getting his chance and developed into a multiyear All-Pro.

Another similarity between Armstrong and Jauron: The offensive scheme and the way the offense performed that year was terrible. And we all knew he was going to get fired at the end of the year.

STICKING WITH RYAN

At least Buddy Ryan was there—and he had guys like Doug Plank and Gary Fencik.

I remember being in New England, watching tape. The Patriots didn't play the Bears, but we watched our next opponent's offense play against other teams, and sometimes it'd be the Bears.

The way Plank and Fencik were playing safety, just killing guys, the Patriot coaches were probably thinking they were the criminal element in the league. I was thinking, "Hey, I'd fit in there."

I think the old man knew it. If it wasn't for George Halas, I never would have had a career with the Bears. If the McCaskeys had been in charge—that isn't their kind of stuff.

And Buddy, I call him the old fat man, now. In the brotherhood of football, there's people like you on every team, and you find that out. That's how you relate.

That dog thing? Most guys, it would have hurt their feelings. I laughed my ass off. I got it. Like I said, before the year was over, we knew the old man was going to fire Armstrong.

Well, Gary Fencik was a staunch advocate of Ryan at the time. I guess since he went to Yale, he was smart enough to see what some folks didn't.

Buddy is a short man. He wasn't fat, but he had a large frame on a short guy. He's country—still lives in Kentucky raising his horses. And what does everybody perceive about someone who has that country slang? Dumbass.

But he ain't. He's a genius, baby. Very intelligent. That's why his defenses were good, because they were smart.

Anyway, Gary brings this piece of paper around, wanting all the guys on the defense to sign it, to give it to the old man, telling him we wanted him to keep Buddy as the defensive coordinator.

Even though Buddy was just playing me as a backup, I signed the thing. I wanted him to stay around long enough so I could finally impress him enough to play me. Then in my mind, I'd done something.

Chapter 16

THE CAST OF CHARACTERS

CLEAN AND—WELL, CLEAN

Everybody's seen *North Dallas 40*. The core of our team might have been partiers and drinkers and maybe took one too many painkillers, but there was nothing like that going on, as far as drugs go.

North Dallas 40 was a negative view. As far as I'm concerned, we loved what we did and we had fun doing it. Nothing but positive, baby.

But like I said, that was the core. From time to time they'd bring a guy in there who you knew was on drugs. There was this little wide receiver we had one year who would carry his Kleenex box around, know what I'm saying?

But he didn't last very long. The day they cut him, Walter Payton, knowing the press was going to be in there and he was going to be cleaning out his locker, dumped sugar in his locker and made lines like they were cocaine for him. We laughed.

Again, those guys didn't last long.

That's one reason why we were a good team, in my mind—maybe we were characters, but we were characters with character.

DOUG PLANK

I only played with Doug one year, 1981, but he's a good place to start. He was No. 46, and Buddy did call it the 46 defense.

Buddy loved him and loved the way he did his business, so that's why it was the 46 defense. That, and it was built around a safety like Doug making plays.

That's why Todd Bell, more or less Doug's successor as a starter after Len Walterscheid got most of the time in '82, was the MVP of the defense in '84. That's why he held out and the McCaskeys didn't give him the money he deserved. Hell, that's why Dave Duerson stepped right in the next year and became All-Pro. The 46 is tailor-made for the strong safety.

Doug was the nicest guy you want to meet in the world off the field. But I guess he's like me when you put that helmet on. Those jaw pads pinch something up there in that soft spot behind your eyes and you just get vicious.

He used to take out guys in practice like you do in games. I guess that's why our offense stunk back then, because nobody was going to catch a pass over the middle. He used to hit guys so hard he'd knock himself out, and that's what eventually ended his career.

I remember his last Green Bay game. A big old behemoth pulling guard—compared to him—came around. Here goes Doug, forcing the play. He came up, the guy didn't try to cut him, so Doug took him on high. Doug took his ass out—boom, hit him as hard he could. It laid out the guard, but it pinched both nerves on both sides of Doug's neck so badly that all he could do was stand there.

I don't know if you know what it feels like to get a pinched nerve, but your arm goes numb and it feels like hot water running down your arm, and it's dead.

Doug hit that guard so hard it did both sides, and he's standing there, can't move either arm, as the running back runs right beside him. In the film room, we gave him hell for that.

DAN HAMPTON

My first recollection of Dan Hampton? He was a bookworm.

Back in college, he was one year ahead of me in school. He played for the Arkansas Razorbacks, and we were mortal enemies. The first time my team was going to play his, when we were in game planning, there were pictures of the individuals. Dan had bad eyes, and I guess that was before he could get contacts. He had these big, coke-bottle glasses on.

Professor Dan By-God Bookworm.

Later, I'd come to find out I was right. Dan was a voracious reader of novels and had a quiet intelligence. Pretty quick intelligence, too. Dan was my best friend in the game, and the trouble we caused together could fill this whole book—but I'll give you one quick taste.

Once we were going out to one of the bars in Highwood near Halas Hall, sometime in the early '80s. Dan brought his classic Corvette up that year, and we were going out in that.

At the time, the bar we were going to was just selling beer and wine, but they'd let us drink whatever we brought in, so we made up a pitcher of watermelons—a mixed drink most people drink as shots—and took it with us.

On the way, Dan wanted to show me how fast the 'Vette could go, so he was punching it through the suburbs. We went down this one straightaway, and we saw an ambulance up ahead with its lights on. Dan, showing off his fast car, passed it.

Of course, a cop saw it and stopped us. We were arrogant enough to keep the pitcher of watermelons right out in the open.

The cop took the pitcher, set it on top of the car, talking about, "Oh, I've got you guys now. Got the evidence right here."

We had to get out of the car, too. So while Dan was getting out, he grabbed the pitcher, tossed the watermelons out, set it back on the car and said, "What evidence?"

Because we hadn't started drinking yet, he had nothing on us. So we got off.

Even with that kind of ability for mischief, I imagine he got the bookworm thing the whole time in school, because he didn't play football until his senior year in high school. He was in the band. The guy's like a savant with instruments—plays like six different ones to this day.

But when he played against me, the Razorbacks never beat the Longhorns.

By the time I got to Chicago, I hadn't really changed. They had this place you might have heard of called Rush Street. That's when Dan Hampton first started becoming my buddy.

I just got to Chicago and didn't know what was going on, the in places to go to. But I promise you, he did, and he was more than happy to show me. Places like Mothers and the Snuggery and those other bars on Rush Street.

I guess we got along because we were both country boys, small-towners, and had a lot in common. The Bears had a bunch

Dan Hampton at his last game at Soldier Field.

of guys from the Southwest Conference at that time—Mike Singletary, from Baylor, was another one. Being from that Texas conference, it was like a brotherhood, a family. That's the best thing a team of guys can evolve into—thinking of each other as family, because you're going to fight your ass off for family.

Danny's just a man's man. His attitude and who he is and what he's about are what impress you. They'd impress any man. It's hard to explain, but he's got the right attitude to survive in this world. If everybody could explain "it," then everybody could get "it." But "it" is indefinable. And he's got "it." Like a movie star.

Thank God he was on the team at the time. He became my big brother, my guide through chaos, really. It especially motivated me in practice to dominate and kick ass. Impressing him was a big factor. I wanted to show him that I was one of the brotherhood, that I fit in with what he considered important about playing football. Every guy who plays that smash-mouth brand of football is impressing other guys who do.

Hampton thought he was in charge of nicknaming guys. His nickname for Brad Shearer was "Snarler," because Brad was this big old guy and when he'd get drunk, you couldn't hear him talk. You'd just hear him going, "Rarrr, rarr."

Dan was the guy who nicknamed me Mongo, because he saw me trying to knock the horse out in practice, figuratively speaking. You know in *Blazing Saddles*, Mongo rides his bull into town, hitches it up by the saloon. A guy rides up on a horse. "You can't park your bull there." I mean, the audacity. So Mongo knocks his horse out.

In practice, there were some things you might let go—if you weren't quite so immediate as me. Say you'd get free of a guy rushing the passer and he'd just grab you and pull you back. With me, after the grab and the pull, wham, a forearm to the head would follow—and the fight was on.

That's how I got Mongo.

Dan gave me "Ming," too. "Ming the Merciless," like in Flash Gordon. That one meant a lot to me, like getting Buddy Ryan to stop calling me by my number. Mongo was something Dan thought was funny. Ming was a sign of respect.

MIKE SINGLETARY

I've heard a lot of people say Mike wasn't much of an athlete, that he was more about film study. Come on. He was a consensus All-American in college, a middle linebacker who could run from sideline to sideline and catch anybody. He had talent. He didn't have the height that Brian Urlacher does—but everybody can see, when Brian has to take on a block, how that height works against you.

I always loved playing against guys taller than me, because I could get under them and they weren't going to move me anywhere.

But, yeah, Mike was a brilliant student of the game, too.

If you know what you're looking for, if you've gone over so much film, you see the tendencies over the years of an offensive coordinator or a coach to do things. When it comes down to nut-cuttin' time, you can decipher a play.

Mike would call out plays in a game when they'd get to the line of scrimmage. He's the only one I've ever known in my football career who was adept at doing that. There were times, when it was blatant, that I could do it. But Mike had a propensity for it.

I've called him the cheap-shot Christian—and I meant it as a compliment, but I think I need to revisit that. I think God Almighty is a football fan. He sits up in the big press box in the sky, drinking a beer, having a hot dog, watching the game. He's not too concerned who's going to win.

Now, you know there's guys who get in the locker room and pray for the win, but Singletary didn't do that. The guys who pray for the win are praying to the devil, you know?

Singletary prayed, too, and then he'd go out there and try to break somebody's neck—which is why I called him the cheap-shot Christian. But when everybody would go in the shower and pray and hold hands before a game, part of Singletary's prayer was, "God help both teams stay healthy."

He was just praying to God that God didn't let him hurt nobody. That's the best part. "I'm going to go out there and be vicious, but don't let me hurt nobody."

Mike and Al Harris were men of their convictions when it came to religion. They weren't selling wolf tickets about it; that's who they were. You can see guys who don't mean it for one fucking minute get in front of the cameras and go, "Oh, I want to thank God and my teammates." That's rhetoric. Mike meant it.

Me and religion? Let's just say I always knew that you can be forgiven. I always talked to my God afterward and said, "I'm sorry."

But I did go to Mike's church one time, just to see what it was about, and he got mad at me because I put it in the papers. Organized religion is about tithing, brother. The first thing out of the box at his church, the first prayer, "Oh, God, please let these people know we need them to put money in the collection plate." I almost got up and left.

Mike didn't like that at all, me talking about his church.

OTIS WILSON
AND WILBER MARSHALL

These two together with Mike were what we called the Bermuda Triangle, those three linebackers.

Otis and Wilber, to me, were the same. They were singular—a vicious brand of howling dog. They'd get on either side of me, and that's how the dog pound got to barking—we did it first in Chicago because of Otis and Wilber.

Everybody sees this on TV—the guys talking smack to each other as the offense is getting the call and coming out of the huddle. That shit wasn't going on, but we'd get the defensive call and Otis and Wilber would be standing there barking at the offense, like pit bulls. Actually, I called Otis the doberman pinscher and Wilbur the pit bull.

If there's one mean dog in the pack, they're all going to be mean. That's what Otis and Wilber afforded us. Sometimes you see teams and one week they're up, the next they come out of the locker room flat. When Otis and Wilber got to playing the game the way they played it, that was impossible.

If the team was flat coming into the first quarter, after a couple of downs of them kicking the shit out of people and barking about it, the team wasn't flat any more.

Don't think Singletary didn't do it either, before the game. Before the game, they'd get together in a three-man hug, and they weren't praying. They were barking.

RICHARD DENT

Nobody wanted him because he was so skinny coming out of college. But Richard set the school record with 39 sacks at Tennessee State—and Too Tall Jones went there before him.

Dan and I recognized it right off in practice. The kid didn't have a clue how to talk football or perceive it, but it was like that photographic memory, that savant thing. You put him out at defensive end, from day one, here comes the play, and he'd make the right decision. Instinctively.

Defensive line coach Dale Haupt surrounded
by Dan Hampton, Richard Dent, me, Jim Osborne,
Mike Hartenstine and Tyrone Keys.

Richard was an amazing athlete. I only see Urlacher jumping over guys in commercials. Richard did it on the field, and we tried to allow for that.

Dan and I and Buddy Ryan, and later Vince Tobin, kind of let Richard play his own game out there. It wasn't predetermined that he had to rush outside. He had the leeway to go inside or out, and we adjusted.

Mike Singletary would call the defensive plays; Dan and I would call the line stunts. That wasn't typical, but the coaches trusted us enough to see things like a coach up in the press box calling down to the sideline. We already knew it.

I knew Richard was going to rush the passer, so whatever line stunt I wanted to call, I had to make sure we had some cover on that side. I just couldn't run Dan and me to the left side and leave a big gaping hole over there between him and Richard—because that's where the quarterback is going to step up in the pocket and have a clear field of vision to throw the ball.

Seems like it worked out most of the time.

GARY FENCIK

They called us the dichotomy of the league, me and the Ivy-Leaguer, the Bulldog from Yale—a guy who was on the cover of *GQ*, for God's sake.

We'd go do that Crain's Quarterback Lunch, a paid speaking gig on our day off during the week, and that's how they billed us. It was theater with the redneck and the conservative Republican. I always told him, though, when Daley's ready to get out of there, I'll vote for him for mayor of Chicago.

But on the football field, he was more like Doug Plank. He had split personalities, a paranoid schizophrenic—and you'd better believe paranoia plays a part of it when you're talking about a DB. I better get my ass deep or I'm gonna get burned—that's paranoia.

Sometimes, though, that Doug Plank in him got the better of Gary.

When we used to have training camp in Lake Forest, we'd go to this row of bars in Highwood. This particular event happened at the Silver Dollar. Dan and I were not too bad at shooting pool, and we were owning the table. Little Gary Fencik was getting pissed off about it.

Finally he came up to Dan and me, pissed off, drunk—conservatives get drunk, too—and says, "You two assholes, if I was as big as you, I'd whip your ass."

We looked at him and said, "Gary, but you ain't." We grabbed him and dragged him out the back exit door into the alley and just started dragging him around. We showed him he's not as big as us, he shouldn't have said it, and please don't ever say it again.

The asphalt left him cut and bleeding, and you know how smart he is. He never said anything like that again. But I love Gary Fencik. There's few men have come through my life who I know have got their shit together, and he's one of them.

LESLIE FRAZIER

Corn—we called him that because he was from Alcorn State—is the best cornerback who ever played whom nobody knows, because of what happened in the Super Bowl. He made the best interception I've ever seen in my life, up in Green Bay.

The Packers were down there close to the end zone and the receiver did a button-hook in front of him. Corn jumped up over the guy and did a jack-knife. His stomach was over the guy's head, with his feet behind him. He grabbed it in front of him without touching him.

He was on the way to being in the Hall of Fame.

Unfortunately, we got a little stupid in the Super Bowl on the punt return team. By halftime, the game was over, and I don't know what the thought process was there, but we ran a reverse punt in the second half. Like we needed to, right?

He got the reverse and blew his leg out on the Astroturf. There went his career.

MIKE HARTENSTINE

I don't know what they do at Penn State, but most of the guys come out of there with huge calves. It's unbelievable. Matt Suhey, Mikey, all the other guys I've seen outta there. Huge calves. Must do a lot of toe raises or something.

I love Mikey. The best friend you'd want in your life would have Mikey's attitude. And he's of the toughest guys, pain tolerance-wise, I ever met in my life. Some of the guys I'm talking about with the Bears—Walter, him, Dan, me, the highest pain tolerances you'll ever see.

The bone in your hand that leads up to your thumb? Mikey broke that once. He didn't miss a game, because they went in and pinned it back together. The two pins were sticking out of his hand like antennae, but he played.

Dan, Mikey, and me, all being defensive linemen, hung out a lot. Dan and I are more the gregarious type. Mikey's more laid back—in other words, he doesn't talk much. But that makes sense. With Dan and me around, how could he get a word in edgewise?

We'd call him Mr. Noncommittal. We'd ask him what he wanted to do, he'd say, "whatever."

On the field, though, he was committed. Laid the best blindside shot I've ever seen on a quarterback—Ron Jaworski of the Eagles. As a result of that hit, he was the first guy I ever heard of getting called to the league office in New York.

The league didn't call the fine down to Chicago. They brought him to the office, put the tape on of him just about killing Jaworski with him sitting there, and said, "This is why we're fining you."

It's kind of out of the ordinary, don't you think? Calling a guy all the way to New York to say, "We're fining you for this. Don't do it again."

What's he gonna say?

"Whatever."

Mr. Noncommittal.

AL HARRIS AND TODD BELL

We played our asses off in '84, finally won that first division championship, got into the playoffs, and lost to San Francisco in the NFC championship game. We knew we were a good team, and the individual guys knew they were good players.

Big Al and Todd Bell's contracts were up. After they've had some success, people are going to start wanting some more money. They were the first ones. That was back before free agency, baby. The teams owned you. The last bastion of slavery in America. If you didn't play for them and they didn't want to trade you or cut you, you sat.

That's what the McCaskeys had them do, I guess to prove a point to everybody else, I don't know. They could've traded them, for God's sake, because they were good players. But they let them sit out the whole year wanting some more money.

We didn't see them the whole year. They were gone. I actually heard Al was living like a hermit in a cave in Arizona—it wasn't true, but I think he kind of liked the story.

When it's all said and done, when it's over, money fades—and fame definitely fades. All you've got is playing the game. Al and Todd, if they had it to do over again, I guarantee they'd have come back and played that year for the money the McCaskeys were offering. Especially since they're not wearing a Super Bowl ring.

To tell you the truth, the defense didn't really miss them. We drafted a kid named Dave Duerson who was sitting behind Bell, and he turned out to be a pretty good player. As for Big Al, well, they'd just drafted the Fridge.

Sometimes that's what happens.

One time Singletary hurt his hamstring and took two games off. Those two games playing behind Dan, Ron Rivera made Defensive Player of the Month in the NFL. Singletary never missed another game.

Ron was good, too. That's what happens when a veteran lets a kid in the door—they find out he can make plays, too.

WILLIAM "THE REFRIGERATOR" PERRY

Fridge was an anomaly back then—over 300 pounds, with a big belly. Today, there's guys playing on every team fatter than him. This guy is more comedian than anybody will ever know. He made me laugh almost every day saying funny shit.

He used to call Ditka the doctor. Not Coach, Mike, Iron Mike—he'd call him the doctor. And I never realized why. Mike Ditka—M.D.—the doctor. Ditka could be on his ass about something, and I guess his defense mechanism was this song. He started singing it all the time.

"Oh, the doctor—cold, bold, and full of what? Soul!"

I don't know why he sang it, but he did.

People have asked me what I thought about the Bears drafting another interior lineman when that was my position. The best way to handle it is you teach the guy what you know and what's going to help you win the game. Any other way, and you're full of shit because you're not trying to win the game.

Besides, the Bears did it all the time. They drafted him, a guy named Fred Washington who ended up killing himself in car wreck, Tim Ryan, Chris Zorich...

You can't have enough good defensive linemen on your team. It just motivates you to play even harder.

Speaking of motivation, the Fridge owes the doctor and the 49ers for making him famous. Commercials, catching a pass and scoring a touchdown in the Super Bowl, none of it would have happened if not for the 49ers rubbing Ditka's face in it when they beat us in the championship game in '84.

They put a guard named Guy McIntyre in the backfield to run out the clock. Like, "We're good enough to play somebody out of position and laugh at you guys." You better believe the next time we played them, Ditka was ready in his mind to show them who'd laugh last. He kept it to himself.

In '85, we went out there and beat them 26-10, one of the best games I played in pro football. Got a game ball, had a guard named Randy Cross jumping offside, I sacked Montana, almost picked off one of his screen passes—just tipped it—had a bunch of tackles. That's when I knew we were going to go to the Super Bowl and win it, when we handed them their ass out in their own stadium.

We were running out the clock, and Mike Ditka, an eye for an eye, puts William in the backfield and lets him carry the ball. It wasn't on the goal line; he didn't score a touchdown. He just handed him the ball and the clock ran out.

But it made such an impact, like a tidal wave over the NFL, it was the only thing anybody wanted to talk about. I guess because a head coach has to be like a carny barker, too, to get a

Relaxing during a practice with the Fridge.

little light shining on his team, Ditka did it again the next week. Plus, he didn't like the Green Bay Packers anyway. So to him, it's, "How can I get everybody talking about my team and stick it in the craw of the Green Bay Packers?"

We got on the goal line, he handed the ball to Fridge, and Fridge scored a touchdown.

In every Shakespearean drama, there's some comic relief. William Perry was ours.

WALTER PAYTON

Emmitt Smith, my ass. That kid ran behind three All-Pros at all times.

Most of Walter's career, until they built a team there in the mid-'80s, he was running behind an offensive line of a bunch of dockworkers. They couldn't blow a fart out a paper bag, and he was still making yards.

Walter was the first guy I ever met who worked harder in the off season than what I'd known. You know how most running backs practice? They get the handoff, it's a brother-in-law thing, they go through the hole, run 20 yards, stop and comes back. Walter would run the whole length of the field, full blast.

In his later years, rookies would come in and try to make a name for themselves by hitting Walter in practice. Who do you think had a problem with that? The bullies' bully—and you don't bully Walter. Plus, I knew he was the show on offense. Without him, we didn't have a chance. Same thing with Earl Campbell down in Texas. That's the franchise. You don't hit the damn franchise in practice.

But the one thing a lot of people don't know about Walter is he was always a prankster.

One of the things he would do—scared the shit out of me every time he did it—he'd get an M-80, low-end dynamite, and he'd tape it to a lit cigarette. He'd go out before practice and plant that M-80 in the grass somewhere around the practice field. Early in practice, it'd go "boom" and it'd scare the shit out of everybody.

Later on, the way he'd show me he respected me, most every day he'd walk up behind me, with me unawares. He'd grab up under my armpits, around my chest, and lock his hands together and squeeze until I'd say uncle. I'm sure he wanted to do it around my neck, but all he could reach was my chest.

I've met Michael Jordan, and of course Walter, and a few other guys people consider superstars. One of the things that defines them is that there's not a stair step to them. There are not different levels of people. They're down to earth. People look up to them like gods, but that's not how they perceive themselves. They don't have the vanity that comes from ego. They know how good they are, but they don't need a pat on the back.

JIM McMAHON

When he showed up in the limo with a beer in his hand, drunk, at his first press conference after getting drafted, I knew our new quarterback was my kind of guy. He wasn't always Dan's kind of guy, which led to the one time I wanted to kick Dan's ass, for real.

It's not his fault, but when people ask me why we didn't win more Super Bowls, I tell them it was Jim McMahon's fault because he was hurt all the time. Jim missed the playoffs in '86. In '87, he got hurt during our loss to Washington in the playoffs. He hadn't played in two months before coming into our first-round win in the fourth quarter in '88, and he wasn't very good and got replaced by Mike Tomczak in the next game, which we lost.

Still, it really wasn't his fault he kept getting hurt. This is what Dan didn't understand. When you're hurt and you're a quarterback and you're getting the shit knocked out of you by guys like Dan and me, if you're hurt already, you're tempting permanent injury by playing against some vicious animals.

I forget what year it was, what playoff game, but Dan stood up in some meeting and said, "Me and Steve are playing on knees that need operations, we're getting them operated on after the season, and we need you to play, man." Calling him out.

I knew right away, man. Anything that can divide a team is better left unsaid. How do you think the offensive guys felt about Dan doing that? "Hey, you defensive cocksucker."

Dan didn't accomplish anything but to divide the team. It pissed me off. I followed Dan up to the locker room and jumped him. It was like a younger brother taking on an older brother—a love thing, you know what I'm saying?

Thing was, everybody thought I was kidding and dogpiled us after that. When William Perry was the last guy on the dogpile, he cracked a vertabrae in Dan's neck—which nobody figured out for years.

Remember Dan's pain tolerance. Years later, somebody X-rayed him and said, "Hey, you had a cracked vertabrae in your neck that healed."

He thought back on it and figured that's when it happened. Dan never knew I was pissed at him. Until now, I guess.

But I knew McMahon had a chance at being nuttier than me when I heard about his retina. He's got a big gash in it—that's why he wears sunglasses all the time—and the story is he stuck a fork in his eye.

Even I won't go there.

You could see in college he was one of those savants—a guy who takes a snap and as he's backpedaling has deciphered where to throw the ball already. It's second nature to them to know where the secondary's rotating to, who's double-teamed, where's man and where's zone. They don't have to go through the progressions like most quarterbacks do.

It's not, "Well, my primary receiver is double-covered," then they start down the line. Who's the secondary? Who's third? It's like photographic memory, and he sees the whole picture at once.

Plus, you've got to like anybody coming in and bucking authority like he did.

THE OFFENSIVE LINE:
Jimbo Covert, Mark Bortz, Jay Hilgenberg, Tom Thayer and Keith Van Horne

I hate to dog the guys who were there before them, but these guys were Walter's first real line. I kind of put them all together, even though Jimbo Covert was the best of them before he hurt his back.

Jimbo's the reason I know anybody can get their ass whipped—I don't care how bad you think you are. He was the only guy in a football practice I ever said "uncle" to.

Something happened in practice he didn't like, and he turned around and thought it was me who did it, so he fired up. Here I come, I'm going to start raining punches on him. Little did I know he was like an All-America wrestler in high school. That's where I learned about the hip toss.

He just grabbed me, turned me, lifted me up and dropped me as he landed on top of me. He wasn't hitting me; he just pinned me there. Well, I couldn't move. Finally I said, "Could you let me up? I give."

You know, this is my book. I didn't have to tell you this. But I just want you to know, there isn't a mortal walking on the face of this earth who can't get his ass handed to him.

Which brings me to Bortzie.

Mark Bortz was drafted at defensive tackle out of Iowa. He wasn't going to make the team until Dan and I mentioned to Mike Ditka that he ought to try this guy on offense. He was pretty stout.

Just going against a guy in drills and he's better than the offensive linemen you're playing against in practice, you should tell the coach, "Why don't you try this guy on the offensive line?" Then he goes on and makes All-Pro.

I kind of did the same thing for Big Cat Williams. You know, "Before you cut this guy, trying to play him at defensive tackle, try him out on offense." And Big Cat went to the Pro Bowl, too.

Practicing is kind of like wrestling sometimes. The body slams are real, but the punches and the kicks are pulled. And you don't go after someone's knees.

So I'm on defense, but it's offensive period. I'm giving Bortzie a picture—a picture of what the other team's defense is going to run against them that week.

It was a rainy day. I found out looking at the film the next day that he didn't do it on purpose; he just slipped in the mud and went down, but when the ball snapped, he fired out and just dove straight at my knees. He hit my legs and just stopped there.

I reached down, and for everybody's enjoyment I was talking real loud, "Get off your knees, son, I'm not God. You don't have to pray to me."

Then I grabbed his facemask and start trying to jerk him up—I'm not trying to help, I'm trying to hurt him. The facesmask, in my hand, went, "bink, bink, bink." All four of the bolts broke off the helmet, and I pulled the facemask clean off.

He jumped up, looking like he's Knute Rockne in a leather helmet, and everybody just broke up.

Jay Hilgenberg gave me the best compliment I ever got in my athletic career. He told a reporter once, "Practicing against Steve McMichael and Dan Hampton, the games are easy."

Jay could deep-snap better than anybody. Because of that, popping his arms back that way, his elbows are terrible now. Can't straighten his arms out at all. I feel sorry for him for that, but I know he'd do it all over again.

He had a great career, especially for a guy who was a free agent out of Iowa, making the Pro Bowl seven straight years for the Bears. Lucky for him I couldn't long-snap when they brought me in for that tryout after I got by New England; otherwise he might not have ever gotten the chance.

Keith Van Horne was a good guy, just a little bit different than everybody else. It's that California cool, the surfer mentality—they just think different.

He was a rock 'n' roller, a live-concert guy. I can't stand live concerts. They don't sound as good as they do in the studio.

But it worked out OK for Keith. He ended up marrying Eleanor Mondale—yeah, Walter's daughter—who was working at the rock radio station in town.

You've got to give Tom Thayer credit for timing. The Bears originally drafted him as a center, but they already had Hilgenberg playing there, so Thayer went to the USFL.

I guarantee the USFL was going to pay more money than the McCaskeys were offering him, so he makes his money for two years, jumps to the NFL just before that league folds and just in time to play guard for the Super Bowl champs.

MATT SUHEY

He's another one of those Penn State guys with the big calves. He was one of the ones who had particular glee in what Jimbo Covert did to me that one day in practice. Offense vs. defense, brother.

The first time I ever met Matt Suhey was the Hula Bowl. Like I said, I was the Defensive Player of the Game and he was on the other team—so he already had bad feelings about me.

But for our team, I just think of it this way. In Dallas, Emmitt had Moose Johnston. Well, in Chicago, Walter had Matt. That's a fair parallel, because Moose was pretty damn good.

Matt was another smart guy. Before everybody was into having their own PC, Matt brought his own computer—a car full of computer, in those days—to training camp and set it up in his room so he could keep up with the stock markets. He was into his postcareer activities that early. I believe he and Paterno got into a bottled water company in Pennsylvania, and it made them a fortune.

Yeah, he's a smart dude. But you look back on any good football team, and that's something you hear about them—they're smart.

I promise you, most of the guys on that football team were football literate. Savants for football. A high football IQ. I don't know about their schooling or anything else, but I promise you they had a high IQ for football.

WILLIE GAULT

Every team has to have that deep threat.

Even in the Super Bowl year, Willie Gault didn't catch 40 balls, but I promise you, he spread that defense out thin running down the field. They had to cover him, so there was always something open underneath. Every team needs a speed receiver, and he was that.

Actually, he was more of a Hollywood actor in need of a stunt man than he was a football player. Because you can't have a stunt man, he did it himself. Didn't want to, but to his credit he did. You better believe he didn't enjoy the contact—but what guy who's six feet tall and skinny as a lizard is going to go, "Oh yeah, I want somebody to hit me?"

He wanted football to get him into acting. Football was just necessary to get him there.

DENNIS McKINNON

Silky D was the best receiver on our team, but nobody ever talks about him. He was smooth—one of those guys who never looked like he was running as hard as he could even when he was hauling ass—had good hands, and went over the middle.

He was also maybe the best receiver I've ever seen when it came to blocking, and toughness, and meanness. Man, I used to love watching him crack back on linebackers—he'd knock the shit out of them. It was a beautiful thing. He was a mean little guy.

He also caught seven touchdown passes our Super Bowl year. Walter Payton and Ken Margerum were tied for second on the team with two each, and Willie Gault caught one. Silky was the go-to guy, really.

Plus, he and I had a lot of little jokes in the locker room. I'd turn around and he'd be looking at me in the shower, toweling off like he's enjoying it a little too much, you know? I'd walk by and squeeze his little butt, like, "Oh, that's firm."

You know, men being men. Having fun.

I'll tell you what I think about guys who are homophobic. It's like, "What are you scared of?" You're homophobic, it's like you're in the closet to me.

EMERY MOOREHEAD

He was good. Sure-handed, and he knew who he was supposed to block on every play. Those guys are valuable.

But an All-World talent like Russ Francis, no.

I never understood that, either. Mike Ditka was an All-Pro tight end, but he never had an All-Pro tight end on his team. You'd think he'd have some coaching there, or some play calling, some thought that there's some value in getting the ball to the tight end.

KEVIN BUTLER

Remember, I was a kicker in high school, so I know how flaky they are. I also know they're usually made to feel like they're outside the team, not really football players, and that just never floated with me.

I made a point to be around Butler, to make him feel like one of us. Besides, he was a good player. He was an All-State quarterback who won the state championship in Georgia.

But, yeah, I took him under my wing, baby. Broke one of his once, too.

There was one night in '93 we were playing the Raiders. All Butler's got to do is kick a field goal and we win. Even Howie Long knew it was over. I was on the field goal team, and Howie was standing on the other side of the line of scrimmage saying, "Steve, I've got a new ranch in Montana. See me after the game, I'll give you my number, you can come on up and visit."

I'm all happy, we're going to win the game. But we line up, Butler hooks the damn thing, we lose.

I walked in the locker room, Butler was sitting there crying in his locker, with reporters all around him like the vultures that they are.

So I spread them apart, yank him up and say, "Goddamn it, there ain't nobody else in this locker room that could even attempt trying to make that field goal. Nobody can judge you in here because you missed that motherfucker. Stand up and be a man, stop squalling."

Well, even afterward, when we went out to dinner, he kept it up. I got so fed up with it, I picked him up and threw him across a couple of tables into a booth. He cracked a bone in his forearm.

He had to wear a cast on his forearm for about a month after that, during the season. Nobody noticed, because he was just a kicker.

Chapter 17

THE DAWN OF DITKA

IRON MIKE SUPPLEMENT

After '81, we knew Armstrong was out, and Fencik's petition got the old man to keep Buddy Ryan, but we didn't know who was coming. Then we heard about Mike Ditka.

I knew of him as a player—how he ended up in Dallas, caught a pass in the Super Bowl and then went straight into being their special teams coach. We all thought at the time, when George Halas hired him with so little experience, that there must be something special about this guy.

It's kind of funny, isn't it? The McCaskeys telling Mike Singletary, when he was trying to get a job there on Dick Jauron's staff, that he didn't have any coaching experience? But just being special teams coach, in Papa Bear's mind, that was enough. Guess he was smarter than his grandson.

Anyway, we found out pretty quick about the fiery competitor that Ditka was and knew why the old man brought him in. What a force.

He was a no-nonsense guy right off the bat. His practices were regimented. The whistle blew for each individual skill. And you hustled to the next drill when the whistle blew. He wasn't about that brother-in-law either, baby. He loved guys going live in practice. He knew that was going to make the games easy.

One day early on, he was out there being Iron Mike. Right out of the box, he yelled, "You guys better hustle, or I'll have your ass out of town with a bus ticket and an apple."

After practice, he says, "Everybody huddle up," because he wants to talk to us. So I yell out, "Hurry up, or your ass is out of here with a bus ticket and an apple."

Ditka was not amused. He wheeled on me and said, "That especially means you, McMichael, if you don't keep your mouth shut."

You can joke with Mike Ditka about most things, but when he has a football mind, he has no sense of humor. He meant what he was saying.

The other thing about Ditka was he was a talented person who'd been through it before, so he knew what to look for in players, what they don't have and what they do have. He had an eye for who was a player and who wasn't, for who wanted to play and who didn't—and he started jettisoning the guys who I knew didn't give a shit.

Ditka started noticing me in practice. His comment was, "He does just enough talking to let you know he's around."

Talking is just kicking ass. The talking goes hand in hand with that. If you ain't kicking ass, you ain't talking. Guys who are getting their ass kicked are kind of quiet.

Ditka made sure he didn't have a quiet bunch.

Ditka patrolling the Bears sideline early in his coaching tenure.
(Photo by Daily Southtown; Tinley Park, Illinois)

HIGHWOOD HOMESTEAD

In Ditka's first training camp, he got an idea what he was dealing with, and we got an idea what we were dealing with.

We were still in Lake Forest at the time, but it didn't take him long to realize that with all the stories getting back to people from the camp there, he better move all the boys out of town.

I'm sure I played my part in those stories. See, after my first training camp with the Bears, I had a house on my own, in Highwood, closer to the bars—just me and the Great Dane; it was a real bachelor pad, baby.

I've always had a level of intelligence when it comes to staying out of harm's way—I mean getting fingerprinted and mugshot and stuff. I realized I could just go to the bars in Highwood instead of going down to Rush Street and driving home drunk.

I hardly had any furniture in it at all. Had a couple of beds, no bedroom furniture, a couple of couches and a TV. I didn't even have a refrigerator. I'd keep the beer out in the snow. But then, there wasn't much cooking going on in the house. In the kitchen, anyway.

It beat my accommodations that first year with the Bears, when I stayed in a hotel right next to Fort Sheridan—the old North Shore military base. They called the place the Blue Room, because all the walls were blue.

When the year was over, I went back to Austin and the house I had there. I sold it, because I wanted to come back up to Chicago and live during the off season, like I should have done in New England.

I think that was part of the problem with the way the Patriots felt about me. Working out in the off season every day up at the complex is what they want.

STRIKE ONE

There were some good things about '82—that was the year McMahon came in, and even though we were still going through some growing pains, it was the start of me thinking there's something going on here.

Funny thing was, it was the strike we went on that helped me realize we had some guys who cared. We ended up going only 3-6 that year, but we lost our two games before we went on strike. When we went out, in September, we still got together and practiced on our own. If you have guys who don't give a shit, that ain't gonna happen.

Fencik was running the defense—but to tell you the truth, the coaches were giving us the game plans, the plays they wanted us to run, a scripted sheet. They weren't supposed to be doing it, but they were.

As far as the strike itself goes, I was young and didn't know what to expect—but I thought we were doing the right thing, and in my mind, it was, "Oh boy, we're really going to get the owners to bend."

Nothing ended up coming out of it except this thing called "Plan B Free Agency." It was so hokey, something had to happen somewhere else for this to happen there, then something could happen for you. And nothing ever did.

We just lost those game checks for nothing. Seven of them.

We screwed ourselves and we really screwed the fans, because they didn't get their football that year.

But we did win the first game back, at Detroit. Practice makes perfect, you know.

TOASTING A SEASON

Because of the strike, they had a cattle call for the playoffs that year, 16 teams. If we won the last game, in Tampa, we'd get in at 4-5.

Ditka decided to take us to Tampa to acclimate us for a couple of days before the game. Big mistake. This was the last game of the year, a hard year, guys were getting away from their families, the drudgery of what they do every day and a Chicago winter.

Dan Hampton was *Pro Football Weekly*'s NFL Defensive MVP in '82 playing defensive end. On the plane, me and Dan were already starting to drink, celebrating his honor.

Let me tell you, a couple days of drinking down in Tampa doesn't lend itself to being in the best shape you can be in to play in the game on Sunday.

You've been playing in cold weather; then you go down to 80 degrees—oh, that's sapping. Every year we'd do that, I'd lose like 15 pounds—and I was in pretty good shape to begin with. I'd always have to have an IV, and I got smarter as the years went on.

Early on, I'd be on the plane and start cramping, and they'd have to rig up an IV solution in the luggage rack above my head and plug me in on the plane. Later on, I'd just go ahead and get the IV, knowing the cramping was coming.

Anyway, we were down there partying, and I really don't think it affected our play, because we played well against Tampa quarterback Doug Williams—until the very end.

FUMBLE! OXYGEN!

They were just letting me get on the field in '82. I wasn't starting yet, but I had four sacks, and one of them was against Williams in that game. And near the end of the game, I had the longest fumble return of my career—a 64-yarder.

We got back and sacked Williams, but they'd been on a long drive and we were starting to get gassed. I was back there to pick up the fumble.

Now, all the receivers were downfield because it was a pass play, so there was nobody back there but me. Plus, Jim Osborne, one of the guys who sacked Doug, was lying on top of him, and besides, Doug had gotten hurt earlier in the game and was limping.

I picked up the ball. Sixty-four yards later, Williams caught me on the five-yard line. He shook off Ozzy, limped down the field and caught me. If I had scored, we probably would have won the game and made the playoffs. As it was, the offense lost yards, kicked the field goal, we went into overtime and lost.

Jay Hilgenberg told me he was on the sideline down on the end of the field where I was eventually caught. He saw me pick the ball up with no one around me and immediately thought he was going to have to snap for the extra point—and he didn't have his helmet. He had to go get it on the bench on the other side of the 50-yard line. He ran, grabbed his helmet and ran back to where he was, and he swore that when he got back there I still hadn't passed where he'd been before.

Ever since then, I don't know if it was in the back of my mind or not, but I always figured it was better to fall on the ball than pick it up and run with it.

A POSTSCRIPT AND A PREVIEW

Y'all remember that story about dragging Gary Fencik through the alley? If not, flip back a few pages. Anyway, Dan and I didn't end our reign of terror when we stopped picking on poor Gary—who asked for it, by the way.

It's training camp, '83, and we were out behind the Silver Dollar in Highwood. Dan was wild. Roughing up Fencik got his blood up—not that it was really about Fencik. It was about how we were going to kick ass playing football that year. Dan turned around and forearm-shivered the driver's side window in my Bronco and just smashed it out.

I knew I better calm him down, so I went around, grabbed him in a choke hold, took him down and held him till he settled down. A minute later, we got in the truck, and he was driving.

Hey, I wasn't going to sit in the glass.

Anyway, we were just late enough to miss curfew. During camp they put us up in the Lake Forest College dorms.

Dick Stanfield was the offensive line coach. I love this guy; when he played with the 49ers he was the only offensive lineman in NFL history to be voted the MVP of the league. But he was a salty old man, and we were always gigging each other in practice.

I'd say, "Old man, you're lucky you didn't play against me. Back then you could head-slap, and I'd have head-slapped you so much your ears would still be ringing."

He'd say, "Well, McMichael, I'd have made sure you got a few more knee operations, 'cuz I woulda cut the shit out of you."

But anyway, it was about 11:30, curfew was 11, and here we came pulling into Lake Forest College. Dick was already walking away from the dorms; he was in between buildings on a sidewalk.

Dan saw him, said, "That motherfucker's going to turn us in. I'll just kill him."

He jumped the curb with the Bronco, started up the sidewalk, hauling ass at Dick. You could tell Dick was an athlete, because he broke down into a hitting position and started shuffling his feet.

Dan didn't slow down. The old man actually had to get out of the way. We passed him, Dan slammed on the brakes, put it park. We left the truck there in the middle of the compound and went up to sleep.

NIGHT RIDERS

When '83 rolled around, I dumped the house in Highwood and moved about a block down and across the street from Halas Hall.

I'd met this kid, Dave Siden, at a Halloween party Dan Hampton had in '81, and we became friends (good friends— Dave ended up being co-best man at my second wedding, to my wife, Misty).

Dave was living in this yellow house right down the street from the fields we had during training camp in Lake Forest. It was like a duplex; the front was an apartment by itself.

Now Dave was a social butterfly, and he had some great parties. At first, he had somebody else living in the front of that house. But the next year, the guy moved out. I was over there so much I was almost living there anyway—waking up on the couch and stuff. I moved in.

So I'm walking to Halas Hall now. Whether I actually slept the night before or not.

One time, Dan, Mike Hartenstine, Henry Waechter and I ended up basically staying out all night. (Henry, by the way, was the second-string guy I let come in during the Super Bowl, and in that series he got a sack and a safety. I tell you, if I'd have stayed in and got that sack and safety, there's a chance I could've been co-MVP with Richard Dent, but I let Henry go in. That's the kind of teammate I am.)

Anyway, Ditka found out about us staying out, because we weren't even close to making curfew. We also weren't even close to sober that morning for practice, come to think of it.

Ditka called us all up on the carpet, up in front of the team, and started, "All right, you night riders..."

He made us do up-downs until we threw up.

Then we went into practice, and Dan was still in pretty bad shape. We went into this nine-on-seven drill, live. The offense came to the line and we all got down; the play started, bodies started moving around, hitting, and Dan was still in his stance. Everybody was boom, boom, boom around him, and Dan was still in his stance.

They got him out of there after that.

DRAFT SPECIAL

The payoff came later, but the draft Jim Finks, Halas and Ditka put together in '83 put us over the top.

Jimbo Covert and Willie Gault in the first round; Mike Richardson, who ended up being our starting left cornerback for six years, in the second; Dave Duerson in the third; Tom Thayer in the fourth; and Richard Dent and Mark Bortz in the eighth.

Unbelievable. Dent and Bortz, All-Pro, from the eighth round?

You've got to ask yourself, "Why did those people make those picks? What was it all about?"

I think they drafted heart.

Those guys were athletes, but obviously they weren't first-round draft-pick athletes. Those guys wanted to play ball.

That's one thing Ditka could do—he could see a guy who had heart.

BUDDY SYSTEM

Playing kids was never Buddy Ryan's greatest strength. If it wasn't for Mike Ditka, Buddy might never have played me—and Ditka finally made Buddy start me, in the eighth game of '83.

Buddy was just an old coach who was loyal to his own—to a fault, really. Dave Duerson was a great example of that.

Dave came in that great '83 draft, and that year they cut Lenny Walterscheid, a veteran safety whom Buddy liked—a backup to Fencik. He knew if Walterscheid had to play, he wasn't going to make any mistakes, because Lenny was smart—and Buddy valued smart so much he couldn't bring himself to trust young guys not to make mental mistakes, a pretty high priority for the success or failure of each defensive play. But they had to cut Lenny to keep Dave.

When that happened, Buddy came in the meeting and just dressed down Dave in front of everybody.

He said, "Look, I had to let a great player go for you, and I don't think you're worth it. I think you're a piece of shit. So you better get after it."

It was Buddy's defense run Buddy's way, but Ditka's influence was forcing Buddy to realize the loyalty to the veterans was going to hold us back because there were some kids who wanted to play and who were busting their asses. He'd tell Buddy, "Because you're coaching them, you're going to make them great."

BREAKING BAD

Early on in '83, Ditka made some bad decisions. The first one was getting his hair done up in that tight perm he had. Boy, he had some curls. I guess that was to show everybody he was tightly wound.

I really wouldn't put it past him. You'd go up in Ditka's office and you'd see psychology books, not football books. I'm sure that perm was just like "an apple and a bus ticket."

Then there was the fourth game of the season, at Baltimore, which was our second straight overtime loss and dropped us to 1-3. If we'd won, I'm sure he would have been happy to be 2-2.

As it was, he broke his hand on a footlocker.

Where Baltimore played, the Coliseum, it was one of those small locker rooms, no place to store the chests all our stuff goes in, so they were just taking up space in the aisles. Ditka was standing by one when he launched into his postgame tirade. When he finished, he turned around and just punched the shit out of one of those footlockers, and then grabbed his hand.

He'd been on a cussing tirade this whole time—and with Ditka, it was clearly a choice. He wasn't one of those guys who, just talking, would go, "This fucking thing," or, "Goddammit." He doesn't use cuss words, generally. He's not casual with it.

When they'd start coming out, though, it was, "Boom-boom-boom, baboom-boom-boom."

So he wheeled and punched the chest. All of a sudden, tirade's over.

Holding his hand, he just turned to our head trainer, Fred Caito, and says, "OK, Freddy. It's time for the Lord's Prayer."

Then he went into the trainer's room.

METHOD TO HIS MADNESS

We should have known that Ditka's arteries were getting clogged back then because of the beet-red face he'd get. Before he'd start a tirade, you'd know he was fixing to chew on somebody's ass when that face was shining like a beacon.

He'd get on individuals; he'd get on the team. Most of the time it was about what the team was doing. But if you saw him ragging on an individual, it was based on his theory about personality types.

Ditka believed in motivating based on what your personality was. Those guys who needed a pat on the ass, you wouldn't see him cussing them. But the guys he knew it would put them in a rage and they'd say, "Well, I'll show you," he got what he wanted. They'd go out, bust ass, come back and say, "See? I told you."

A START, AND THE BEGINNING

I started the last nine games in '83 and finished the year with eight and a half sacks. We went 6-3 over those games, and 5-1 in last six.

Coincidence? I think not.

No, seriously, a lot of things started to come together.

Willie Gault really started to open things up on offense, and they were starting to catch up to the defense. When he was streaking down the field, it opened up underneath; then you've got Walter—uh-oh, gotta watch him.

All of a sudden Jim McMahon was completing 60 percent of his passes, Willie was catching eight touchdowns on the year and Walter was still Walter, running for 1,400 yards.

Everybody loves talking about our defense—but remember, in '85, our offense was the highest-scoring offense in the league. I know that we on defense were setting them up and scoring some touchdowns ourselves, but Chicago hadn't known that kind of offense before. Not since that 73-0 game against the Redskins for the league championship in 1940.

A great old guy from the '63 championship, Ed O'Bradovich, still talks shit about how bad the offense was on his team. He was a defensive end, and he claims that whenever he'd run off the field when the offense was coming on, he'd say, "Just hold 'em, boys."

WHERE'S MY KICKING SHOE?

One thing from '83 that won't be going on my resumé was the resumption of my kicking career.

In college, I kicked some extra points and field goals when our kicker, Russell Erxleben, was hurt, so when the Bears' Bob Thomas tweaked his back, the put me into duty on kickoffs.

I did it for two regular-season games, so somebody got the bright idea of seeing if I could get a little something for the effort. Everybody was saying, "If I were you, I'd go up there and ask the McCaskeys for a little bump for doing this."

I went up there and they said it was covered in my contract under "football."

Maybe so, but they got more than they paid for. For my two names of glory, I averaged deeper kicks than Eddie Murray, the All-Pro kicker that year. Kicked his little ass.

THE PASSING OF AN ICON

In the middle of the '83 season, George Halas died. It wasn't expected, but he was 88 years old, so it wasn't a surprise either—but in Chicago, you'd better believe it was a very big deal.

I can't remember how many people showed up at his funeral, but it was almost everybody. The whole team went to the funeral. Everybody in the football world went to the funeral.

The multitudes of people, the respect for George Halas are things I'll never forget.

I hope nobody forgets he was the man who invented pro football, the man who had the first team in the league—no matter what they say up in Green Bay.

DIE, PACKERS, DIE

One truly great thing happened in '83. I got my first win over Green Bay.

I'd been around for the second of two losses to the Packers in '81—at Lambeau Field—and we didn't play at all in '82 because of the strike. We lost again at Lambeau in '83, and by the time we got ready to play the Packers in the last game of the year, I was getting a pretty good idea how much it meant.

I mean, I knew the animosity the fans had for them, but I didn't know the depth of hatred of somebody who'd played against them and known the rivalry. Ditka had it. He hated them.

I hated them, too, but I loved the game. It's like in wrestling—there's no show, the fans don't care, unless there's a feud. Without that, it's just another match.

Plus, being a student of the game, playing in Lambeau Field and Soldier Field, that was the shit to me. It's like you're unbound. Like living in every age. Ditka said it once about me, and I think he applied it to anybody he considered a true Monster of the Midway: He could've played in any age.

Playing in a Bears-Packers game made you feel that way.

ALL KNEES ARE NOT CREATED EQUAL

The last game of the year, against Green Bay, my knee was hurting. I got a sack at the end of the game, and instead of landing on the quarterback, if you're watching the film you just see me kind of spin him down by his shirt and limp off the field.

I needed an operation at the end of the season, and it was probably the first example of Mike Ditka working on me.

There was this great surgeon in East Lansing, Michigan, named Lanny Johnson—he was like the keynote speaker at orthopedic surgeon conventions, that kind of thing.

That's where they sent Hampton, who, as usual, needed a knee done at the end of the season. I mean, the guy ended up with something like 12 surgeries. I look like a piker with my eight.

The guy they assigned to operate on me was the team surgeon up in Lake Forest we called Butch, short for Butcher. I go to Ditka, "Coach, can I go to the good one?"

He says, "Steve, you're just not one of our stars."

In the off season, working out, I felt something in this knee. Butch went in there and cut some out, but he didn't look around and find everything.

Ditka understood the intensity of the Bears-Packers rivalry.
(Photo by Daily Southtown; *Tinley Park, Illinois)*

When I got to camp, two-a-days, pounding it, the knee started to swell up again. With tears in my eyes, I said, "Coach, the season's fixing to start and my knee's already bad. I've got to get it worked on."

They sent me back to Butch again—and three weeks later I started in the first game of the season.

But don't think I'm complaining. There's a line from D.H. Lawrence that goes, "I never saw a wild thing sorry for itself."

That hits me pretty hard. I'm talking about all these injuries, but I ain't sorry for myself. I had to play. Come hell or high water.

Especially in 1984.

FIRST STOP, NOWHERE

I know why Ditka did it. He was thinking, "We're gonna get these guys away from their norm so they can really concentrate on football." So he brought us out to Platteville, Wisconsin, population 9,708, in territory that's not only more Packer than Bear country, it's more Iowa Hawkeye, too.

Not that it mattered. We got real popular in town, real fast. All Ditka really did was let married guys loose from their families. In Lake Forest, you might see the night riders down on the bar row in Highwood, but in Platteville you started to see married guys out, too. Before, everybody was going home to their family. You'd go to Platteville like you were on vacation from all that.

It was all good, healthy fun. Boys will be boys, you know?

Every year we'd have a post-training camp party at one of the bars in town. There'd usually be some hijinks going on in there, baby. One year, this place had a tile floor, McMahon just soaked the whole floor with a couple of pitchers of beer and says, "All right, we're having McMahon Olympics."

Everybody took their pants off, naked from the waist down, and we had a butt-sliding competition across the floor. I believe McMahon won—but then, the guy who picks the competition has usually done it before. He was adept at it.

Some people claimed Platteville was boring, but not to me. Practice was a joy, baby. I love every aspect about that game. Preparing for it and playing it are the same. When they say I even loved wind sprints, it's kind of the truth, because when you were tired after practice and Ditka still ran you, it was like measuring up to yourself.

I'm tired. I make myself take another step. I'm proud of myself. Pushing through the limits, that's what makes the games easy.

BEWARE THE SAVAGE ROAR

Even before the 8-8 year, we thought of ourselves as a lot better team than that already. Heading in, we knew we almost went to the playoffs in the strike year, so we expected to do better than that and be in the playoffs. For whatever reason, we didn't... but we knew we were a good team. Not a great team, but we knew we were competitive. And we came ready to compete in '84.

That was the year we set the sack record—72 sacks—that no one has even gotten close to and no one will. With the West Coast offense, there are no more seven-step drops. Until they get back to the seven-step drop and the pocket passer, nobody will have a chance to get to a quarterback 72 times in one season.

Buddy Ryan realized we had the guys on the defense to attack the offense whenever he chose. Whatever stage of the game, bring 'em, attack the quarterback.

Most coordinators run a blitz so somebody will be set free; there won't be anyone to block him. Buddy would run a blitz for the opportunity to get one of us one on one with a blocker.

He used to tell Dan and me in the meeting rooms, "Why the fuck didn't you get to the quarterback? We ran a blitz and got you single-teamed."

People assume it was Buddy's system that did it, but we were system and personnel. That's why nobody's been able to duplicate what we did. We had the personnel to run it up front, which means at least three defensive linemen who can get to the quarterback.

Without that, you'd better sit back in zone coverage and wait for the offense to make a mistake. All the great attacking defenses had at least two ass kickers on the line. The Fearsome Foursome had Deacon Jones, Rosey Grier and Merlin Olsen. The Steel Curtain had L.C. Greenwood, Dwight White, Mean Joe Greene and Ernie Holmes. Even the Purple People Eaters had Alan Page at tackle and Carl Eller and the guy who ran the wrong way, Jim Marshall.

Three guys up there kicking ass, that's what we had, with Richard getting 17 1/2 sacks, Dan 11 1/2 and me 10. We called it a jailbreak. Three or four guys just running at the quarterback—it looked like cons jumping the fence and hauling ass.

It wasn't arrogance. We weren't full of ourselves, but we were confident. The other team played our game.

And here's the proof that we had the personnel: We set the sack record with Buddy Ryan in '84, he left after '85, and Vince Tobin come in with his scheme and we set the scoring record.

SALLY, DICK, JANE AND BUDDY

Buddy Ryan's plans were easy to read for everybody. While most defensive coordinators have all these hand signals, Buddy Ryan most of the time would just clap his hands. That meant AFC—Automatic Front and Coverage. We had to be more intelligent and more responsible to play in Buddy's defense.

During the week we studied up on the opposing formations and what plays they ran out of those formations. It was understood that we already knew the best defense to get in based on their formation instead of the coach calling something on the sideline and hoping they'd come out in that formation.

That was the genius of Buddy's defense. The guys on the defense got into the best defense possible to go against the formation that came out of the huddle. Most defensive coordinators are guessing when they call a defense on the sideline. Buddy didn't have to guess, because, in all instances, when they came out of the huddle and got into a formation, we would shift.

For example, if the other team got in a "blue" formation—the fullback on the tight end side—in our automatic front and coverage, the defensive line knew to shift over from a 4-3 into an "over." That's the defensive end on the tight end, a tackle in the guard-tackle gap, a tackle over the center. Buddy didn't have to call it. But everybody's got to know their shit, because if one guy reads it wrong, you're fucked.

Of course, it helped Buddy that we were all pretty versatile players, so he didn't have to use the personnel groupings most defenses do today.

On the line, I called stuff and so did Dan. Mike Singletary was in charge of making sure the linebackers were in their place. Fencik handled the secondary.

AIR DALE

Dale Haupt was our defensive line coach. Usually he wasn't a wild man, but there was this one time in '84 he figured he needed to fire Dan and me up. He still has a scar on his bald head because of it.

We were in warm ups before a game, basic stuff. You come out, split into your groups, and the first thing Dale would do was hike the ball and we'd take off, getting our legs warmed up.

This day, Dale didn't think we were spirited enough, I guess. He looked at us, he looked down at the other team across the way, and says, "Look down there. See those guys? They're going to whip your asses."

Dale learned the unmitigated rage Dan and I carried into each game. We look at each other like, "Oh yeah? Let's teach this old man a lesson."

Next time he got down like the center between us at defensive tackle and snapped the ball, with my right forearm and Dan's left, we hit him at the same time and flipped his old ass over so hard that the back of his head was the first thing to hit. The Astroturf turf-burned his head.

He got up, and Hampton and I said, "Now say something about the other team again."

GETTING AHEAD OF OURSELVES

In '84, we went 10-6, we won that first division championship. That was our expectation. I think that's why we lost to the 49ers in the NFC championship game. That wasn't our goal. We'd done what we set out to do.

Beating the Washington Redskins the game before was kind of like the highlight, the culmination of everything we worked to do. They were the previous Super Bowl champions, and we went to their house and whipped their asses.

Joe Theisman was the quarterback, John Riggins was at running back, the Hogs were on the offensive line—and we stuffed them. In the fourth quarter, especially, they had a chance to beat us, but we stuffed them and we won, 23-19.

In the locker room after the game, it was an emotional high. We were jumping around like we just won the Super Bowl, because we'd just beaten the defending Super Bowl champs in their own stadium.

Plus, we'd just pulled off the Bears' first playoff win since that '63 championship. Nobody was saying, "Slow down." Everybody was caught up in it. And as high as we were, we should have known there'd be a low to match it.

It happens to this day. You've got to really be conscious of that and defend against it, or you're going to be an up-and-down team and you're screwed.

HEY, GATORADE, WHERE'S MY CUT?

When Ditka first came to town, he was going around drinking with Hampton and me. He was like a buddy. He hadn't gotten into the state of mind where he had to separate himself from the players yet. We were drinking buddies, talking about the future. After a while, he separated himself.

But in '84, we were still in that mindset, and that's when Dan and I came up with the Gatorade bath—and it's time we got the credit. You always hear the Giants invented it. Credit the obvious East Coast media bias in this country. But it was us; they just followed suit.

At the away game in Minnesota, where we clinched the division, our plan was basically, "All right, Dan, you go get the Gatorade jug and I'll stand in front of him and keep his attention." So I stood in front of him as the game was still going on, and he was protesting, "Get away from me." He couldn't figure out why I was talking to him when he was trying to run a game.

I actually had to grab his shoulders and hold him, and Dan came up from behind and just doused him. That's when the Gatorade baths started. Hampton and I invented it, but we only did it once. Then Harry Carson and the Giants started doing it every game—and oh boy, what a splash it made. If you ask me, the Giants were fabricating character and we had it.

THE POX RETURNS

Coming into the '84 NFC championship, we really thought we were going to dominate physically in that game.

But like I said before, Joe Montana is a pox on my football career. He started in college, when his Notre Dame team beat our asses when I was a sophomore, and this was the next time he got me.

It could've been worse, though. I could've been beaten by someone I don't consider to be the best quarterback of all time. Joe Montana does something I've never seen anybody else do, and I've watched enough film to know. In a three-step drop, not a seven-step, he reads four receivers.

Anybody else you can mention, the most they'll do is three before the rush gets to them or they run. He reads four, and the fourth check down would usually be Roger Craig. He'd dump it to him—not a bad place to check down, considering Roger Craig had better than 1,000 yards catching the ball. That made him hard to get to and harder to rattle.

In fact, I really only tried to rattle him once, and it was in that game.

We were in the 46, and the guard and the tackle blocked on me. I knew it was coming, and I knew they were trying to show us they could be physical, too, so I used it to my advantage.

I leaned my shoulder in there like I was going to try to split them, but when the tackle came down hard I spun around, with my arms spinning too, and caught him head-high with my forearm. Now he was out of my way and blocking the guard for me. I came around free, there was Joe, I sacked him.

It was the first series of the second half, still a close game, so I tried to intimidate Joe into being a pussy the rest of the game. I got up, looked at him and said, "Suck on that, motherfucker." He didn't get intimidated. He got pissed off. He didn't say anything; he diced up our defense.

Six different guys on the 49ers that day caught a pass of at least 10 yards.

I never talked shit to Joe after that.

REMEMBER HOW BAD THIS HURTS

After we lost in the NFC championship, we came in on the plane and the core of the team went to Z Sports Tap. Fencik, Hampton, some offensive guys—all the boys. About 10 or 12 of us altogether.

There were some steps inside the place, and we were all sitting on them like it was a team photograph—a pretty sad one at that. It could have been a trip downtown to drown our sorrows. It could have been a party—most people, if they didn't have the goal to get where they did, so what if they get beat? It's like, "Party time. So what? We got beat. We went farther than we were supposed to."

Nobody expected us to be playing the San Francisco 49ers in the NFC championship game, including us. And it probably didn't bother anyone but us that we lost.

But boy, it hurt. Crushing. That's one of the first instances I knew we weren't going to be a one-year deal. It mattered to these guys. I remember Gary Fencik saying, "Remember how this feels. How bad this hurts."

Chapter 18

THE SUPER SEASON

THE PRESEASON

I don't know what this says about how hard Ditka's training camps were, or how bad our backups were, but our preseason was hardly a precursor to greatness, that's for sure. We went 1-3, and we lost the first three.

It did seem like teams were starting to treat us differently—like we were everyone's homecoming game. We'd see teams running their goal-line offense or their No. 1 field goal team to get the points.

But even if we weren't playing like it, we were starting to get treated like stars. Because we'd won in '84, the training camps were starting to get ridiculous with how many people would show up every day—I'm talking thousands of people.

We were proud of the crowds, but it's hard, man. After practice, when there's little kids standing around and you know your day is still full of meetings, and you've got to eat lunch or get a nap—it's hard to not walk by them.

I'd stand there for a while and sign a bunch of autographs, but when you leave you always leave somebody behind. That's just bad. I never liked doing it. Whenever I do an appearance now, I'll stay until the last person standing there gets his autograph.

I can't stand it when an athlete or a celebrity has a two-hour appearance, and when that two hours is up they get up and leave. If there's people still standing in line, that guy's an a--hole.

Then again, the celebrity isn't always the only one.

We were guys who liked going out and having a good time, brother, and it started getting where you couldn't go anywhere. That's when I realized not everyone's your fan, even though they come up with a smile on their face. Being young and immediate, sometimes it was hard not to hit some condescending shithead right in the face.

For instance, there was one time when I was at the pool hall, playing doubles with my lady, a friend, and his lady. By now, out in public, I'm like the Terminator, always looking around—and I could always see the guy who's going to come up and say something. There's a little clique, they're all looking at you, and sooner or later one of them's coming up with a smile on his face. You know, the red-horned devil can't steal a soul if he comes up looking like that, you understand?

They won't come up and say, "Steve McMichael, nice to meet you." They'll come up and say, "Steve McMichael, what's your secret? I always see you with women." That's what this one guy did.

Most guys might take that as a compliment. But this guy meant it like, "I don't give a shit who you are, but if I had your secret, I could have beautiful women, too."

I told the guy, "Grow six inches taller so you don't look like a midget. Get your hair cut so you don't look like a Chernobyl victim. Change the way you dress, because girls don't like that lumberjack look, and change your rap, because you didn't even fool my ass."

The guy walked off with his tail between his legs.

The fans and the people who care about you aren't the only ones coming out of the woodwork. The jealous ones do, too. Fans aren't condescending. They might want to come and meet you, but they say hello then leave you alone. The jackasses come to get a bite, like a shark feeding.

Now, I'm not the kind of guy who thinks I'm better than anybody else. But then, the opposite of that is ain't nobody better than me, either.

I had to learn to stop being immediate, because there's haters out there.

GAME 1: BEARS 38, TAMPA BAY 28
September 8, Soldier Field

I remember getting booed at halftime at Soldier Field, walking into the locker room down 28-17. Some great start, huh?

I really believe we came into the year with dead legs. I loved Ditka's training camps, but they were brutal. That might have had something to do with giving up four first-half touchdowns.

The Bucs did, too. They had a good team back then, really. James Wilder was at running back, and Steve DeBerg, their quarterback, could decipher a defense.

But we came out after the half, Richard Dent tipped a pass thrown out to the flat and gave Les Frazier just enough time to break on it, catch it and score—a 29-yard interception return. With that we went ahead and ran them out of the stadium after that—we shut them out in the second half.

On the other hand, Wilder had a huge day—166 yards on 27 carries. He just ran all over the field on us.

Ditka and Buddy Ryan, people say they were different coaches, but they adhered to the same standard. You're never as bad as you look when you lose and you're never as good as you look when you win.

When you win, they're going to come in the meeting bitching about plays you didn't make—and we didn't make plenty that game.

GAME 2: BEARS 20, NEW ENGLAND 7
September 15, Soldier Field

My first crack at my old team.

Back then, I downplayed it, but inside there was a fire. These guys had told me I wouldn't be any more than a backup in the NFL—that's if I were to catch on with another team. You better believe I wanted to show them they were wrong.

We all had something to prove, really. The week of meeting speeches might have had an effect on us. We might have come out a little pissed off after getting our asses chewed on for a week.

They had 27 yards rushing, we had six sacks—but I'll tell you, the biggest stat that stands out to me was they only spent 19 seconds over the 50-yard line all day.

That's domination.

OK, so I didn't get a sack. Mike Singletary had three, and Otis Wilson, Wilber Marshall and Richard Dent had one each. But listen, baby, the position I played in the 46 defense, it was pretty tough. I was right in that gap between the guard and the tackle, and those two guys make sure you don't go nowhere first.

Anyway, we beat a good team—shit, they went to the Super Bowl.

GAME 3: BEARS 33, MINNESOTA 24
September 19, Metrodome

Ah, the Vikings game on Thursday night, baby. Everybody remembers this one because this is the one McMahon came off the bench and led us to victory on national TV.

They're beating us 17-9, McMahon is hurt, he's not gonna play. Seems to me it was a kidney or something—I don't know, with him, take your pick.

I don't know if I should tell this on him, and I don't want anything negative about the boys in this book, but he wasn't supposed to play, remember. So, yeah, he'd been out all night. Smelled like alcohol, you know? Might have been why he got in the game. Allegedly, I mean—because I was in my room fast asleep, getting ready for the game the next day.

Anyway, we were losing and he was over there in Ditka's ear so much that Ditka was tired of having him on the sideline, so he put him in the game so he wouldn't have to listen to him no more.

The first three passes he threw were touchdowns—70 yards to Gault, 25 yards to McKinnon and 43 yards to McKinnon. We went on to win the game. I think that was the beginning of the Jim McMahon folklore.

Fuller was 13 of 18 for 124 yards in that game, and he was a good quarterback, but every great team's quarterback is *somebody*, you know what I'm saying? Except for maybe a Bill Parcells team that wins the Super Bowl with a Jeff Hostetler or something.

A commanding presence. When I talk about the difference between Jim McMahon and Steve Fuller, I'm not talking about athletic ability, I'm talking about presence—the kind of person who everybody knows is around.

It's like when you're at the high school dance and the most popular girl walks in the gym, all eyes turn to her.

I always seemed to play better against the
Vikings, Packers, and Cowboys.

Besides McMahon, Kevin Butler had four field goals that night. It was like all phases were starting to come together.

Kevin never made All-Pro as a kicker because he kicked so often in Soldier Field. But the All-Pros realized how difficult it was to kick there, because when they'd come in, Kevin would out-kick them.

And I got two sacks. Finally!

You know, there were some teams like the Vikings, the Cowboys and especially the Green Bay Packers, where usually I'd have some stats. I don't know what that's about, but most players have certain teams they play better against.

Besides, statistics are for losers, baby, and this game was a great example. Tommy Kramer threw 55 passes that day. Of course there was an opportunity to get a sack or two.

On the other hand, take a look at the defensive film of the Super Bowl sometime. The first half, there's hardly any film on the reel.

I mean, I had 44 tackles in '85. In '89, when we went 6-10, teams were on the field all day against our defense. I had 108 tackles. In '85, our defense was so good and our offense was good, there were about 50 plays for the other team's offense on the field while ours was out there 75 or 80. You don't have the opportunity for stats.

GAME 4: BEARS 45, WASHINGTON 10
September 29, Soldier Field

The year before, they were the defending Super Bowl champions when we knocked them out of the playoffs in their place; now they came to ours and we gave them their worst beating in 24 years.

Because of that game in the playoffs the year before, we had them beat down. Of course, I think because of those two games, they beat us in the playoffs the next couple of years because they had their dander up.

There's a shot of me from that game, just freight-training Joe Theisman, that ended up on a bubble gum card. I'm on my knees, pushing him down, and he's on his back with his legs up in the air.

Sorry, Joe.

You know, I'd like to tell every quarterback I ever played against it was just that thay had the other uniform on. That's the way I built up my rage, by hating them. But that's all over now. They don't have to hate me still.

Anyway, they got up 10-0 right off the bat, then Willie Gault ran a kickoff back 99 yards for a touchdown. That's kind of the way it went that year—teams would play with us, then we'd start making some big plays and they couldn't keep up. We set the team record with 31 points in the second quarter, seven of them on a pass from Walter Payton to Jim McMahon, which was kind of fun.

As a team, we were kind of like a school of sharks, always fixing to frenzy. One of 'em gets a bite, then all of a sudden everyone's swimming real fast and bitin' stuff.

GAME 5: BEARS 27, TAMPA BAY 19
October 6, Tampa Stadium

Another game, another come-from-behind win. That's why we weren't really getting a lot of attention yet, because we were always coming back.

The Bucs were up in this one 12-3 at halftime. I guess we still had dead legs from training camp; I don't know. We were actually losing 12-0 at one time, but all the details of the game have faded for me except one.

Walter was already 31 years old this season, in his 11th year in the league—an awful long time for a running back. But he made a move in the fourth quarter to score a touchdown that you don't see anybody except maybe a young Barry Sanders make.

They pitched the ball out to him going left, he was going outside, stopped and dipped a shoulder, the Buc out there took the fake, and boom, that quick, Walter was around the corner outside. Unbelievable.

It was the kind of running play that could only have been Walter Payton. He looked like a Royal Lipizzan stallion out there, doing his stuff—with those high-leg kicks, running stiff-legged.

You know, I don't think he would do that to show off. When you've got fluid on your knees, you run stiff like that. He never said anything to anybody about it, but I knew because when I was in the training room getting my knee drained, he'd be there standing in line.

We had another couple of interceptions that day, which goes to show you what pressure can mean. Sacks and interceptions are byproducts of the pressure you get.

If you're getting back there and the quarterback is throwing off his back foot, that pass doesn't have much zip on it and the cornerback can break.

Oh, yeah. This was our rematch against James Wilder, and you better believe Buddy made him our special emphasis.

After that first game, only one running back all season had a 100-yard game against us, and that was Gerald Riggs in Atlanta, who carried it 30 times in a game we won 36-0.

The Bucs knew we were going to stop Wilder. They threw the ball a bunch, and it made sense. When you play a team twice a year, and the first time they run the ball like they did,

I promise you Tampa Bay's offensive coordinator knew we were going to put emphasis on shutting that shit down the second time.

So they went away from Wilder, who only ran it 18 times for 29 yards. On the other hand, Steve DeBerg threw for 346 yards. Not that it mattered.

GAME 6: BEARS 26, SAN FRANCISCO 10
October 13, Candlestick Park

Did I say we weren't getting a lot of attention? Not after this one.

I'd like to say it was because I had one of the best games of my career, which I did. But it wasn't.

This game was big for a lot of reasons. Walter started a streak of what became a record nine straight games with at least 100 rushing yards. We sacked Montana seven times. We got payback for the NFC championship.

And out of that payback, the darling of the media, William "the Refrigerator" Perry, was born. But I'll get to that in a minute.

I always loved it when we'd go to somebody else's house and hand it to them, just like with the Redskins. And we really wanted to do the same thing against the 49ers in Candlestick.

Once we did, I knew we were going to the Super Bowl. We'd just beaten the defending Super Bowl champions in their house, with no excuses. They were there in all their glory—Montana, Jerry Rice, Roger Craig—nobody on their team was hurt, they couldn't bitch they had jet lag because we were in their stadium, and we handed it to 'em.

Before the game, I walked up to Jim McMahon and said, "You get us an early lead, we're going to win this game."

First possession, he went out there and drove us 73 yards in six plays for a touchdown. McMahon came back to the sideline, looked at me and said, "Was that quick enough, Steve?"

We scored three out of the first four times we had the ball and were winning 16-0. Their only touchdown came on an interception return.

All day, I went against their All-Pro guard, Randy Cross, and Keith Farnhorst, a tackle. It wasn't a lot of fun, because they weren't exactly the Marquis of Queensbury—in fact, the 49ers were the worst team I played against as far as high-low blocking you.

The only thing I'd do where I was kind of askew of the rules was I had this pass rush where I'd fade outside to get the guy leaning over thinking that's where I'm going, then I'd slap the shit out of his inside shoulder. Sometimes that slap would ride up and hit him in the ear hole. Of course, the head-slap was the thing Deacon Jones used to get to do legally that they outlawed.

Even with those devious double-teams, I actually had the 49ers' plan down so much, I was having one of those Singletary days where I knew what was coming. One play started and I knew it was going to be a screen to Roger Craig out in the right flat. The ball was snapped; I didn't rush Montana. I started shuffling down the line to my right to get in the middle of the screen. I was out there so fast, he had to try to lob the ball over me. I jumped, almost intercepted it, tipped it and got a pass defended.

I also sacked him, for once had a great day against the pox on my career, and got a game ball.

Eventually, we all got our sweetest revenge for the NFC championship game. All week, Ditka was motivating us, reminding us how they'd used Guy McIntyre to run out the clock.

He's saying, "They not only beat our ass, but they rubbed it in running out the clock with a guard in the backfield."

It was good motivation, but putting a guard as your lead block in short yardage is kind of smart. Why have a small fullback when you can have an offensive guard leading in the hole? And Bill Walsh was an offensive genius.

But even a genius can do things that will hype up the other team.

So we were up 26-10 at the end of the game, running out the clock. Ditka trotted out William Perry, baby.

Walsh didn't give the ball to Guy McIntyre. But to one-up that, Ditka handed the ball off to William. They stacked him up at the line, he didn't get any yards, but the legend was born.

We all loved it. We were yelling and screaming in the locker room, but none of us knew it was going to take off to the tune of him making like $6 million in endorsements after the season's over—hell, it started before the season was over.

One of the first things Fridge did was a McDonald's commercial during the season—with me, Dan and Dave Duerson. We're all sitting at the table eating our cheeseburgers and Fridge is like the comic relief.

GAME 7: BEARS 23, GREEN BAY 7
October 21, Soldier Field

OK, it's not like Mike Ditka and Forrest Gregg were buddies before this.

I remember in '84, in the preseason, when I was out with that hurt knee, we played Green Bay in Milwaukee, where both teams had to stand on the same sideline. I was in a hospital bed with my leg up watching it on TV, and I could see during the game the two coaches cussing at each other on the same sideline. I was just waiting for the first punch.

But, my God, this turned into a war—and they were Patton and Rommel while we were tanks.

It was *Monday Night Football*, we were a week after the Fridge's debut on offense, and Ditka didn't bother waiting until we were running out the clock to bring him in.

I'm not saying there wasn't a legitimate football reason to do it. Practicing with William, Ditka realized what a juggernaut he was in the backfield.

Remember how Walter always had to jump over the pile in short yardage? Well, in this game, William being the lead fullback blocking, Walter walked in for our first score.

You could see in the film, there was this big pile of Packers on the goal line, and when William hit into them, they moved back. George Cumby took a direct shot and went backward like a car hit him.

Then William scored our second touchdown, and there was no denying he was a phenomenon. You'd better believe he only got the chance to score because it was the Green Bay Packers and Forrest Gregg.

Even our punter, Maury Buford, threw a pass that day. We were pulling out all stops.

It was amazing, the way Mike Ditka came through his football career just absolutly hating the Green Bay Packers. You could see the ramifications of it every time you looked at a game plan for the Packers.

I promise you, if you had been watching Mike Ditka after that first touchdown by the Fridge, you'd have seen him thumbing his nose at Forrest Gregg.

The rest of us? We couldn't help laughing.

Everything that came out of the Fridge kind of tickled your funnybone. The fat guy scoring the touchdown; the cheerleaders he had, the Refrigerettes, none of 'em being under 200 pounds; it was all comical. We all loved it.

GAME 8: BEARS 27, VIKINGS 9
October 27, Soldier Field

We were at the halfway point now, and this, I think, was where we really started rolling.

After we beat Green Bay on *Monday Night* and our fat guy scored, everybody wanted to know about the Bears.

The media could always come into the locker room during our lunch hour, and the first day back after Monday, there was more media in the locker room than football players. And it wasn't just media from around Chicago; they were from everywhere.

But you'd better believe we were ready for it.

There's a saying I've heard, "When you take the characters out of the game, you take the character out of the game." Our team was chock-full of characters in their own right. Every guy was a freaking sound bite for any media who wanted to talk to him. It wasn't like you had to fabricate something to make it more colorful—it was just verbatim what one guy said making an article.

You might run into a team nowadays that has a couple of guys who are good sound bites, but our team was full of them. Hell, you just had to follow McMahon around—you didn't even have to ask him a question.

Anyway, the Vikings were one of the teams I always played well against. And they were always the worst team I can recall in terms of being front-runners. They're hell on wheels when they've got a lead, but you get up on them, they'll quit before anybody else.

We got up on them 10-0 that day, and the rest was a jailbreak. Even Fridge, feeding the legend, got his first sack. We got four all day, to go with five interceptions, while Kramer and Wade Wilson went 21 of 46 between 'em.

GAME 9: BEARS 16, GREEN BAY 10
November 3, Lambeau Field

This game just furthered the legend of William Perry, who caught his first touchdown pass. Beautiful. What a way to foster hate in an arch-rivalry. How much more can you rub it in?

But it's still Green Bay, and no matter how bad they are, they're still gonna play us tough. Actually, they played us dirty. This was the game one of their DBs, Mark Lee, took Walter way out of bounds and over a bench on the sideline, and Kenny Stills got ejected for a really late hit on Matt Suhey.

In the fourth quarter, we were losing 10-7, but for whatever reason they got back by their end zone and I could see by the way the offensive linemen were sitting back, they were going to throw a pass.

When both Walter and Jim were clicking, we were pretty hard to beat. (Photo by **Daily Southtown; Tinley Park, Illinois)**

So I got up in my track running stance, and it was so loud, when the ball was snapped, the guard got off later than I did. I ran around outside him, hardly touched, and I got back to the quarterback before he got back to set up.

I got back and sacked Jim Zorn for a safety.

That made it 10-9, and they had to punt the ball to us from the 20-yard line. We got the ball on their 49, Ditka handed the ball off to Walter three times—Walter had 192 yards that day, his best game of the year—Walter scored on a 27-yard run, and we won.

GAME 10: BEARS 24, DETROIT 10
November 10, Soldier Field

At this stage of the year, the defense finally really had its shit together.

This game was a classic example of how you get to be the No. 1 defense. It doesn't have to do with points. It's the yardage you give up rushing and passing. We held the Lions to 106 yards of total offense. With Walter and Matt Suhey both running for over 100 yards, we held the ball for over 41 minutes to not quite 19 for them.

Steve Fuller played that day and for the next couple of games. That was fairly typical of what happened most years in Jim McMahon's career, except most years he was hurt and couldn't play in the playoffs.

Like I said, that's a major contributing factor to why we didn't win another couple Super Bowls. We were playing in the playoffs with Doug Flutie, Steve Fuller and Mike Tomczak instead of Jim McMahon.

But playing with a second-string quarterback didn't stop us from dominating, not against the Lions.

GAME 11: BEARS 44, DALLAS 0
November 17, Texas Stadium

The turning point, baby. This was a good Dallas team, not some red-headed stepchild. They had Tony Dorsett, Danny White, Randy White, Too Tall Jones, the Doomsday Defense, all that BS.

They were talking a little bit before the game, too. One of their corners, Everson Walls, said something like, "They're 10-0, but they ain't played nobody yet."

Hah!

After we beat 'em 44-0, Dan Hampton told all the reporters, "You know, Everson Walls was right. We still ain't played nobody."

That was one of those days we could've beaten them 3-0. Right out of the box, we crushed them on defense, a ball got knocked up, Richard Dent grabbed it and scored a touchdown. They weren't gonna do nothin'.

It was the worst defeat in Cowboy history. It was so bad, their running back, Tony Dorsett, was taking snaps right before halftime after we knocked out Danny White.

Remember, I'm from Texas, and football is a religion down there. I've never heard a quieter stadium in the state of Texas during a football game, and I never will.

One thing I regret from the game was I cussed one of my heroes. In college, we ran the flex defense like the Cowboys, so I watched hours of tape on Randy White.

I saw him quit in the third quarter, and it crushed me.

We were all about the shutout, so even when it was 44-0, the starters were still in there. And Tony Dorsett was still in there, because I guess he had incentives and wanted to lead the league in rushing or something.

So in the third quarter, we ran Tony out of bounds on their side. There was Tom Landry standing right next to me, and behind him was Randy White, and he already had his baseball hat on, he was through for the day. I couldn't hold it back.

I said, "Randy, I've always looked up to your fuckin' ass, but look at you over here. I don't care if the score's a hundred to nothin', I'd never quit. You pussy."

Right in front of Landry.

Randy still hates me, and I'd like to apologize. It was just something I said in the heat of the battle.

Anyway, we were 11-0 now. We clinched the division and the playoffs earlier than anybody else in a 16-game schedule ever had.

We were on a "going to the Super Bowl" roll now and getting pretty cocky, too. In fact, I started doing something I got from Dick Butkus, reading his book in junior high.

You know how in pregame warm ups, after everyone warms up with their position, everybody comes together and the offense runs plays against the defense?

I stopped doing that. I'd go stand at the 50-yard line and stare at the other team.

Talking about it later, I found out other teams got out of it exactly what I wanted them to. Some guy on another team would say, "Yeah, we used to see y'all standing there staring at us like crazy motherfuckers."

Nice to know it had the desired effect.

GAME 12: BEARS 36, ATLANTA 0
November 24, Soldier Field

Like I said, we were on a roll now, baby. Second straight shutout, Walter's seventh straight 100-yard game. For Pete's sake, Henry Waechter got three sacks.

Oh boy, we're going to Miami and we're going to kick some ass.

Of course, that attitude can come back to bite you on the ass—and I'm glad it did. Miami was the wakeup call we needed so we didn't go into the playoffs and get our asses beat before going to the Super Bowl.

GAME 13: MIAMI 35, BEARS 24
December 2, Orange Bowl

The whole week leading up to this game, all we heard was, "You guys are the greatest ever. What are you going to do next? What do y'all got in store for us as you go undefeated through the Super Bowl?"

Ditka was more up on this stuff than we were, because at the time we were about to become the youngest team ever to go to a Super Bowl. We thought we were going back every year.

Ditka knew what we cost ourselves when we went down there and fucked up our undefeated year. Of course, the Dolphins knew it, too, because they called in all markers to try to keep their undefeated season protected. Every old Dolphin they could find was in the stadium for that game. They knew how good we were—that's why they were there.

One reason we got beat was McMahon didn't start. Another was that on the Dolphins' first five possessions, they scored five times.

We should have known it wasn't our night when one of Dan Marino's first touchdown passes bounced off Hampton's helmet. A ball bouncing off a helmet is supposed to die, but this one somehow flew farther, like a rock skipping off a lake. Nat Moore was behind the coverage, the ball went right into his hands, and he got a 33-yard touchdown.

At halftime, Buddy Ryan and Mike Ditka had to be pulled apart before they started throwing punches.

With five possessions, five scores, you better believe Ditka was wanting to know what was going on. Walking into the locker room, he was on Buddy's ass. That chapped Buddy good, and he'd be the first one to throw a punch at you—as Kevin Gilbride found out a few years later in Arizona. Don't question what Buddy's doing.

So the argument started on the way to the locker room. Once they got in, they were in each other's faces. The guys on the team had to separate them—the offense getting Ditka away from Ryan and defensive guys holding Buddy.

It didn't exactly bode well for the second half.

But then, I don't know what we could have done. It was sort of like any golfer, any pool player, I don't care how good you are, how consistent, there's gonna be that day you miss that two-foot putt with the game on the line, or there's the eight ball, right in the pocket, you can't miss, and somehow it doesn't go in.

Plus, every year, it was like a curse. We'd have two *Monday Night* games a year because we were a good team. One, we'd be great, the other, we'd get our asses blown out. Every year. I don't know what it was about. There was a curse. Somebody had a Bears kewpie doll and it was full of needles one Monday a year.

There was no doubt in my mind, if we'd have played the Dolphins at 12 o'clock on a Sunday, we'd have beat the shit out of them. I was so sure at the time that, when the Miami Dolphins were playing in the AFC championship game, I was rooting for them. I wanted some justice.

And like I said, we were more than a little full of ourselves.

Being 12-0, we were already in the playoffs. We got down to Miami, and I tell you, I don't know how the Dolphins or the Tampa Bay Bucs can ever field a winning team. You're down in the tropics where everbody goes to vacation. Every time we had a game in Florida, some Bears fans were going, too—and the Sunday night before that Miami game, I think I saw just about all of them out somewhere.

I think we started out at Hooters and it just degenerated from there. We were thinking, "We've got plenty of time to recover. It's not a 12 o'clock game, we don't play 'til late."

THE SUPER BOWL SHUFFLE

Sorry, I've got to take a timeout from the game by game to get something off my chest—the goddamn "Super Bowl Shuffle."

I was pissed off about this from the inception until—well, I'm still mad about it.

Everybody had known for a couple of weeks that, on Tuesday after we got back from Miami, the guys were going to start shooting the "Super Bowl Shuffle." If you don't remember, it was a music video about how we were going to the Super Bowl. Nobody's team had done one before, and I didn't think we should.

I could see it if we'd been there the year before and lost, saying, "We're going to go back and win it this time." But we didn't even get close. We got out asses run out of the stadium by 'Frisco in the NFC championship game in '84.

My opinion, how often do things work out for you when you brag about doing them before the fact? Hardly ever. I thought the sumbitches had jinxed us.

I wasn't happy about it; neither was Hampton. Talk about bulletin board material. Any coach who wants to get his team fired up to play against the Bears in the playoffs or the Super Bowl, all he's got to do is put that fucking thing on the night before the game.

But the thing that really chapped my ass was, after the loss, I couldn't believe they were still going to do it. I actually assumed it wasn't going to be done. I was mistaken.

We got into Chicago about 3 a.m. These guys were going to start filming at 7 a.m.

So after they got their asses beat, they had to go on no sleep to some studio and start shuffling about how they're going to the Super Bowl.

Gary Fencik shouldn't have done it, because he showed everybody how horseshit of a dancer he was. And Steve Fuller, everybody knew he was bluegrass, redneck country when he opened his mouth.

Anyway, I don't think it worked out quite the way the guys who did it expected. They got paid five grand apiece for it; the rest of the money was supposed to go to charity, but after it became a gold record and was up for a Grammy, they found out most of the money didn't go where they thought it would.

Anybody who reads this book, please, know one reason why I'm so pissed off about it: When I do appearances to this day, people come up to me and say, "Weren't you in the 'Super Bowl Shuffle?'" I've got a Super Bowl ring on, and the thing they remember is that "Super Bowl Shuffle." I go to appearances, and they're playing that song like it's the Bears fight song or something.

I loathe it.

And now, back to the season.

GAME 14: BEARS 17, INDIANAPOLIS 10
December 8, Soldier Field

It was a close game. I think we were all playing tight because of the Miami loss.

Still, the game wasn't as close as the score. We dominated them. They had a long score late.

But we did maybe play a little close to the vest. Most big plays—and we were nothing if not a big-play defense—are made after a guy takes care of his responsibility, then goes outside of that and makes the play.

After you get your ass handed to you, guys are about making sure they're taking care of their responsibilities—so those big plays don't happen.

GAME 15: BEARS 19, NEW YORK JETS 6
December 14, Giants Stadium

The Jets were a good team. They made the playoffs that year, and Ken O'Brien, their quarterback, was the league's top-rated passer when we played them.

They had 122 yards passing that day, 89 after you subtract the lost yardage from four sacks.

The first thing you've got to do is predicate every game plan on the best thing your opponent does. They're going to get to it sometime during the game. You just hope they can't do anything else.

It's like with John Elway. He goes to two Super Bowls and loses, but he gets Terrell Davis behind him and they win two.

Now, you can't just stop Elway. You've got to stop Davis, too. And because you've got to stop Davis, it opens up for John Elway.

The only bad thing from the game was it instigated my fourth knee operation.

It was a cold game, so the Astrotruf was frozen. Another jailbreak, we went after O'Brien, somebody wiped him out before I could get to him. The first thing that hit was my knee on the turf, and I tore cartilage.

Every week from then on, until I got it operated on after the Super Bowl, I had to have it drained.

GAME 16: BEARS 37, DETROIT 17
December 22, Pontiac Silverdome

The one thing I'll never forget about this game—mostly because they're still showing it on highlights—is Wilber Marshall hitting Joe Ferguson and just knocking him out.

You could tell, just like a boxing match where a guy's been hit so hard he's already out before he hit the ground, Joe was out like a light.

Remember in the old days, how they'd pick a guy's arm up and if it flopped down, he's out? Richard Dent walked up to Joe, picked his arm up, let it go and it just flopped back to the ground. I shouldn't have been laughing about it, but I was.

The play itself was a thing of beauty. Joe took the snap in a passing situation, and here we came. Wilber was actually in the flat in coverage, not even rushing, but because we flushed Joe out to my right toward Wilber, Wilber's job was to come up and force the play.

Joe saw him coming, and he got the pass off, just dumping it somewhere. But he had to straighten up, turning to his right, to throw the ball, because he was right-handed.

You've got to understand how fast Wilber Marshall was. If the perception is he was linebacker fast, that's wrong. He was defensive back fast—and that's what cost Joe Ferguson. He thought he had time to square up and get rid of the ball before Wilber got there, but Wilber hit him right in the mouth with his helmet.

Wilber didn't even have to dive. Most great shots, the guy lays out like a missile, hits his target and goes down with him. But Wilber just ran up and boom! Then he was standing there while Joe goes out.

Now we were on to the playoffs, and we didn't care at all that we lost to Miami. We thought because we were a young team we had plenty of time to have an undefeated season and go back to the Super Bowl.

Chapter 19

BEAR WEATHER: THE 1985 PLAYOFFS

THE WINDY, COLD CITY

I don't know how it came as a surprise to anybody, except maybe that it had been so long since there was an NFL playoff game in Chicago—1963 to be exact. But this was January. This was Soldier Field, right on Lake Michigan, back in the days when the columns were taller than the stands.

It was cold, and it was windy, and those things became a prevailing factor in our playoff games. Hell, they were a factor most games, considering it seemed like nobody but Kevin Butler could kick in Soldier Field. Every other kicker and most quarterbacks who came in would have something to say about the wind gusts, and the later in winter it got, the worse it got.

We wanted a rematch with Miami in the Super Bowl.
(Photo by Daily Southtown; Tinley Park, Illinois)

At least we were acclimated to it. It didn't bother us as much. Like the Denver Broncos playing up in that thin air at Mile High Stadium.

We knew the teams coming in there, it bothered the shit out of them, especially the teams from warm-weather cities.

LIKING OUR CHANCES

I knew we were just one play away from McMahon getting hurt. But as long as McMahon stayed healthy, we were pretty confident—really on the side of arrogant. We felt like nobody could beat us, and if they did it was a fluke.

To us, the Miami Dolphins were the clear No. 2 team, our main challenger. I couldn't wait for them to win the AFC championship and meet us in the Super Bowl so we could rectify that one defeat. I know most people don't think that way; they'd be scared to play them in the Super Bowl because they beat us. They'd want to play someone else.

Cowards.

DOING FOR RICHARD

So we got the regular season out of the way and were rolling into the playoffs. All of a sudden, Richard Dent and his agent came up in the press and said they weren't going to play unless they got a new contract.

Seems like their reasoning was the year's over, he doesn't have a contract, he's not going to play. Something like that. Or maybe it was he wasn't going to play the next year.

Either way, in my mind, that didn't make sense, so we set it up in practice to turn him loose, to set him free in the game, make him the Defensive MVP so the Bears would have to deal with him.

We set up this line stunt called the Echo, where Dan and I slanted to the right toward Richard, and he came around both of us, to the outside of me. The guard blocked me, I held the center, and the tackle was out blocking on Mike Hartenstine or whoever the defensive end was, and Richard would come in that gap.

It seems like a long way to go, and the way they run those games now in pro football, it is. They almost never run three-man games, because there's no time, and even when they run a two-man game it takes too long because the second guy coming around is rounding it off instead of running on an angle to the quarterback, because the first guy is just stopping his man at the line of scrimmage.

You want to penetrate, like a fullback blocking on a run.

Now, what we were doing wouldn't work so well with the West Coast offense and quick drops. But back then, the seven-step drop was still in vogue. It worked.

We set Richard free about three times and he was knocking the shit out of Phil Simms all the time. He ended up with three and a half of our six sacks that day.

It just happened that that game, the Echo was tailor-made for what they were trying to do, and we didn't even realize it when we were thinking about running it. But after we ran it the first time, I knew it was going to work whenever I saw they were going to drop back to pass.

It was called at the line of scrimmage, and the first time I called it, it was a long-yardage play. With that long-yardage play, we had the chance for this Echo to get home because Simms was going to seven-step drop. It came clean, real fast, too. It happened quick. For the rest of the game, I knew their game plan was going to be to try to bust a long play on our defense. Because we blitzed a lot, there was a chance to get a long, successful play—but that takes time.

Richard knew. I told him. I said, "We're going to make you a hero." In the fourth quarter, we'd already beat them, but we stayed in there because we wanted to shut them out.

Richard was looking down the line of scrimmage, actually trying to call it out himself before I could read what the offensive line was going to do. You had to see if it was going to be a pass. You had to see by the strength of the formation whether they were going to east or west block it.

I'd have to basically wave him off—just wait a second, Richard. And he's "more, more, more." Like a little kid.

It wasn't like we were taking a chance of losing the game for Richard. A few plays out of every game wasn't a big deal. Dan was still outside where Richard was supposed to be in containment, so we weren't fucking the defense to help Richard. The jobs were all covered, just switched.

We went through the whole playoffs set up like that. Richard was the Super Bowl MVP and he got his money.

FEEL THE BREEZE

Poor Sean Landetta. The guy stayed in the NFL longer than just about anybody this side of George Blanda, and he's still remembered mostly for whiffing on a punt.

Being an old kicker myself, I have some sympathy—but how Landetta punts the ball is not conducive to punting in high gusts of wind. Some punters cradle the ball on their hand; others grab the tip of the ball—Landetta cradled it.

Having hold of the ball is the best way to punt when you're dealing with the wind. The way Landetta did it, you actually have to get your hand out of the way before you punt the ball, so it's suspended in midair, and if there's a gust of wind it blows it. That's what happened to him. The wind turned the nose of the ball before he could punt it, moved it out of his way.

Shawn Gayle picked it up and ran it in from five yards out for our first score. That was the first big play he made in his career—and he went on to become All-Pro.

WAIT TILL NEXT YEAR

Even though we ended up winning, you could see the Giants had a good defense—and it turned out to be a great defense, because they won the Super Bowl the next year.

I think our game turned out to be their Waterloo like we had with the 49ers the year before. They realized how that felt and that they hadn't raised their goals or their expectations high enough. They were happy just to be where they were, and they got their asses whipped for it.

One thing's for sure, though, Jimbo Covert completely took Lawrence Taylor out of his game that day. Shut his ass down.

Not too many people realize what the worth of the offensive line is. I promise you Lawrence Taylor was trying to be the MVP himself, but Covert shut him down. There's one clip in the official '85 highlight film that shows Covert just splattering Taylor, boom, flat on his back.

Just goes to show you Covert was the best offensive lineman in the league, before his back got hurt. If he'd had a long career, he'd be in the Hall of Fame no question, just like Taylor is.

FEVER PITCH

In some ways, it was just another Bears win that year—we held them to 32 yards rushing, got a bunch of sacks and held the ball most of the day.

But if you're talking about the fan fervor, it kicked up another step higher, which was natural seeing as there hadn't been a Bears playoff game in Chicago since the 1963 championship game.

I always stayed in the locker room a long time after games—so long that whoever was there from my family would be mad at me for making them stand around. After we beat the Giants, I took my time as usual, but the mob of people, the fans, were still there waiting to get a glimpse. Not standing around inside the stadium, but outside. They were almost groupies.

You know how you hear the buzz above the din? That buzz was all over town. Like electricity.

It was a distraction. Everybody was looking for their piece. Media, fans, even people who weren't fans—imagine that, there's lots of people in Chicago who aren't Bears fans.

Everybody wanted a piece, and for the most part we were pretty happy to accommodate them. That was when we started coming into our own about being flamboyant personalities and characters, finding out that sells.

BULLETIN BOARD MATERIAL

Going into the Rams game, Buddy Ryan kind of pissed me off.

It wasn't like the "Super Bowl Shuffle" was enough motivation for anybody we were going to play to get into the Super Bowl. He had to go challenge the leading rusher in the league.

Buddy said, "We're going to make Eric Dickerson fumble three times." God, you don't know how that irritated me.

I mean, Ditka would do it on occasion—like the time a couple of years later everybody in Minnesota raised a fuss when he called the Vikings' stadium the Rollerdome. I believe they beat us that day, but anyway...

Buddy was cocky and arrogant and he said we were going to make Dickerson fumble three times and win the game. I don't know for sure why he said it, but I blame it on the media gigging him.

You know how it is. You keep asking the question until you get the answer you want. They were probably telling him, "Eric Dickerson, the rushing champion of the league, how can you possibly stop him? Nobody can stop him." I can just hear Buddy saying, "Ah, we're going to make him fumble three times and shut his ass down, that's how."

Buddy was not far from wrong, though. Dickerson fumbled twice and we shut his ass down. He had 17 carries for 46 yards and on one short-yardage play, Mike Singletary met him head on, stood him up and pushed him back.

LET IT SNOW

The biggest play of the game, at least in terms of making you wonder if somebody up there in that press box in the sky was scripting the whole thing, came late.

We were already winning 17-0. We already know those L.A. boys were shivering in their boots, them with their long sleeves on and us with our bare arms acting like we don't feel a thing.

Hell, in the highlight film from that game, one of their defensive linemen looks over at the camera and says, "Why the hell don't they put a dome over this thing?" And that's before the game. So you know the Rams were out of their element.

To tell you the truth, it was colder in the Giants game. But the wind was blowing harder for the Rams.

Anyway, the Rams were trying to make something happen. Their quarterback, Dieter Brock, dropped back. We sacked him, he fumbled, Wilber picked it up.

Regular season or playoffs, we loved stopping a great back like Eric Dickerson. (Photo by **Daily Southtown;** *Tinley Park, Illinois)*

And in the middle of his 52-yard runback for a touchdown, it started snowing.

Bear weather. A sign from God that we're the chosen team.

At least, that's the way the fans reacted to it.

Hey, I think it's all head games, and if that works in a positive sense, well, then I'm all about head games. It's all psychology, baby.

We were already winning the game 17-0. Maybe if we were losing the game 23-17 and that happened, I'd think God was shining down on us or something, but no. We won 24-0. We could've played 'em on the beach and won.

There was no big celebration. It was understated in the locker room after the game. We remembered the feeling of the year before, going into the locker room with our asses handed to us.

We were in it to win the Super Bowl, not to get there. Hell, we were in it to win the Super Bowl, then three-peat. We were pretty cocky.

Of course, we had reason.

Two playoff games, two shutouts. Bring on New Orleans.

Chapter 20

THE BIG EASY

HIGH ROLLERS

I'm not a gambler, but I do happen to know that after the conference championships, we were made 21-point favorites for Super Bowl XX in New Orleans.

But when the oddsmakers saw how much we were partying on Bourbon Street the week before the game, the spread went to 10.

HOMEBODY

We had two weeks between the conference championships and the game, so we spent the first in Georgia at the Falcons' training facility. It was just like a regular-season game week—practice and go home.

To me, it wasn't out of the ordinary, because back then I wasn't into the media hype and stuff I got into later in my career. After a while, I realized nobody knew who I was, so I'd better start talking about myself, but that first week I was just going home, staying to myself.

Well, more or less. It wasn't like I was a priest that week. We were young and brash and we were going to play in the Super Bowl every year as far as we were concerned. To slow down would be to become a hypocrite.

On the other hand, things clearly sped up in New Orleans.

LAISSEZ LES BONS TEMPS ROULER

You'd think a good old southern boy like me would've been out on Bourbon Street in New Orleans sometime in his life, right? Not until the Super Bowl, baby, and when I got there it was like all the cajuns say, "Laissez les bons temps rouler."

Let the good times roll.

Our last day in Lake Forest, we had a walk-through at Halas then got on a plane. When we got off the plane, we went straight to Bourbon Street—didn't even check into the hotel—and started partying.

Well, we went to the hotel on the team bus, but we were staying in the hotel attached to the Superdome, and that's walking distance to Bourbon Street, so right out of the box we walked over and started drinking.

Actually, I think we were already drunk when we got off the plane.

Back then, Hampton and I would carry around a liter of Crown Royal in our bags. Really, we'd been doing it ever since we met.

It usually wasn't to drink going there, but to drink on the plane coming back from a game. We'd sit beside each other on the plane, have our little country & western music going, usually some Hank Williams Jr., and had our bottle to drink. Beer's fattening, you know, and I had a waistline back then.

In fact, it was our superstition to go have two Crown and 7s in the hotel bar the night before a game. Something for the effort, we called it.

As you get older, some of those superstitions wear you down and you don't do them anymore. But this was the Super Bowl—and with plenty of time to rest up.

Bourbon Street was everything it was cracked up to be. Bars up and down the street for blocks, people walking down the middle with drinks in their hands. And we were basically VIPs—carte blanche everywhere.

That first Monday night, I fell victim like most tourists do to the Hurricanes at Pat O'Brien's. It's this big old umbrella drink with about seven shots of different kinds of booze in it—and when you walk in the place already drunk, one of them is going to put you over the edge.

So that Monday night, I left a little dissolved Hurricane juice in the alley behind Pat O'Brien's.

But it helps when you're a finely tuned athlete. Your body recovers in a few hours and you're able to drink again.

AWAY FROM THE ACTION

I don't want you to get the impression we went out and partied every second of every night we were in New Orleans. That second night after practice we went over to a hospital to visit kids in the terminal children's ward.

That's tough to do. Always has been. Holy Christ, that'll put everything in perspective.

How do you go in there? I mean, what do you say when you first meet somebody? "How are you doing?" I know the answer. They're dying.

What do you say to a little kid like that? I'd say things like, "Everybody looks up to me, but I'm looking up to you because you're going to be in heaven before me. You're going to be on God's football team, all practiced up and ready to whip my butt when I get up there."

Half the little kids didn't know who we were. All the parents did, all the hospital staff did. It was like more of an appearance for them than for the kids, from what I saw. But I might've pissed a few of them off, because I was there for the kids.

Just the sheer presence of huge individuals sometimes is enough to make a kid smile, so at least I could do that. That's what I think wrestling is all about, just these cartoon characters that wrestling fans look at like, "Wow."

FAMILY MATTERS

My mother tells the story of me taking her and the family—I had 30 family members there—out the first night they were in.

I think it was Thursday. The next night, getting closer to the game, I didn't go out with them. But this night, free drinks, free food, no standing in line. The next night, they don't go out with me, they're back at the end of the line with everybody else.

Actually, that first night, she might not have minded being left outside the first bar we went to. In those first few nights drinking, I hadn't been all the way down the end of the street yet, so I said, "Let's start all the way down the end and work our way up front."

Well, we found out the first bar was a gay bar, with transvestites in it. Wasn't too long before my mother wanted to get out of there. Didn't bother me. Shoot, they're fans, too.

Something did bother me relating to family during the week, though. In one of the team meetings, Ditka came in and told us that after the Super Bowl, the Bears were going to have a party in the ballroom of the hotel if we win, and we'd all get 20 tickets to the party.

Now every player had gotten 30 Super Bowl game tickets each. I stood up and said, "Well, Mike, what 10 family members do you want me to tell they aren't important enough to me to come to this fuckin' party?"

He figured I was talking for the whole team, which I was, really, and said, "You young fuckers haven't been to a Super Bowl, you don't know what it's like, you don't know the privileges and how you should be treated." Basically, he was saying, "Suck on it. The McCaskeys are screwing you out of the 10 people you had coming." And we found out later the sumbitches closed the party down at 10:30.

It was no time after the game. The party was over in a couple hours. That's chicken shit. That's why I believe that story you hear about George Halas to his daughter on his death bed:

"Please, Virginia, anybody but Michael."

AND ANOTHER STORY I BELIEVE...

Pretty famously, Jim McMahon got in trouble during Super Bowl week for supposedly telling a radio reporter that all the women of New Orleans were sluts and the men were nuts.

OK, so he never actually said it. At least not to a radio reporter.

But let me tell you, I understand the impression.

When you go out and every minute there's some groupie wanting to give you a piece of ass, and you're in New Orleans—even if they're not from New Orleans, what's your impression going to be?

I tell you what it is:

"Every woman I met in New Orleans was a slut."

McMahon (here ignoring Vince Tobin later in his career) got himself into some trouble during the Super Bowl week. (Photo by Daily Southtown; Tinley Park, Illinois)

Even if McMahon never said it, women ain't going down on Bourbon Street to try to become nuns. They're there to get theirs. Even if it didn't happen, I could see McMahon saying it, because that was my perception.

You can go down there the deadest time of the year, and you'll still have guys down there with beads wanting girls to show them their titties. Boy, I didn't even have to have beads back then. Things were getting thrown at me I didn't even want.

Anyway, people were wondering if it was going to be a distraction. Come on.

It was hilarious. It was entertaining.

IT'S MY PARTY

When I went out during the week, it was with the night riders—me, Hampton, Mike Hartenstine and Henry Waechter. But that didn't mean we didn't see our teammates.

We'd be walking down the street and somebody would say, "Hey, so-and-so's in there." So we'd go in. Every bar along the street, it was like a different Bear was having a personal appearance, or at least different cliques of Bears. It was like a block party—our block party.

It damn sure wasn't the Patriots' party. You'd see their fans here and there, but they were getting squelched. They were getting freight-trained.

THE SATURDAY SERMON

One thing people always want to know when I'm out making appearances is what Ditka told us the night before the Super Bowl, what fiery oratory he used to stir our passions.

This is usually where I tell them a joke about Ditka's speaking prowess, but since it calls into question the sexual preference of our quarterback, I think I'll let it be. After using it so many times, I'm getting tired of telling that joke, anyway.

To tell you the truth, Ditka was calm that night. The total opposite of what people think he's about.

People think he's about boiling up, cussing, and ranting and raving on the sidelines.

He just told us, "This is hype, it's another level, but don't let yourself go there, because then you're playing out of your norm. That's when guys start making mistakes and start forgetting what you're supposed to do. That's the first thing that beats you. That's when you see a big play happen."

He was just trying to keep us on an even keel, knowing that we were about to blow up.

OF BUDDY, GOOD-BYES AND CHALKBOARDS

The story was around all that week that the Philadelphia Eagles wanted Buddy Ryan to be their head coach.

Of course, we knew all along that it was not only the Philadelphia Eagles, but most every team that needed a head coach. Buddy Ryan was on their hit list. But during that two-week span before the Super Bowl, it was apparent that the Philadelphia Eagles were going to be on the forefront. Even so, it was all kept quiet, because it's disruptive to the team if they find out their defensive coordinator is leaving before the game.

I know, it's hard to believe that would be disruptive considering the way sports are covered and rumors are spread. You'd think we'd be used to it. But never underestimate the ability of an NFL jock to be stupid.

We know how much truth is in most press coverage—if you see something in the media saying this is the way it is, it ain't always that way. So as long as Buddy was with us, he was with us. He's on our side, he wouldn't be talking to the enemy—right?

But he did.

The night before the Super Bowl, after Ditka gave us his pep talk, we split off into offensive and defensive meetings. It's the same before any game, really, a meeting to find out, in the 13th hour, if everybody knows their job responsibility. Buddy and Vince Tobin, who came to be the defensive coordinator after him, both would give us a handwritten test on our responsibilities in whatever defense was going to be called.

At least, that's what we'd usually go over in these meetings, but that ain't what happened the night before the Super Bowl.

Buddy Ryan normally would get up, talk about what he wanted to talk about, then leave the meeting. He'd leave it up to Dale Haupt, our defensive line coach, to run the projector while we watched some more film on the other team.

Everything was going down the way it always had until Buddy got to the end of his talk. I can't even remember now what he'd said to that point, but I'll never forget the last thing he said, with tears in his eyes:

"Guys, no matter what happens, you guys will always be my heroes."

I knew he was gone right there.

He walked out of the room. It pissed me off so much, I couldn't sit there in my rage. I jumped up, grabbed the chair I was sitting in—a metal chair—and there was a chalkboard up in the front of the room, which I was pretty close to. I wasn't one of those guys sitting in the back. I grabbed my chair, and to sound off as loud as I could about my angst about this, I grabbed my chair and threw it at the blackboard, thinking it was just going to shatter.

I threw that chair and somehow it had the right spin so that all four legs hit the blackboard first, went through and stuck there. Hampton saw that, jumped up from his chair by the projector, smashed his big club of a hand into the projector and just destroyed it.

The offense was sitting across the ballroom, on the other side of one of those sliding divider things. They heard all this commotion.

The whole defense sounded like "Rarh!" like you hear fans in the stadium when the team walks out. The offense heard "Boom! Crash! Rarh!" then saw us all filing out of the meeting.

They talk shit to us to this day about how we got to get out of the meeting first. 'Cuz you know we all went back to our rooms and had milk and cookies and went to sleep.

ALONE WITH MY THOUGHTS

I always had this superstition involving coming out a couple of hours before anybody came out even for warm ups before a game, already in my cleats and football pants but not my shoulder pads and my helmet, to just walk around the field, stretch and get in the necessary state of mind.

It was no different for the Super Bowl, except for the fact that it was the Super Bowl, which made everything different.

At first, I was a little distracted by the stadium. I don't know why the NFL doesn't do it all the time, maybe it's too expensive or something, but it's impressive the way they get a Super Bowl stadium decorated up. It's just 10 times more pomp and circumstance than a regular-season game with the banners, the painting on the field and stuff. Little things count.

It didn't take long, though, before I was trying to get down to business. But in taking my usual walk, I kept running into some of the people I'd known in New England.

The equipment guy, the trainer, guys like that, were all trying to come up and talk to me. I fucked 'em all off, like, "Get the hell away from me, fucker." Vicious. Looking back, they were trying to acknowledge the Patriots were wrong about me, but I didn't even let them get the words out.

I sort of regret it now, but don't go up and screw with a predatory animal, you know?

SHUT OUT OF HISTORY

We shut out the Giants. We shut out the Rams.

If we'd have shut out the New England Patriots in the Super Bowl, we'd have pitched a shutout for the playoffs—no points—and that hasn't ever happened.

We were serious about it. Sure, we partied all week, but the business of football was attended to. There was not one mental mistake made in that game—by the defense.

Not that it mattered.

Walter Payton fumbled on the first series, which you can blame mostly on the offensive set being wrong.

In the huddle, they call the offensive set—which is where the tight end's supposed to be—and the backfield set with the play. They were called two different ways. The strength went one way and Walter went the other, opposite the blocking, and he got crushed.

Walter fumbled the ball, we stopped them right there, but it was so close they kicked the field goal. Three points, right at the beginning of the game. If that hadn't happened, we'd have shut them out, because it was a bunch of reserves who let Steve Grogan throw a touchdown pass at the end. No way we'd have let those guys on the field if we were working on a shutout.

A MOMENT OF DOUBT

After Walter Payton fumbled that ball, I had a little consternation, like, "Aw, shoot. They're going to be in the game with us."

It didn't last long.

New England beat Miami in the AFC championship by running the ball and keeping Dan Marino off the field. Against us, they decided to come out and try to trick us by throwing.

But I was always adept at reading offensive linemen by how they set whether it was going to be a run or a pass. When they come to the line of scrimmage with all five of them sitting back like they're taking a dump in the woods, it ain't going to be a run, baby.

Since I knew it was going to be a pass, I looked up at their starting quarterback, Tony Eason. Now, what does a quarterback usually do that gives away whether it's going to be a run or a pass? He looks down the field to see what the coverage is. But Tony Eason was wide-eyed, like a deer caught in the headlights, looking at our front four thinking, "Who's fixing to kill me when I drop back?"

That's when I knew we were going to win the game.

It ended up all three plays were passes, they completed one of them and ended up kicking the field goal.

THE EARLY KNOCKOUT

It was 3-0, we got the ball back and tied it with a field goal set up by a long pass to Willie Gault.

Then we traded punts; they got lousy field position. That's when they dropped back and neglected to double-team me. I beat their guard, Ron Wooten, and sacked Tony Eason. While I was in the process of taking him down, Richard Dent came in from the back and hit the ball. Eason fumbled, Dan Hampton recovered, we got another field goal and were up 6-3.

On the next series, they pitched the ball out to Craig James. Richard hit him, made him fumble, we get the ball back, again on their 13. Two snaps later, Matt Suhey scored on an 11-yard run.

That was big. If we'd have let them stay in the game, who knows? The longer you let that lesser team stay in the game, the more you build them up and there's a chance they're going to hang around until the end. You have to discourage them during the game, and a turnover deep in your own end, followed by a quick touchdown, is discouraging.

After that, the floodgates were open. It's like we were scoring every perceivable way. Reggie Phillips, a backup defensive back, had an interception return for a touchdown. Of course, the Fridge had to get in the act. It was just one of those games where it's your day, baby.

But then, it helped that the Patriots gave up after the first quarter. You could see it in their eyes and in their performance. They weren't on an emotional high; they were struggling.

HALF EMPTY

The Patriots had minus-19 yards of offense at halftime. My God, man. The reel of film, it's half-full. It was three-and-outs.

Our offense was controlling the ball and scoring. We went out, it wasn't just three-and-out, it was minus yards and out. I mean, minus-19 yards of total offense? It's amazing.

You'd think, winning 23-3 and rolling, we'd have been happy. We weren't. It was more like a frenzy. "More, more. Eat, eat." It was more of an adrenaline rush at halftime than it was before the game, and we were killing them.

We wanted to blow them out; 23-3 wasn't enough. Even for the coaches, considering they decided to run the punt return reverse that ended Les Frazier's career.

I mean, we're going to reverse-punt with a starting corner when the game's already blown out? That shows the fervor that was in the locker room at halftime.

Sure, the little special teams coach, Steve Kazor, was wanting to call it. But it was ultimately Mike Ditka's call. Ditka wanted to punctuate that victory with a blowout. What blew out was Les Frazier's knee.

I think Astroturf is more dangerous inside a dome. They don't crest the field in the middle for the water to run off like they do on an outdoor field. It's more conducive to hurting your knee when it's flat. When it's crested, your next step outside, toward the sideline, is kind of downhill. Both Les and New England's tight end, Lin Dawson, hurt their knees in that game without any real contact and were never the same.

GENEROUS TO A FAULT

After the third quarter, we were starting to get a little unfocused on the sidelines. Hell, I was high-fiving fans in the stands.

Maybe I should've stayed in the game. I gave up a chance to be the co-MVP with Richard Dent and a chance to be in the record book when I let my backup, Henry Waechter, go in.

I'd had some nice plays—the game's first sack, another they stole from me right before halftime where, three-man rush, I beat a double-team, swiped Grogan's legs, and he stumbled down, fixing to fall. Richard came along, fell on his back and got the sack.

To this day, most people tell me, "Ah, your Super Bowl, I quit watching it by halftime. I was bored." Well, so was I.

So I let Henry go in, Buddy ran a blitz when they dropped back in their end zone, Henry got a safety and a sack.

That safety is in the record books, that's what kills me. There have been other guys to get one, but is anybody ever going to get two safeties in a Super Bowl? Henry's always going to be in the record book. But I don't regret it or think I did wrong. By God, my teammate got some.

HEAVY CELEBRATING

During the game, Hampton and Otis told me they were carrying Buddy Ryan off the field. Dan told me and Fridge, "Y'all carry off Ditka."

When I came up to Ditka, he said, "No, no. You leave me alone." But I knew they were carrying Buddy off. Was he going to be the only coach up on shoulders? Oh, no. So I actually jerked Ditka up—he didn't want to go—until he was up there and finally having a good time.

It was the first time two coaches ever got carried off the field at the Super Bowl.

That was a nice moment, but the rest of the postgame celebration didn't seem like any big deal.

I remember going to the locker room and being disappointed. No champagne. There's still a Coke splash on the jersey I wore; it's in a glass frame, and everybody thinks it's blood or champagne or something. I tell 'em, "Nope, it's Coke, because the NFL didn't allow alcohol in the locker rooms."

I've always been short-changed, my whole career, in shit like that.

What was really strange, though, was that we stressed out and focused so much, and it was easy. Handed to us. It's like what most people tell you about the mountain top. It's the climb up that defines a man, not the top.

We'd gotten up there. We'd done it. What's next?

TAKING THE TROPHY HOME

You know what? I've never gotten to touch the Lombardi Trophy without a pair of gloves on.

For some reason, it never made it into my hands in the locker room or on the plane back, and it wasn't until the 15-year reunion party that I ever held it. They had the trophy there, but they had white gloves for people to put on to touch it. Something about the oil in your skin tarnishing the metal. So my skin has never caressed that trophy.

Michael McCaskey's has, though. Talk about tarnishing.

I can still see him getting off the team bus back in Chicago, holding up that trophy like "I am responsible for this."

My ass. It was George Halas, Jim Finks, Jerry Vainisi and Mike Ditka. Michael McCaskey had no input whatsoever in having that trophy in his hand.

Anyway, Chicago hadn't had a champion to celebrate in a long time, so they had a parade for us. Most of us. We set a team record with nine guys making the Pro Bowl, and all of those guys—Jimbo Covert, Richard Dent, Dave Duerson, Dan Hampton, Jay Hilgenberg, Jim McMahon, Walter Payton, Mike Singletary and Otis Wilson—went straight to Hawaii from New Orleans.

I made the AP and UPI All-Pro teams, but I definitely wasn't in Hawaii. It was about three degrees in Chicago for our parade.

There was still a multitude of people out along LaSalle Street, packed in like sardines—I guess to keep each other warm.

The street was so crowded that the people wouldn't let the buses through. The cops had to get them out of the way each foot of the way. The buses were at a crawl.

Of course, it didn't help that the windows of the buses were tinted, and people were crowding up close just to try to get a glimpse of us.

I remember this one lady, in such a fervor, jumping up on the front of the bus like she was going to try to stand on the front bumper and scream at us through the front window. She couldn't keep hold, she was slipping, and the last we saw of her was her sliding down, the bus was still moving, and her purse was still hooked onto the windshield wipers.

Like I said, nobody could see us. The fans were getting so pissed off about that, I think, they started climbing on top.

After they did that, we thought, "Why don't we get up there?" So we pulled the hatch, climbed out, and the crowd went nuts.

It gave them what they wanted—and it gave me something, too. I was cold up there, wearing just a tweed sports coat, and every other foot of the way somebody was trying to throw me a bottle of booze. Every now and then I'd catch one, drink out of it and throw it back to them.

Then we got up to the stage, and for years I got hate mail over what I said when it was my turn to talk. The only thing I said was, "That's right, Chicago, we got fucking bragging rights over the whole goddamn country now."

Because I used the Lord's name in vain, those cheap-shot Christians reared their heads again. They loved how I'd go out there and cripple another player, but don't say God's name in vain.

Chapter 21

A FAREWELL TO KINGS

STARS AND BARS

After the Super Bowl, here comes the big time. When you win, I don't care how bad or good you really are, you're a star—and you can capitalize on that name recognition.

Hell, even Mike Tomczak, the third-string quarterback on the Super Bowl team, bought a place—T'n'T's, with Tom Thayer, out in Joliet, the far west suburb of Chicago where Thayer's from. Let the good times roll. Everybody's a hero, especially the real heroes.

Walter Payton had a couple places out in Schaumburg, and it was a drive, but I'd still make it out there.

I was a regular at Ditka's City Lights. Still am at his current place downtown. And I went to all of them, from Fencik's place, the Hunt Club, to McMahon's. Even Butler had a joint.

A lot of guys got into places that didn't make it, but no matter what, most everybody made their money. Most places have a lifespan of three years anyway, then people go somewhere else because somewhere else is cooler.

Most of the deals guys had were along the lines of "Let us use your name for some of the cut." If they're just using your name, you're getting proceeds. It doesn't matter if the place goes bankrupt down the road, because you're getting checks before it does.

All I know is every time I went into one of those guys' places, they were packed—and like I said, I went in all of them. Help out the boys, you know?

Now I really believe this: To have a winning team, you've got to have some intelligent guys. And that doesn't just mean intelligent at football. You use your intelligence to be a good football player, but that intelligence works in society, too.

Ditka was always relating his team speeches to the real world. He'd talk to us like a father to his sons, laced with, "Men, you're going to find out in life..." There's a lot of aspects of life that are relatable to football—making a game plan, having a goal. That's all business. It's a natural extension to want to get into something.

NO SHOTS AT SCHOLTZ'S

Me, I fought off the entrepreneurial spirit until '89—when I bought a piece of Scholtz's Beer Garden, the oldest tavern in Texas. Eventually, every guy who gets a little money in his pocket succumbs to the dream of standing behind his own bar and pouring his buddies a free drink.

Free my ass.

I poured so many drinks on the house for me and other people that we had to take liquor out. Beer and wine only after that. Couldn't keep Crown Royal in there.

At least it was fun. Some of the boys even came down to the grand opening, too—Keith Van Horne, Tommy Thayer.

MONSTERS OF A NEW MIDWAY

After '85, Platteville became a carnival, literally. When we got big, they'd put the county fair there when we were in camp, and people from all over the area would come for a barbecue with us as the honored guests. Live bands, me and Dan would get on stage and sing with them—our staple was "Up against the Wall Redneck Mothers," and entertain the crowds.

The whole camp became the way I always envisioned George Halas's barnstorming trip with Red Grange to be. In 1925, Halas made pro football when he signed Grange for $100,000 and then took him on a coast-to-coast train ride where the Bears played 16 games in two months. It must have been a real traveling carny.

In Platteville, it wasn't like they were showing up for football any more. They were showing up for Great America. We were the Bears Theme Park.

We'd get thousands of people at every practice—more for those than for my high school football games, and that's saying something considering Texas high school football.

Everywhere, it was little kids sitting there with their big eyes looking at you.

They were there to be entertained, and I have a loud voice. All I'd have to do is say something sarcastic, and they'd roar. I was doing it for them.

There were other things, too, like when it wasn't my turn to run drills. I'd just stand over by the Gatorade bucket, and there'd be cans of the stuff sitting there. To live up to the Mongo moniker, I'd turn around toward them with a can of Gatorade and bite into the side of it with my canines, like a vampire. While it was spewing, I'd drink it down like that—oh, they'd hoot and holler.

That's when I started becoming an entertainer.

I've always been a fan of that kind of entertaiment, anyway. I like the end zone dances. Terrell Owens is a funny motherfucker to me. When he grabbed those pompons from a cheerleader? I fell on the floor. That's part of the experience to me.

Me being a fan of that, I wanted to give the fans some of it as well.

SPEAKING OF THE CARNIVAL

In the off season after we won the Super Bowl, I got a taste of wrestling. Jim Covert and Fridge did *Wrestlemania*, Covert because he was the Offensive Lineman of the Year and a former wrestler and Fridge because he was the Fridge. He was the biggest thing going.

I went and sat in the first row, because I was a fan.

Anyway, a Battle Royale is when all the wrestlers get in the ring and the last guy who doesn't get tossed over the top rope is the winner. They both got tossed over—but I'm pretty sure it took more than one guy to get the Fridge—and Andre the Giant won.

Those wrestling guys remembered me coming down to sit in the front row. Later, when I was in Green Bay and Lawrence Taylor was going to do another *Wrestlemania* against Bam Bam Bigelow up there, they asked me and Reggie White if we wanted to be his All-Pro backups. Had to have the All-Pro moniker, you know.

It worked out well for me. I did the Monday show before the pay-per-view to pub the match because Lawrence was out playing golf and wouldn't do it. That led to me doing announcing one night with Vince McMahon on another one of their shows, *Raw*, and that led to me getting the announcing job on *Nitro*. I was hired to be an announcer that year after I retired, but if I wrestled I got more money.

After I wrestled and they saw how good I was at it, I just became a wrestler full time.

It was a traveling carny. You're just a sideshow dancing chicken. People paying a quarter to say, "Look at this chicken dance." They don't see the guy with the hot plate under the table turning the heat up on the chicken's feet.

But that's probably a whole 'nother book.

LOOSEN UP, GINNY BABY

The year after we won the Super Bowl, before training camp started, the Bears rented out this banquet hall for a ceremony to give all of us our championship rings. We all showed up; it was a suit-and-tie affair.

They sat Ditka with all the McCaskeys, a millworker in the middle of Martha's Vineyard. By the time the night was over, after we all got our rings, he was face-down in his plate, dead drunk.

That's the difference between the boys and the white collars the McCaskeys brought in. Heck, it might be one of the reasons the McCaskeys wanted to go white-collar.

LOOSEN UP, GINNY BABY II

The McCaskeys being the tight-ass conservatives they are, they frowned on T&A, so they fired the Honey Bears—our version of the Dallas Cowboy Cheerleaders. They told them during our Super Bowl season they wouldn't be coming back the next year. Word was they didn't think girls in short-shorts showing lots of cleavage projected a wholesome enough image for the franchise.

Of course, there were stories about the girls cavorting with the team, too. You'd get busybodies calling Halas Hall, ratting people out—allegedly.

I didn't see anything.

Wait, I didn't get married until the off season of '84, and they got rid of the Honey Bears in '85, so I suppose it's OK to say that at every level—high school, college and pro—I've always liked to have the cheerleaders around. Let me put it this way: I've dated a few at every level.

WELCOME, VINCE

Coming into '86, there wasn't a whole lot to be worried about, except for the fact that we were changing defensive coordinators, and all the talk was that the new guy, Vince Tobin, was going to change things a bunch.

Vince was the little brother of our personnel director, Bill Tobin, and hadn't coached in the NFL. He had had a couple of pretty good defenses in the USFL and Canada, and he played a style Mike Ditka liked.

Ditka always wanted to play a reading, blitz every now and then, zone defense. Let the offense make a mistake instead of Buddy's way, which was going and making the mistake happen before the offense has a chance to do something good.

Not that Ditka's way wouldn't work. There's a few philosophies out there that have won Super Bowls. It's just that I'm a fan of go get 'em.

There was some apprehension. I didn't know how this was going to work—taking attack dogs and making them sentry dogs. You don't teach an old dog new tricks, right?

But as soon as we got into the defensive meetings, Vince fixed that. He said, "We're still going to run the '46,' we're just going to call it the 'Bear defense' now."

We did some other things, too. Vince gave us the first example of a zone blitz I'd seen in the league. You're still attacking up front, but playing a zone behind it. Buddy was man-to-man, with a blitz.

Really, it was still the same attacking defensive front for us, and I loved it.

It was tough at first getting used to the terminology changes. We'd been in Buddy's system for a few years, and learning a new language wasn't easy.

Maybe it doesn't sound like much, but when the middle linebacker comes in the huddle and says, 'Bear defense,' you better not be having flashbacks or you're not going to know what that is. In the heat of battle, just that little introspective reflection of, 'OK, this used to be that and now that's this...' there's that half a step and now you're fucked.

But there's good reason for changing the terminology. The coordinator and his coaches have to be the first ones in line to know what's going on. They've got to flash quick in their minds, too. They can't be up in the booth going, "This is what we used to call it, but Buddy calls it this, so..." Too late. You've just got to get the players, through intensive meetings, to know, "This is what we're calling it now."

Most of the coverages around the league are the same anyway.

To tell you the truth, I think Vince's situation was just like when Barry Switzer inherited the Dallas Cowboys from Jimmy

Johnson. Stay out of the way. Do your best not to fuck up the machine, brother, cause it's running fine.

Vince was a genius at that. I imagine he had different ideas of what he wanted to incorporate, but if something's already working, why blow up the factory? He turned us loose, too. We got some sacks in Vince's defense.

WELCOME, AL AND TODD

Al Harris and Todd Bell came back in '86 after holding out the Super Bowl season. The way they were treated, it took their football out of them. They weren't the aggressors anymore. They were the defenders. I felt sorry for them—not for the money, but for the fact that they didn't get to go to the Super Bowl.

Of course, when they came back, we were just gonna go get another one, so they'd have theirs.

GREAT EXPECTATIONS

Heading into the season, everybody thought we were going to win another Super Bowl, me included. I didn't think there was any way we weren't going to repeat—until McMahon went down. He only played six games all year and went out for good in December after having rotator cuff surgery.

When I saw how bad the offense was struggling in practice under different signal callers, I knew we were in trouble.

I mean, you've got to recognize the signs. You know this might not work out in a game when you hear the head coach yelling constantly during offensive drills, "Run it over." You know you're in trouble.

Ed Hughes was the offensive coordinator then, but our offense was really Mike Ditka being smart enough to run Walter Payton and Jim McMahon being smart enough to know what to audible off of that. Without McMahon, no audible. It was tough. With him, we had an offense. Without him, we were just running plays.

As it would turn out, every year we went to the playoffs and we didn't have Jim McMahon starting at quarterback, I knew we'd be sucking hind tit.

The defense was enough to carry us through the regular season, but the playoffs were something different. You've got to have that stability.

I don't care if it had been Joe Montana taking his place. That offensive line trusted Jim, loved him and wanted to perform for him. It's like part of the reason I busted my ass was liking Mike Ditka and wanting him to glow about me.

Here's the best example I can give you of Jim McMahon's value. When he first got drafted, we still had training camp in Lake Forest. We had a scrimmage one day over at Lake Forest High School. It was Ditka's picked team against Buddy Ryan's picked team.

They did like a schoolyard, "I'll take him. I'll take him," and we scrimmaged.

Buddy's first pick, he didn't take Mike Singletary or Dan Hampton. He took No. 9.

WELCOME, BAMBI

Doug Flutie was supposed to solve our quarterback problems—hail the conquering hero, the Heisman winner, the guy who hadn't really been given a chance to prove himself in the NFL because he was only about five foot nothin'.

It wasn't the easiest deal for him. They brought him in late, taught him the system and threw him out there in the playoffs against the Redskins, who gave him fits.

Of course, some of his teammates did, too.

There was a lot of talk that nobody on the team liked Flutie, mostly because he had Thanksgiving dinner with Ditka, but really it was all the offensive side of the ball. I think they felt like he was the usurper to Jim McMahon's throne, so he wasn't going to be accepted.

Somebody even started calling him "Bambi," not the manliest nickname in a football locker room. I don't know who started it, but I have to admit it fit. You know, the little baby deer, how deers run around—he was kind of a prancer back there.

Me, the only problem I had with Flutie was him was throwing two fucking interceptions and fumbling the ball twice against Washington in the playoff game. I don't give a shit if he eats dinner with Ditka. If he'd have gone out there and won the Super Bowl, I'd have been fine with him being the quarterback. But he didn't.

Four fucking turnovers. We lost 27-13 to Jay Schroeder.

Of course, I don't know if Sid Luckman would have helped us against the Redskins that day. Sometimes things just don't go your way.

I mean, some days you have to beat a double-team to get free, but the quarterback holds the ball too long, so you get a sack. There was a time in this game, Schroeder's first touchdown pass, where we ran a blitz. I was on the line of scrimmage, got off with the ball, the line parted, blocking other guys, and I was set free. I ran back there as fast as I could, nobody touching me, he backed up, threw it falling over backward as I hit him. Touchdown pass. Shit happens like that, it ain't your day, baby.

FOR THE RECORD...

If I'm running the team, I'm looking around for a quarterback, too. Maybe not a midget like Flutie, but somebody.

Jim getting hurt and us having to play Flutie in the first place, that's why I love Jim, but I say it's his fault we didn't win three Super Bowls in the '80s. He was getting hurt all the time. It ain't his fault, now. But, dammit, every dynasty had one quarterback.

Ours could have been Steve Young, as I recall. Back when Tampa Bay offered him up as trade bait, Dan Hampton and I politicked to get him for the Bears, but it fell on deaf ears.

Why? Where was he from? Brigham Young. I think Jim McMahon scared them off of BYU quarterbacks.

Dan and I knew, though, from playing against Young in Tampa. We beat them, of course; they had a terrible team. But you could see the guy was good, a playmaker.

Of course, playing for us, those concussions that drove Steve out of football might have come on a little sooner—for the same reason I think it was a little bit our fault Jim was getting beat up pretty good.

Playing quarterback for the Bears, you were a marked man. Our defense hurt a lot of other teams' quarterbacks, so you know they were out to get ours.

WELCOME, BUDDY

Sometimes, I think the schedule makers just can't help themselves. They see the chance for a ratings blockbuster and they go for it, which I'm sure was one of the reasons Buddy Ryan's Eagles came to visit us in the second week of the season.

There was a lot of hype in the press, and it was a little strange having to face Buddy—but only for the defense.

I think the offense kind of enjoyed it. If I was an offensive lineman, playing against a coach I'd practiced against for years and knew what he was in the habit of calling, there'd be some things to look for, you know? Even an old shaman like Buddy had his habits. Vince sure had his. Once he got to town, if we had somebody backed up behind the 20-yard line, everybody in the huddle knew a blitz was coming.

The Eagles gave us a good game, took us to overtime before we won, and you could call that a victory for Buddy. After all, the Eagles were one of the worst teams in the league, that's why they needed a new coach in the first place, and they played the world champions to an overtime game. That's pretty good progress two games into his first year in Philly, don't you think?

To be honest, there wasn't a whole lot in the way of interaction with Buddy. I had blinders on, baby. And here's one thing about Buddy—the whole time he and I were together on the Bears, the only time he stuck around on the field after the game was when we won the Super Bowl and we carried him off the field. Buddy Ryan, after the game was over with, walked straight to the locker room every game.

You know, I didn't really shake hands much after games either. It's hypocritical to me, to get out there and go to war with somebody, not exactly being his friend if you know what I mean, and at the end shake his hand? When you've, you know, done things all afternoon? It ain't the Marquis of Queensbury out there.

TOO CLOSE FOR COMFORT

One thing we should have learned from beating the Eagles just 13-10: We were going to be in a lot of close games that year.

That's what happens when you run a read-and-react defense. When you play it safe and don't go try and make a play, the games are going to be close in the end the majority of the time. Keep the game close and in the last possession try to win it. It does work, you've got a chance, but man, why not try to make it so the game's over in the third quarter?

We went 14-2, but it wasn't an easy 14-2. Seven games were decided by six points or less and of the three times we won by more than 14, two came against Tampa Bay.

SAY WHAT?

Losing to Washington was unbelievable to me. We lost? What? I was beating shit up in the locker room afterward. Everybody was, which was a sign of how surprised we were. Most of the time, after a defeat, guys would be introspective, not showing emotion outwardly. This time, there was shouting, stuff getting hit—my locker caught hell, I know.

I think the Redskins were really up for that game as a direct result of getting their asses beat by us a couple times in the two previous years. In '84, we came in and handed them an ass-whipping in the playoffs when they were the Super Bowl champs the year before, and the way we beat them in '85, 45-10, we'd humiliated them two years in a row. That will get you up for a game, and they were ready to play.

Thing is, even with all that, nine out of 10 days, even with Doug Flutie quarterbacking, we beat them. That was their 10th day.

The one thing it didn't hurt was our confidence. We still felt we were the best team in football. We had a good year, even with the new defensive coordinator. We figured Doug Flutie wasn't going to be quarterbacking and turning the ball over six times the next time we played. What the hell, no big deal.

HULA SCHMOOLA

In '86 I made my first Pro Bowl. I went in '87, too. Didn't much like it, to tell you the truth, even with the return to the site of all my monkey bowl-grabbing glory in college, the Hula Bowl.

The Pro Bowl is scary, really. Playing on Astroturf in a game that don't mean shit, that's the time people get hurt. A freak

We always sent a number of players to the Pro Bowl,
but I wasn't a big fan of the game.

accident, somebody falling on the side of your leg in a pickup game, more or less, might wreck your career.

That game is almost like my Harley. I'd always wanted a Harley Davidson, but I never got one until my last year in the league, up in Green Bay—that's how much I cared about being a Packer, I guess, I got a Harley in October on my birthday when I was still playing for them. I'd never got one because you wreck, you fuck your leg up, there goes your career—how stupid is that?

BACK IN BLACK

After the playoff loss to Washington, Mike Ditka decided, "OK, we're going back to old school, we're going back to black shoes." God, how I hated those things.

Old-time religion. Black shoes. Man, those damn things made you feel sluggish, like you were slogging around in black work boots.

You know, you look in the mirror and you look sharp, you feel sharp. It gives you that bounce in your step—and that bounce is important playing football.

Dan and I tried, though. We always taped over our shoes, even though a lot of guys don't—which I think is a mistake. Put your shoe on over the tape, it's easier to roll an ankle, I think. Put tape on over your shoe, there's no way your ankle can roll as much. Anyway, once we got those black shoes, Dan and I would always have the tape cut special, so the shoes looked like Italian loafers.

POT, THIS IS KETTLE...

Ditka had one other great example of trying to keep our focus on football. He came into a morning meeting one time in '87 and—I'll never forget it—says, "You fucking guys are doing too many commercials. You need to concentrate on football."

Shit, he was doing more than anybody.

DITKA PICKS HIS SCABS

It might have taken five years, but I believe Mike Ditka laid the groundwork for getting himself fired in '87.

We went on strike that year, and they hired other players, paid them and called it NFL football. Most of the world called it scab football. During that time, Ditka lost ground with some players I don't know if he ever got back. He sided with those scab players—called them the "real Bears"—and the McCaskeys over the guys who were on strike.

There is a type of player who needs a reason to push beyond what they think is their limit—for whom? for what? Ditka ceased to be the who and the what for those guys when he sided with the scabs. Whatever part of them that played for his approval was gone.

I understood Ditka's point of view. In his mind, you sign a contract, you live up to it. We had individual contracts, but we went on strike.

The first scab game the Bears had was in Philadelphia, and it didn't draw at all—barely 4,000 people. At Soldier Field the next week, there were 32,000-plus to watch those guys.

Of course, some of them were there for us, too. We had an autograph session outside the stadium. I wasn't going to stand there holding a stick with a cardboad sign saying we were on strike.

I understood the fans who showed up were just football fans. One thing you learn after you retire is to appreciate the fans.

I was a Bear, but being a Bear wasn't mine to own. I was part of the history. The team really belongs more to the people who cheer for it than the people who play for it.

Most of the guys around the league resented the fans who showed up for those scab games. Not me. They're Bears fans. I came out to have fun with them. Here's an autograph from a real Bear, thanks for coming out.

I was there to entertain them. You know how they call some guys a players' coach? I like to think I was a fans' player.

CAN'T BLAME McMAHON

We still had a good team in '87, damn good, really. We had 70 sacks; the only guy we really lost from the year before was Gary Fencik, who retired.

But Washington caught us. They beat us in the playoffs 21-17, then went on to win the Super Bowl.

This time, it wasn't Jim McMahon's fault. He played, and the Redskins barely beat us with a punt return by that little Darrell Green, their DB, who was the fastest player in the league. We were ahead in the fourth quarter, punted the ball, and Green actually tore a cartilage in his rib cage vaulting over the top of Jim Morrissey, the last guy he got away from, scoring the winning touchdown.

We were still the local heroes, though. I wasn't hearing boos yet. Around Chicago, it was still early enough that people still remembered the Bears being not worth a shit. Here they were

getting to enjoy a winning season and a playoff game, where
before they never sniffed the playoffs.

I think leaving football was tough on Walter.
(Photo by Daily Southtown; *Tinley Park, Illinois)*

FAREWELL, WALTER

The saddest thing about '87 was that it was Walter Payton's last year—not for what he did on the field, but for who he was. That's what I was sad about. Not being around him in the locker room, on the team bus, at hotels. It was like living in the same house with a brother, then he gets older and moves on with his life. He was around every now and then, but I wasn't able to enjoy him every day.

It's the nature of the business to get used to guys coming and going. But I'll always remember Walter, when we got beat by Washington that last game, sitting on the bench until the stadium was just about empty.

He sat on the end of the bench, like he was trying suck it all in and remember that little microcosm of where he was right then in his life. Just sitting there with his head down, reflecting, like the statue, *The Thinker*.

When what you're about your whole life, every waking second, is now over—man, that's a big change. That's the change large people need to make in their life to become skinnier and healthier. It's something you don't know how to do, but it's flat changing who you are.

I think that's what Walter was reflecting on: Who am I now? Who am I gonna be? And Walter had himself more together than most of the people on this planet.

WELCOME, NEAL

I have to say, the Bears really found a gem when they drafted Neal Anderson out of Florida. We were coming off the Super Bowl when we got him, so it wasn't like we had any expectation of landing a star with our low pick, but Neal was the shit.

That spark Walter had when he ran? Neal had it, too. They shared duty in '87, and Neal actually outgained Walter even though Walter got more carries.

For three years after that, Neal always gained over 1,000 yards and caught around 40 balls.

That's lightning striking twice. Neal was good. He wasn't as good as Walter, but by God he was a playmaker.

I don't think people appreciated him, though. People got spoiled with all those years of Walter. All of a sudden there's Neal carrying on. They didn't realize they'd caught lightning in a bottle twice—but there's been nothing like Neal on the Bears since.

That's what I tell people about our whole team. We spoiled you guys. Now you appreciate us, because there hasn't been anything like us since.

FAKE OR REAL?

Heading into '88, the Bears did something else I think ended up costing us.

They took the Astroturf out of Soldier Field and put natural grass in—and didn't put a heater under it. That's why in the playoffs we'd end up playing on painted green dirt. It's not like they couldn't have put a heater in, either—Green Bay'd done it, and it wasn't all that expensive, either.

Even Green Bay would turn that heater off sometimes, when a team like ours was coming to play. They'd rather have us playing on ice, so we couldn't get any forward push.

That was the mistake the Bears made with that grass field. I'm convinced it cost us winning games in the playoffs. They were thinking we were going back to the good old days, old-time football, even though we'd kicked people's asses on Astroturf.

Most people won't believe this, but I'll say it anyway. I'd have given up years off the end of my career to keep playing on Astroyurf like we'd won the Super Bowl on. I'm sure we'd have won a few more playoff games if we'd have been playing them on turf, and I'd have gladly traded the wear and tear on my body of playing on Astroturf for another shot at the Super Bowl.

In '88, it cost us playing against Montana in the NFC championship game. The field was frozen. We couldn't attack the line of scrimmage. Their offensive linemen just sat there and waited for us to come to 'em on ice skates. Our front seven, that's how we won football games, baby. We got into the backfield. You can't do that on ice. For whatever reason, on Astroturf, you wouldn't get that ice on top—even though it was hard as ice underneath.

PAGING DR. HAMPTON, DR. McMICHAEL

On November 2, 1988, Mike Ditka had a heart attack.

I'm tempted to say "allegedly," because the way he came back, you could almost think it was a ruse to get the team fired up. Vince Tobin assumed the couching reins, but not two weeks after it happened, Mike was standing there on the sideline in Washington, just watching—with his heart specialist making sure he was not going to go overboard, I guess.

He took over from Tobin the next week in Tampa.

It was like he had no convalescence. But then, based on what happened the day he fell ill, he might have figured he needed to get back quick.

The day it happened, it was big news, and we were watching on the monitors in the locker room. The cardiologist came on and said, "No more drinking and smoking." That was our cue, baby.

Up in his office, it was more of a cigar bar than a coach's office. Ditka had nice Cubans, whatever you wanted, in humidors up there. He had nice sipping whiskey and brandy and stuff like that. Dan and I went up there and barged into his office while he was lying in the hospital bed, stealing his cigars and his bottles. But we didn't steal them for ourselves; we went and handed them out to the team.

It was all out of concern for the coach, pure and simple.

FOGETABOUTIT

I've seen some crazy shit in my time, but one of the craziest was something just about everybody else couldn't see, no matter how hard they tried. Too bad, too, because it was our first playoff win in three years—against Buddy Ryan, to boot.

In '88, Buddy started spouting off about how great his defense was—better than his Bears defense, he was telling folks. Now any defense with Reggie White rushing the passer was going to be good—but they weren't monsters like us.

So here come the playoffs, on New Year's Eve no less, and here come Buddy's Eagles.

Then the lights went out. I think it was God's way of putting a pall over the whole thing.

You could tell it was going to be a weird day. The weather was real funky, but when this fog came in off Lake Michigan just before halftime, it was like nothing I'd seen. It just started settling down, lower and lower, until the people in the stands

*We beat Buddy in the fog bowl, but that pox
Montana finished our season a week later.*
*(Photo by **Daily Southtown; Tinley Park, Illinois**)*

couldn't see a damn bit of what was going on on the field. On
TV, it was like watching no channel—snow. Unbelievable.

From my point of view, though, it looked worse than it was.
On field level, you could see the guys on the other sideline. Fog,
you know, it's a little off the ground.

But a long pass? Forget about it.

Randall Cunningham had one picked off by Maurice
Douglass, but I never saw it. I just heard the fans cheering, and
I still don't know how they saw it.

However it happened, we beat them, then played San Francisco in the conference championship.

You can thank the frozen grass for us losing 28-3. It would have been a different story on Astroturf or even with a heater under the grass where we could sink our cleats in and try to get Joe. Years later, when I was with Green Bay, one of the Packers coaches who was with San Francisco at the time told me Montana was so cold he couldn't feel his hands, and he still beat us.

Damn pox.

TEXTBOOK TACKLES

There is one thing from '88 I'm pretty proud of. When Dan Hampton was being inducted years later into the Hall of Fame, he said, "There was a point in time when my friend Ming and I played the best ever."

That was in '88. Dan played defensive tackle that year, and there were no two defensive tackles playing side by side who ever played better in tandem than we did that year.

It was the only year I ever led the team in sacks, with 11 1/2, and Dan got nine and a half. We both had 88 tackles, tied for third on the team behind Singletary and Duerson.

That year, they were double-teaming both of us. The center and one guard would turn on one of us, and they'd leave the fullback in to help the other guard with the other one. You don't ever see that—the fullback just stepping up to help the guard every time. It was unbelievable.

We had one better year sacks-wise, in '84, when he had 11 1/2 and I had 10. That's when he was playing defensive tackle again. When we played tackle together, we fucked shit up.

Dan never really liked playing tackle before that. I had to talk him into moving from end in '84. When they suggested it, he rebelled. I convinced him that, out on the end, you only make the play when it comes to your side of the field. At tackle, you're like the middle linebcker; both sides of the field are open for you to make plays.

Even after '85, when they brought Fridge in and moved Dan back to end in the base defense, he was inside in the 46 defense—which, of course, we played a lot.

Most of the time, the 46 would look like this: Otis and Wilber would be on the same side, the left, either both outside the tackle or one of them on the tight end and the other outside of that. I'd be in the gap between the tackle and the guard. Dan was over center. William would be in the other guard/tackle gap and Richard would be on the outside, like Otis and Wilber, usually on the weak side, while Mike Singletary would be stacked up right behind Dan.

The strong safety would always make a lot of plays in that defense, because he'd be more or less a baby linebacker on the strong side. There was always an open area between Mike and the linebackers on the line, or between Mike and Richard, that the strong safety would step in and fill. The strong safety would make plays because the running back, on his cutback, usually perceived that area to be open.

Whatever. All I knew was, when Dan was at tackle, it was like I was free. Because he was so good, they had to worry about him, it set me free to do some things I wanted to do.

There were times when the center had to turn to him. I knew that gap was going to be open for me to come inside that guard and get up in the quarterback's face.

There were games in the 46 that were almost like magic. They couldn't stop us. Dan would hit to my side and hold the center; then I'd loop around. The tackle would always try to block down on me in the 46, to make sure I wasn't going to try to come around outside. So I'd go at the tackle like I was going outside of him, then the guard would think he's free to pick up Dan.

All Dan had to do was grab the center and hold him; I'd fake outside the tackle and come around Dan free while he shielded three guys.

The difference with Fridge was his sheer presence, taking up that much space, I knew the ball wasn't going to go there. The run, the quarterback stepping up in the pocket, or having an open field of vision, none of that was going to happen through Fridge.

LAST MAN STANDING

Look, you get used to people leaving in football. Happens every year. I mean, Fencik retired after the '86 season, Walter after '87. Otis Wilson tore up his knee in '87 playing defensive end in the nickel package on a muddy field in Green Bay—he came back after that and played for the Raiders, but it wasn't the same old Otis. Wilber Marshall and Willie Gault were on other teams starting in '88.

But '89? Worst year of my football life.

McMahon was gone, to San Diego, and with him went our offensive heart. We went from moving men on a chess board to running plays. But that was just the start.

Even so, the year started out great. Dan played in the first four games, we went 4-0; then he hurt his knee.

Dan missed the rest of the season, and we won two more games.

At one point, we were 6-4, Ditka said, "We might not win another game," and we didn't. I don't know why he said it, but by God it was prophetic.

As the injuries mounted, our season began to unravel.
*(Photo by **Daily Southtown**; Tinley Park, Illinois)*

There were reasons. William broke his arm. Richard broke something in his leg and was gone. Dan hurt his knee and was gone. Hell, Singletary and I were the only two guys on the defense to start all 16 games. We were the last men standing. I was looking around the huddle not recognizing anybody.

Like I said, worst year of my football life. Capped by a 26-0 loss at San Francisco to finish 6-10.

Chapter 22

RANDOM NOTES FROM TRAIL'S END

MAKING CONCESSIONS, RATINGS

When Dave Duerson went to the Giants for the '90 season, I took his TV gig. In the old days, that would've been impossible—football blinders on, got no time to do something so frivolous.

It was me making concessions. My football career was on the down side. Here's another avenue. I could be an entertainer.

I should probably still be getting a cut of Mark Giangreco's paycheck. Eventually, he became the highest-paid local TV sports guy in town, but when I joined his Sunday night show—everybody did extra sports on Sundays during football season when we were big—he was more or less low man on the totem pole going up against guys at the other stations who'd been around longer—Tim Wiegel and Johnny Morris, who was an ex-Bear and had Mike Ditka on his Sunday show.

The way Giangreco was trying to gain his notoriety was by being the negative, sarcastic fuck of the media. Ditka hated him. Probably still does.

One of the reasons I took that job was the heel always needs to get his. Before it was ever seen on TV, I'd already seen in my mind these flashes of brilliance, these pearls I was going to cast before swine, of the things I was going to do to him live on camera.

Weekly, I'd do something slapstick to him, and the people loved it. I imagine Ditka was getting a chuckle out of it himself, even though he was doing his show over on Channel 2. In fact, Ditka's show won a local Emmy one year, but once Giangreco added me, we'd beat him in the ratings as often as not.

My personal favorite thing I ever did to Giangreco was one that went along with the old expression about having egg on your face when you've talked out of turn.

In '90, he picked us to go 8-8. Well, we won the division, and we're in the playoffs, and the night we won the division, I took a raw egg into the studio and slapped it on his forehead. I said, "Don't you have egg on your face now?"

There were others, though.

I used a chainsaw on him—a fake one given to me by this comic, the Amazing Jonathon. He was a fan of the show and had all kinds of gimics, and he sent me a fake chain saw that, when you pressed a button, squirted fake blood all over the place. So I fired that thing up and it looked like I was cutting him up, cutting him up.

There was whipped cream, the spitting snake, cutting his tie off, holding him down while my wife at the time put makeup on him. What didn't I do to that poor man?

I'd wait for the inevitable sarcastic, negative comment, then I'd blast him.

Giangreco was OK with it, because he knew it was working for ratings, and he knew I was making a joke out of myself.

The heat was on me. He had a line with the station that I wasn't going to shit on. The integrity of him reading off the teleprompter, that was off limits.

Besides, there was always a method to my madness. I knew there was a cliff, a line I could go over and fall straight down. The juggling act is to get right there and make people think you were fixing to fall off, then not. The time the little red light was on me, that's when they got the juggling act. He didn't know it was coming, but he more or less trusted me.

Station management wasn't always so sure, right from the start.

The first show, I'd had a pretty good game in the opener, we beat Seattle, so before the red light came on I said, "Mark, ask me how I'm doing."

He did, and I launched into, "Well, Mark, when I went to take my constitutional after the game, I didn't know if it was hemorrhoids dripping blood in the water or the wife's Lee Press-On Nail finally dissolved."

I heard the producers yell from the booth, and those are sound-proof. The first break, there's the phone ringing off the hook under the desk.

What did I say that hadn't been said on TV? You get commercials for hemorrhoids and Lee Press-On Nails both.

I ended up getting fired, as I recall, for something along the lines of, "This is what I think you meant by saying that."

Of course, I did get accused by Jenny Jones, the talk-show hostess, of spray-painting a mustache and a goatee on her big picture in the lobby. All I can say is boys will be boys after a football game and one too many toddies. Might have been Kevin Butler along with me, instigating.

I did happen to have spray paint along with me to use on the show.

To tell you the truth, I was kind of glad it was over. It had become a weekly thing; what was I going to do next? It was almost a distraction from football.

In the end, that show was sort of like Marilyn Monroe. It died an early death and left a pretty corpse.

AGING WELL

When you get away from it after a time, the things you most remember, the things you're most proud of, are the things you did in the game as an old man. You've really got to be knowledgeable, you've really got to be on top of it, to make the plays as an old man that you did as a young man.

I had that talk with Reggie White, when we did a wrestling show when I was with the Packers. He was getting ready to quit, but he came back, played a couple more years and did some great things. He wasn't the Reggie White of old, but I guarantee you he enjoyed every minute of it.

Actually, I told the same thing to Jerry Rice. My wife, Misty, was with me when I was wrestling, doing a card show in Dallas. They had football players too, and Jerry Rice was there right after he'd hurt his knee. He knew from years of scouting reports I'd had my knee problems, so I was a guy he could talk to about it. Backstage he came up and said, "I've probably lost a step now. Should I retire?" I said, "Jerry, when you've got two steps on everybody, you can afford to lose one."

He's still playing and scoring touchdowns. I guarantee you he's prouder of himself for what he's doing now than if he'd retired after he'd thought he lost a step.

PRESIDENT WILLIAM, SERGEANT MING

Women sometimes say men only grow older, they don't grow up, and I guess you might could prove it by some football players.

William Perry and I, for example, had a clubhouse sitting beside Halas Hall. It was a groundskeeper's shed, but it was like our little kid's fort. William was the president, I was the sergeant at arms, and if somebody didn't belong in there it was, "Get out." Think of Spanky and Our Gang, "No Girls Allowed," but with the "s" backwards, that was about our mentality.

After practice we'd go in there—me and William and whoever we deemed worthy. We'd tell the old stories, have our little bottles of booze hidden around, have a couple drinks. We'd end up making the equipment guys wait late, because we'd still have to take our showers and change after our meetings.

William was the president because he was like the groundskeeper's assistant, like Bill Murray's character, Carl, in *Caddyshack*. William seriously liked to cut grass. Every once in a while he'd just have to tend to the grounds, so he'd head for the shed.

One time, there was no key to be had and William wanted to cut some grass. There's the riding lawnmower, and I said, "Now, Goddammit, William, don't mess up that lawnmower. Wait for him to come tell you where the key is."

He said, "Don't worry about it, I'm a MacGyver," like the TV show where the guy could build a bomb out of a paper clip. He started that mother up—hot-wired a lawnmower.

STARTS AND FINISHES

Dan Hampton had gotten hurt in '89, I want to say his 12th knee operation as a result. We all knew right away he was coming back for his last hurrah in '90.

I came into that season with 101 straight starts, but it was a little crowded on the D-line that year with me, Dan and William at tackles, plus Richard Dent and Trace Armstrong, coming off a decent rookie season, at the ends. My starting streak got screwed up because we went with a three-man rotation at tackle, which meant half the games I didn't start.

So my starting streak got messed up, but I still ended up setting Bears records for most games and most consecutive games played, both 191.

It says in my bio in old Bears media guides my start streak ended in the first game in '90 because I missed training camp with a contract dispute, but it was really about the rotation. They can say what they want.

Dan and William had been the ones in camp doing the work; they deserved to start in the rotation that first day, in my mind.

MONEY MATTERS

When I held out—and I did twice, in '89 and '90—I always used to catch hell in the press about "the sanctity of the contract." My ass. Where the hell is the sanctity now that there's a salary cap, and instead of honoring the contract management says, "We'll cut you and bring you back for less money?"

There's no sanctity there. Fucking hypocrites.

At one point, the Bears had enough and decided to threaten me with a trade. The Houston Oilers were willing to trade for me, and that didn't sound too bad to an old Texas boy; then all of a sudden the Bears came up with some money.

To that point, I believe Larry Csonka and I were the only two guys in NFL history to hold out, with a contract, two years in a row.

They doubled my salary after I went to the Pro Bowl in '86 and '87. I was making $500,000, but there were still guys making a million while I was making all the plays. I didn't care what contract I signed. I wanted them to show appreciation to me the only way ownership can show a player appreciation—with money.

Ditka was even kind of on my side. I knew how he felt about contracts and holdouts, but he told the press something like, "In this case, I think Steve McMichael deserves it."

I did a lot of the negotiating myself, not always with the most pleasant circumstances, but I think it was the right way to go. Most players find out agents are the biggest scam since two-man beach volleyball got put on television.

All an agent does is go to the owner and say, "How much you giving him?" Then he goes to the player and says, "This is the offer, do you want to take it?" Player says no, agent goes back, "He said no."

He's just a go-between. You can do that yourself.

Even so, when I started out, I had an agent—the same guy as Dan. When I became an All-Pro, having the same agent as another All-Pro defensive lineman on the same team wasn't a good thing. I dropped him. My friend Larry Bales and I went into partnership in a bar in Texas. He was a lawyer and a politician, and he wanted to take a stab at being an agent. So I let him come along in these negotiations.

He'd meet with Ted Phillips, the Bears' money man in those days before he replaced Michael McCaskey as president and CEO, when I wasn't around. When I'd come back, things would get said.

Ted still talks about it to this day, and I swear I don't remember it, but he says when the negotiations ended on the last contract I signed, I got up, leaned over the desk and said, "I'd like to hit you right in the fucking mouth."

A lot of people might have liked to do it, but I'll take Ted's word for it that I was the one who actually said it.

A FINE USE OF FINES

One of the times I held out, the Bears extended my contract and bumped it up a little. They gave me a signing bonus, which made up the difference of the fines I was accruing not being in training camp.

One of the favorite things I ever did in football was with that money from the fines. I got to select which charity it'd go to, and it was $70,000 or $80,000.

Part of it went to refurbish the terminal children's ward at a hospital on the West Side of Chicago. They got new TVs, carpeting, games for the kids and things. Another part went to our team preacher's church. Father Nick's church had a little kindergarten on the side of the church, and a tornado wiped it out. They got the money and rebuilt the kindergarten.

It wasn't about the money. There wasn't a press conference. I had a chance to give, so I did. I think most players in the league are like that. Most guys don't need a celebrity golf tournament with their name on it. Most of the guys I knew in football were good guys who wanted to do good things.

DAN'S LAST STAND

It became apparent pretty early in Hampton's last game that it was gonna be Hampton's last game. We were playing the Giants in the playoffs, the year Jeff Hostetler took them to the Super Bowl. Sometime in the first couple of series, I actually got back there, sacked him, and caused a fumble that Trace Armstrong recovered. But I knew we were going to get beat that day when the offense ended up getting down to their goal line, went for it four straight plays and didn't get in. I knew our offense wouldn't do shit against their defense that day.

Comes down to the end of the game and the Giants, for whatever reason, were trying to rub it in. They already had the game in a blowout, but it was 24-3, last minute of the game, and they were still trying to score a touchdown.

We were in a huddle in our own end zone. Dan was usually quiet in the huddle, but this time, before Singletary can call out the defense, Dan stood up and said, "Guys, don't let 'em score on the last play of my career."

Touchdown.

I apologized to him afterward in the locker room on behalf of all the guys.

HOT NUTS, ANYONE?

We all know football is an emotional game, and anyone can tell you sometimes emotions blur—laughing at a funeral, crying at a wedding, that kind of thing.

Similar things can happen when attempts at inspiration take a wrong turn into comedy. It could really happen to Mike Singletary, who was never funny unless it was on accident, and the accident usually happened when he was trying to be his most serious.

Knowing he wasn't trying to be funny about it made the stuff that came out of his mouth the funniest things you could hear somebody say.

One year, the year after that second Redskins loss in the first round of the playoffs, we're getting ready for our first playoff game. Mike's up there and he's just lost it. He's fixing to lead calisthenics, but that's the time the spirit moves him to give a team speech.

The guy considers himself a minister—and I've got to give him his props for his convictions, he means it when he's carrying his Bible around—but he's really lost it this time. Expletives are flowing out of his mouth, he's preaching up a storm, screaming, "I refuse to go home early. Get your goddamn nuts hot!"

I fell out laughing. Get your nuts hot? I still give him hell about that. I think it means get fired up and have some balls, but he just put them together.

PULL UP A CHAIR, KID

Mark Carrier, a safety out of USC, was a rookie in '90, and he was in awe of me and Hampton. Strangest thing was, the first thing we noticed is how bad his hands were.

It's strange because when Mark was a rookie he set the team record with 10 interceptions in a season.

But it's like Fencik found out—with our pass rush, most of the passes that came down the middle were floating passes that most of the time you could catch like a punt. We'd come in, the quarterback would throw off his back foot and throw up a floater. Brett Favre was the only guy who could throw it off his back foot and still zing that thing in there like he was stepping through it.

That year, Mark saw a lot of floaters he could close in on.

He saw a lot of things, sitting around our team breakfasts like a groupie. The day of the game, we'd do a lot of what I'm doing right now, sitting around the table telling stories, and Mark Carrier would be sitting around wide-eyed, taking it all in.

Actually, it was nice to see. Not all of the guys the McCaskey regime brought to the team, but more than I'd care to recall, were more business than football. It was their job, not their love.

I didn't have a lot in common with those guys.

That's why I appreciated the Mark Carriers.

Anybody you saw on the field busting their ass, doing whatever they could to win that one game that day—not saving themselves for the year, not waiting to turn it on in the playoffs—those are the guys I appreciated.

THE ARMSTRONG OF THE LAW

Trace Armstrong was one guy who knew it was a business—hell, we called him the clubhouse lawyer, and he eventually became the president of the players' union—but he could separate himself from that on game day.

Trace was studying to be a lawyer, so talking to him in the locker room was to talk about the law, the judicial world, the courtrooms of America. But on the field, he was different, a pure player—after a fashion.

At first, he was gangly, clumsy even. He was like a marionette, how they dangle and flop around—that's what he looked like in practice to me when he first got up here after we drafted him out of Florida in '89.

Dan and I looked at each other like, "Oh, no."

But even the most intelligent guys in the world like me can be wrong.

Now, though, I'm proud of his career. I helped teach him football, him playing left end right next to me.

REFRIGERATED FEAR

Donnell Woolford was quite a little striker when he first came to us as a cornerback out of Clemson in '89. But one day he found out firsthand how heavy William Perry was when he fell

It was my pleasure to help Trace Armstrong
become an outstanding player.
(Photo by Daily Southtown; Tinley Park, Illinois)

on you. I have to say, it kind of crushed the physical right out of Donnell.

Donnell came up to force the play on a quick throw in the flat. William Perry broke out that way and got there just in time to pile on without getting a flag. Donnell was underneath, and William just about squished the life out of him. It actually hurt him somewhere, and Donnell was never quite so physical after that.

THIS ONE'S FOR YOU, COACH

During the '91 season, Mike Ditka won his 100th game in his 10th season as our coach. After the game, in the locker room, I stood up and gave him the game ball.

He had always been the one in the locker room handing out the game balls. He gave me a few, for sure—I think I've got 30. But that was a milestone that needed to be recognized.

I got up and said to everybody, "Think about that. One hundred wins in 10 years—that'll get you in the playoffs every year, won't it?"

Somebody needed to say something about him and I did. He played it down. Didn't want to show anything. Didn't have to, I knew how he felt—even if I only heard it once.

The year he got fired, '93, I walked in the locker room after a loss and the guys were kind of nonchalant. To me, you show the loss some respect by being somber, not laughing. I walk in, there's some guys over on one side laughing, guys over in another corner saying, "Where we going tonight?" Another guy's standing with the press, talking to everybody about what he did.

My locker was all the way across the room from where I was standing. I took my helmet, threw a strike into it. Boom! the noise reverberated through the room. For the rest of the time I was in that room, it was somber, and in the quiet I heard Ditka from the coach's office say, "I love that guy."

I feel the same way. I don't just like Mike Ditka, I love him—he was the coach I was supposed to play for, you know?

McCASKEY FAMILY PLANNING

I'll say this for Michael McCaskey's tenure as president of the Bears: I promise you, during that time the Bears made money, and what else would a businessman want to put on his resume?

As far as the business part of the Bears goes, he did a hell of a job. But when it came to knowing football, knowing the mentality and what makes up all the different facets of a football team, Mike came up a little short. You need pawns and knights and castles on a chess board, not all pawns; everyone has to have different talents, and I think Michael McCaskey was in love with scouting combine types. Run fast, jump high, score well on the psychological tests, you're his guy.

But here's some scouting wisdom: I don't care how fast or how high you jump. If you didn't make a play in college, you damn sure aren't gonna make one in the pros.

There's got to be heart to go along with God's physical gifts.

I don't know why Michael underestimated heart, because there was plenty of it in his family. His grandfather, George Halas, had it. His mother and George's daughter, Virginia McCaskey, had it—and I'm sure Virginia, in her time being around the team in the earliest Monsters of the Midway days—saw something besides these Marquis of Queensbury, white-collar guys Michael favored.

God bless Virginia's husband, Ed McCaskey, who was the team's chairman of the board from the time George Halas died until 1999, then was chairman emeritus until he died in 2003. I liked that old man. He knew what was going on. He'd come through the locker room, basically the owner of the team as Virginia's husband, but he was a players' owner.

He'd talk to the guys, come into the training room with me and Dan and say something like, "OK, I'm going to the track today, I've got a winner. You guys want in on it?" Stuff like that.

That stuff was always out of Mike's realm. He's not personable like that. He's dry.

THE DEATH OF DITKA

Seems to me Mike Ditka should have gotten more rope than the McCaskeys gave him at the end. Sure, we went 5-11 in '92, but we'd been in the playoffs seven of the previous eight years.

I believe Ditka wanted more control over who was being brought to the team, and by this time he was getting less. Jerry Vainisi, his good friend and the Bears' general manager after Jim Finks resigned in '83, was replaced in '87 by Bill Tobin—a McCaskey guy.

I promise you, Michael couldn't wait for an excuse to get rid of Mike Ditka so the team would be his.

In '92, Ditka finally gave him that excuse—the tantrum that just about broke Jim Harbaugh.

We were in Minnesota, winning 20-0 in the fourth quarter. Ditka called a run and Harbaugh audibled to a flat pass. He threw an interception for a touchdown, and we went on to lose the game 21-20.

Jimmy wasn't a bad quarterback. It took some time for him to adjust to the pros after getting drafted out of Michigan in '87, but he had some pretty good years for us and went to the Pro Bowl later with Indianapolis. He just called the wrong audible that day.

This is why Ditka went off on Jim: When you're up 20-0 in the fourth quarter, you run the damn ball. You don't audible to a pass. I promise you, Ditka had gone over that in meetings.

Harbaugh audibled to a pass, it got picked off and run back for a touchdown, Ditka went off.

I don't think Harbaugh completed another pass that day. I'm sure, after the Vikings went up 21-20, that Ditka wanted him to.

If you look at it from the McCaskeys' point of view, it's like, "He cut my quarterback's nuts off and he didn't complete a pass after that."

That was the death of Ditka, basically, the last time he lost a Bears player after he started losing them during the '87 strike.

TRUE CONFESSION

To tell you the truth, the stage my career was at when Ditka left was almost becoming drudgery. The sheer repetition of every day—Monday come in and watch the previous game, Tuesday you're off, Wednesday you do what you've always done on Wednesday for years. Now Dave Wannstedt comes in with new terminology, new philosophy, it rejuvenated me in a way. It was a new challenge.

Setting goals is a big thing to do in life. It's the climb up the mountain that defines the man, not the time at the top. Hell, you get to the top and what do you see? Other mountains—and you say to yourself, "I want to climb that one."

WANNY'S WORLD

Dave Wannstedt was the hot candidate, and Michael McCaskey went and got him. Dave was the defensive coordinator for the Cowboys, who had just won the Super Bowl, and their defense was a big reason they started their decade of dominance in the '90s.

The fact that they got that decade started against us with a playoff win in '91 probably didn't hurt Dave's chances any.

Dave's scheme was about putting guys in the gap and getting up the field. At first I thought, "Great, this puts me in automatic pass rush mode. I don't have to read offensive linemen anymore. I just get in a gap and go."

What it did was get my ass double-teamed. Offensive linemen are going to squeeze you, make sure you don't get through the gap, then they've got time to go get somebody else.

I'd sort of get away from the system, though, by doing what we called holding the jump-through for the linebacker.

It was something Dan and I had done constantly in the old days.

Mike Singletary had a habit of coming up to me before every game and posing me a question: "Who's the best middle linebacker in the game, Steve?"

He'd expect the response, "You are, Mike, go show 'em today."

Then he'd say, "Take care of me today." That meant hold the offensive linemen so they couldn't get off on him.

All I had to do was grab the guys double-teaming me and Singletary's running free.

Wannstedt was about getting up the field, don't hold anybody, because the linebacker's job is to get in his gap. His idea was get in that gap, and when somebody gets off you, you make the play. I kept holding the jump-through, and look at how many tackles Dante Jones had that year—189.

We were 7-9, and I figure we lost nine games where the other team was running the ball. A middle linebacker makes more tackles in a losing season than a winning one, because teams are running at you, winning the game.

RIDDLE ME THIS

I liked Dave. I didn't like what he and just about every other defensive coordinator to ever get promoted to head coach did.

What's the thing he did to get the job? Coach defense.

Why not hire an offensive coordinator to run the offense and stay on the headset running the defense? Why do they all start thinking, "This is what I want to run on offense," when that's not their expertise?

Bob Slowik was his defensive coordinator, and he just left it up to Bob. I'm sure he and Dave went over it during the week, but in the final analysis it was Bob on the sideline calling the defensive plays. It should've been Dave doing that.

BACK TO YOU, JOHN

We played three Thanksgiving Day games during my time with the Bears and didn't win one until the last of them—but that's the one you might say left a bad taste in my mouth.

We were playing the Lions; John Madden's crew was there, so that meant he was going to make a big to-do of giving a turkey leg to the game's MVP.

We held Barry Sanders to basically nothing and won 10-6, so John decided he was going to give his turkey legs to the four defensive linemen—me, Trace Armstrong, Chris Zorich and Richard Dent.

We were already in the locker room, and they had to call us back out onto the field for them to talk to us after the game. They had only two headsets, and Madden told them, "Give the headsets to Dent and Zorich." That hurt. So I was just standing there eating a turkey leg while he was trying to talk to those two.

John's humor—Chris Zorich and Richard Dent were just not getting it. Finally, they were standing there mute long enough and Madden said, "Well, give the headset to McMichael."

Naturally, I've got to retort, "John, these turkey legs are as dry as your humor." And I flung it away.

John's had a problem with me ever since.

But then, I've had a problem with him longer. In '85, he picked the whole defense to make his All-Madden team—I've still got the poster—but every year after that I never made it. I always figured I was a blue-collar guy, down in the trenches, a tough guy who kind of seemed like an All-Madden annual pick. And he never took me.

Sharing the Madden Thanksgiving Turkey with my teammates.
Coach Madden didn't appreciate my "dry" humor.

WEARING THE GREEN AND GOLD

God forgive me, but I ended my career as a Green Bay Packer. Hey, I began it as a Patriot, and don't tell me I wouldn't have heard that a little more often if the Super Bowl had gone the other way.

But I want to tell every fan in Chicago that when I went to Green Bay in '94, the Bears had fired me. They said, "We're not giving you any more money." The Packers called up and said, "We'll give you a half million dollars." Is anybody in the habit of giving back a winning lottery ticket? I don't think so.

After '93, Dave Wannstedt gave me two choices. He said, "Steve, salary cap reasons, if you come back, we'll bring you back for $300,000." I was scheduled to make $1 million that year. He said, "You'll be in the rotation, but you won't be starting."

Then he said, "Or you can come be my defensive line coach."

I said, "Coach, I still got the fever, I still want to play ball, so I'm going to see if somebody else wants to hire me."

The Bears found out the Packers were offering some money; they just said, "Let him walk."

It wasn't bad, outside of playing the Bears twice. I still got to play the whole NFL. We made the playoffs—Dallas beat us, but it was still a good year.

Green Bay really only got half of me. I tore a knee ligament off in training camp, so I was playing on first down, didn't hardly ever get to pass rush.

Call it karma, or kismet, or whatever, but old immediate Steve made a concession, and it cost him. I wanted to show Brett Favre and his teammates I was one of the boys, so I brother-in-lawed it in a practice. Never did it in Chicago. Do it one time in Green Bay and I tore ligament in my knee, right off the bone.

In a drill, I beat the guard, and he was off balance after I ran by him. He was scrambling, down low, trying to keep up with me, and right in front of me was Favre.

Most of the time in Chicago, I'd run by and just slap the shit out of the quarterback, let him know I'm there. This time, I started shutting it down to slow down in front of Brett. He saw me coming and started to reverse pivot like he was going to spin and run outside. He was going slow, making a joke out of getting away from me, and I saw that, so I stopped, and I was going to turn the other way, because I knew on the film it was going to look like we were dancing. But when I stopped, that guard caught up with me, pinned me back over my leg, and I heard that ligament snap.

Even so, I told the head coach, Mike Holmgren and the defensive coordinator, Fritz Shurmur, "Hey, I'm probably gonna lose a step, but this is my last hoo-rah, so I ain't gonna get it operated on. My legs are strong enough to make the season." They're like, "What?" So I took them down to the weight room, put 725 pounds on the bar and did three reps squatting with that bad ligament. Holmgren said, "Well, I guess you can do it." I played the year, my last one.

I was still being hard-headed, thinking I could still play, until Barry Sanders went the distance on me in Detroit. A play I'd always made just wasn't there.

Granted, Barry was a guy I could miss three times on one play when I was healthy. He could back up faster than I could chase him.

He cut inside, then cut back into the gap where the defensive end should've been, but wasn't. The play I'd always made, to come back out and make the tackle, the knee wasn't there, it gave. He was gone. That's when I knew it was over.

SOLDIERING ON

The most enduring memories of that last year, naturally, came from Soldier Field. At one point, the Bears ran a fourth and one play right at me and I stuffed it. I never felt more guilty.

I shouldn't have. We—the Packers, I mean—ended up winning 33-6.

The cosmos was crying, baby. That was the Monday night they finally retired Dick Butkus's jersey. I came back to Soldier Field as a Packer, and it was like a hurricane. A monsoon. Water was just standing on the field, coming down too quick to run off.

It was like the heavens unbound. Add in the throwback jerseys we were wearing—the Bears had these striped deals, just about the ugliest things I'd ever seen—and it was like a timeless game, one for the ages.

And I was a Packer. God forgive me.

PACKER WHACKERS

All this talk about my time in Green Bay makes me think back to how much I hated those bastards at one point.

In the Ditka-Forrest Gregg heyday, I'd heard through the grapevine that Gregg told his players something along the lines of, "I don't care if it's illegal. Take them out."

That's when the rumors started hitting that we had had personal bounties out on guys. But I'm not going to confirm or deny it.

If anybody wants to pay heed to it, fine. But I'm not confirming or denying.

A sight that probably still burns the eyes of most Bears fans.

I will say, never put a bounty on a guy who's wearing your same number on the other team. There was a Packer named Brian Noble who went down in a game and he wore No. 99.

I'm not confirming or denying, but there could have been a guy named Dan Hampton standing up in a meeting going,

"Brian Noble, fuck him, bounty on him." I believe the records will show Dan went down in that game, too.

Let's just say there was a possibility Dan went down that game.

I'm telling you, when the commissioner heard about this, there was an investigation into criminal charges.

It was seriously ugly back then. That was the year Kenny Stills hit Matt Suhey about a year after the whistle and some nobody named Mark Lee took Walter Payton way out of bounds over the Bears' bench—though, really, Walter knew he was going, and he was so strong he held onto Lee and took him with him.

Then there was '86, when Charles Martin had his "hit list" towel, with a bunch of Bears names on it. Martin body-slammed Jim McMahon on his shoulder and right out of the lineup, and guess whose name was on the top of Martin's list?

Part of me takes that as a show of respect, like, "We can't beat you guys legal, so we've got to do it dirty."

On the other hand, body-slamming McMahon did lead to Flutie in the playoffs that year...

Chapter 23

MONGOISMS AND
OTHER FLOTSAM

MONGOISM #1

A coach isn't somebody who just tells you where to go in a defensive scheme. He shows you how to get there.

STRONG MEN

If I hadn't been as strong as I was, I wouldn't have gotten near as far as I did.

I had a reputation for bending bars in the weight room, but there were some others.

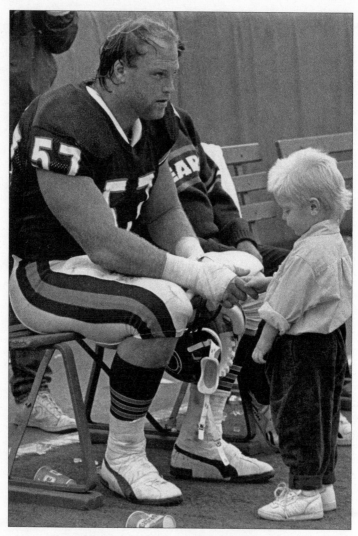

Tom Thayer was one of the stronger guys on the team.
(Photo by Daily Southtown; Tinley Park, Illinois)

Jimbo Covert, doing squat reps at like 800 pounds, had the strongest legs of anybody before he hurt his back. The Fridge never put the time in weight room because he was so naturally strong, but the things I had to work my ass off to get to, he'd come in there and just do naturally.

Tommy Thayer was plenty strong. I saw him in Atlanta, where we were training the week before we went to the Super Bowl, bench-press over 500 pounds. During the season, that's pretty damn strong. In the off season, I'd be benching over 500 on occasion, but as the season wears on, damn...

Really, we had four or five guys on the team who would bend bars, literally. I was always doing it because I benched with a close grip. You don't go out on the football field and do a nice, slow press with an offensive lineman; it's as quick as you can do it.

So I used to pound reps out with that close grip. Quick-twitch muscles are what football is all about. Doing that with 500 pounds on the bar tended to leave a few of them bent.

A FINAL THOUGHT ON THE POX

Joe Montana, for all his mobility, might have ended up being one of the easiest quarterbacks in the league to sack. Fat lot of good it did.

After playing Joe for a couple of years, he knew we were coming and we were trying to hurt him, to hit him hard. He'd see you coming and he'd just fall down. Now it's second and 17, he stands up and throws a pass to Jerry Rice for 20 yards, and that sack didn't mean shit—and he didn't have to take any punishment for it, because of the way he'd gone down.

Outfoxed by the pox.

MONGOISM #2

I'd always had a love-hate relationship with the fans in Chicago. You get enough of walking in at halftime getting booed. And I'm not talking because we were losing; I'm talking because we weren't covering the spread.

ATTENTION TO DETAIL

OK, I might have had a slight problem with obsessive-compulsive disorder when I was a player. Everything about my uniform, I was concerned about, down to the tape on my hands.

I'd actually hold my arms up to the mirror, and if they weren't even, I'd get 'em that way. My thumbs had to be taped exactly the same way, my socks had to be pulled up the same height and the stripes in the same spot.

I would even stress out during the game if I sweated so much the tape would start coming loose. If that happened and we lost the game, I'd be in the locker room going, "That fucking tape came loose and we lost the game."

IT'S MILLEN TIME

You might not expect Matt Millen—former TV guy, now the Lions' general manager, looks comfortable in a suit—to be much like me.

But we both played defense, and I liked him. I respected him because we were kind of in the same vein as players, with the sarcastic sense of humor.

We played the Raiders this one time, there was a TV timeout when he was on the sideline and I was on the field. Man, I hated those things, waiting around for ages during a commercial—that's when you'd get the coldest in one of those frozen games we were always playing.

When you're playing the Raiders, invariably during a TV timeout there's going to be a wisecrack coming from somewhere.

This particular game, we beat them 6-0 in Los Angeles. Millen's about the same size as me, and Hampton and Dent always called me the midget. I'm sure he got that from his team, too.

Anyway, I heard him call out, "McMichael, you're so short I could eat pea soup off of your head." I looked back at him, and Tom Flores and Al Davis, the coach and the owner, were standing there. I cracked his whole team up with my retort:

"Millen, I've seen longer legs on a coffee table."

MONGOISM #3

If you practice full speed, you know the speed of the game. If someone tells you the big adjustment for him is the speed of the pro game, he's practicing half-assed.

COVERT OPERATIONS

Jim Covert had the best technique at run blocking I've ever gone against. Most guys make the mistake of trying to get their head and body into you at the same time as their hands. That's compact. You can get around that. Jimbo led with his hands first to grab you. There was going to be contact, but his hands were on you straight up out of his stance before the body contact.

WORLD TRAVELERS

Because we were such a big draw after winning our Super Bowl, the league was always sending us to play in those American Bowls, preseason games in Europe. The first one was in '86, when we played the Cowboys in London, and our last one was against the 49ers in Berlin in '91. In between, we played the Vikings in Sweden—kind of appropriate, don't you think?

Europeans may not have known American football very well, but they did appreciate the contact. Every time there was a big hit, there'd be a big roar—well, with one notable exception in Sweden.

Right out of the box, Kevin Butler should have known Sweden wasn't for him. First night there, we had a drink with Ditka in the hotel lobby. Maybe more than one drink. We were relaxing. Butler got so drunk, he just leaned over and threw up right on the hotel lobby floor, right in front of the coach.

He was out of it. I had to pick him up, take him back to his room and throw him on his bed. So I did that, then I ripped his shirt open, poured baby powder all over his chest and stomach and wrote "pussy" in the powder. There's still a picture of that floating around somewhere.

That wasn't Kevin's lowlight of the trip, though.

The hotel had a little outdoor bistro—you know, al fresco dining—and Kevin and I and our wives were sitting at a table having something to eat. This bum walked by on the sidewalk, stopped at our table, leaned over, and we didn't understand what he was saying, because he was talking in Swedish. Finally, I guess he got frustrated, and he spit on the table. Butler stood up and hit him right in the face with a nice jab. Bam! Knocked the guy down. Well, Kevin got scared because we weren't in America. He ran up in the hotel. He shouldn't have worried, because the bum got up and walked off—actually, I was kind of disappointed he couldn't knock the guy out. Anyway, I went up to try to find Kevin, and when I got to his floor, he was hiding behind a plant in the elevator lobby. I was laughing my ass off so hard I could barely tell him he was off the hook.

MONGOISM #4

Guys come up to me to this day and say, "I was going to play pro ball, but I hurt my knee." Look, pal, I had eight knee operations and that didn't stop me.

MUSCLE VS. BULK

When I played, I was listed at 6'2", 268 pounds. That would just about make me a linebacker today. My heaviest was 284, and I always had a waist. Seems like every tackle in the league is at least 300 pounds, and Ted Washington, who went to the Pro Bowl with the Bears in 2002, was pushing 400.

Put it this way—Fridge, at 305, used to be an anomaly. Now he'd be undersized.

I think it's stupid. Now, you've got situational pass rushers— little, fast guys who aren't that strong—and big fatasses to stop the run.

I took care of both of those. I didn't weigh a ton, so I was fast enough to get to the quarterback. But I got in the weight room and made my ass strong, too, so I could handle the run.

SEEING THROUGH THE HAZE

One of the reasons I got "Ming the Merciless" was because I was so merciless breaking down a guy's weakest point with my sarcastic humor. "Boy, you got your ass toasted that time, didn't you, pal?"

I could tell other guys were thinking, "Why'd you say that, you insensitive so-and-so?" I didn't care how sensitive a guy was. Get him over that, he becomes a player.

Most rookies in training camp, you'd have the rookie show, make 'em get up on stage.

The big thing about that was how we reacted. It wouldn't be hazing them. It'd be ignoring them. We'd walk by without acknowledging they were standing there.

They'd be like little puppies, looking for affection, for acceptance. Our thinking was if they couldn't get it that way, they'd try to get it by busting their asses on the football field. Then you'd go, "Atta boy."

MONGOISM #5

I don't care how much you try to deny it or hide it, it's always in there festering—the defense hates the offense and the offense hates the defense. Can't help it; we're all just brainwashed that way.

GAPS IN THE STORY

I think a lot of old athletes are like me in one respect.

Sometimes it's hard to remember details—not because we got hit on the head too many times, but because of the way we had to approach our jobs.

The worst thing about it is family and friends got neglected because of this. It sounds chicken shit, but in my mind I had to do it to get where I did, I had to put the blinders on and

Being retired from football has allowed me to spend more time with my wife, Misty. (Don Rogers Photography, Austin)

focus on what was in front of me, not what was off to the sides. I probably had to do it because of the negative the Patriots had planted in my mind in the first place. I needed the blinders, the concentration, to get it done.

My family and friends missed out on a lot of me—because I was neglecting them for that focus.

Friday night, Saturday in particular, they'd come in for the game. Well, I didn't have time for them. It's the day before the game, you know?

There have been bad feelings, and I resent myself for it, but it's what I had to do.

WHAT BRIAN LACKS

I always hear people saying Brian Urlacher, the new darling of Bears fans, can't take on a block. I say he doesn't spend enough time in the weight room to be strong enough to take on a block.

In my estimation, you should be the one striking the blow on the offensive lineman. He's standing there letting the blow come to him instead of taking it to the blocker.

MONGOISM #6

Football is fun. The job part is getting ready to play four or five hours a day in the weight room. You better work harder to get your ass ready to play than you actually play on the field. Then the games are easy.

There's an equation for you: Practice hard, easy game.